Regional Products and Rural Livelihoods

Regional Products and Rural Livelihoods

A Study on **Geographical Indications** *from India*

N. LALITHA AND SOUMYA VINAYAN

OXFORD
UNIVERSITY PRESS

OXFORD
UNIVERSITY PRESS

Oxford University Press is a department of the University of Oxford.
It furthers the University's objective of excellence in research, scholarship,
and education by publishing worldwide. Oxford is a registered trademark of
Oxford University Press in the UK and in certain other countries.

Published in India by
Oxford University Press
2/11 Ground Floor, Ansari Road, Daryaganj, New Delhi 110 002, India

ISBN-13 (print edition): 978-0-19-948969-5
ISBN-10 (print edition): 0-19-948969-6

ISBN-13 (eBook): 978-0-19-909537-7
ISBN-10 (eBook): 0-19-909537-X

Typeset Dante MT Std 10.5/13
by Tranistics Data Technologies, New Delhi 110 044
Printed in India by Gopsons Papers Ltd., Noida 201 301

In memory of
Dwijen Rangnekar, whose work on GI inspired us to explore this area

Contents

Figures, Tables, Appendices, and Boxes

Figures

Tables

Appendices

Boxes

Foreword

Diversity in languages, food, crafts, and arts enrich Indian culture set in agro-climatic variabilities. It provides a crucible for experimentation, innovation, and emergence of region-specific creative identities. Historically, many of these cultural identities have been given labels signifying the region all over the country. Patan patola, or kanjeevaram sarees from Kanchipuram village, Banaras sarees from Benaras, or Pochhampalli sarees are just some illustrations. These products woven with the culture, heritage, and tradition prevailing in the place are based on the knowledge and skills that have been preserved over generations. These origin-linked products have come to be protected by the *sui generis* framework of Geographical Indications Act of 1999, which came into force in 2003. In this book, N. Lalitha and Soumya Vinayan have chosen to study a few handicraft products from southern India which are registered with the GI Registry in India. GI protects a product within a specified geographical location and, therefore, is linked with that area either through human skills, cultural practices, or via natural resources/factors, or a combination of all these.

Though GI is a community-held intellectual property right (IPR) compared to the individually held intellectual property rights like patents or copyright, the bundle of rights that come with the individually held IPRs, like defining who may use the resource and at what conditions and importantly the right to exclude, are also applicable to GI. However, creating widespread awareness, often among economically poor artisans and craftsmen, is a challenge. Therefore, infringement is widespread and, as yet, hardly any specific benefit has accrued to the genuine producers due to GI. The artisans are dependent on these products for their livelihoods and find it difficult to devote time and resources to fight infringement. A mechanism which runs on public support is needed to nurture such communities. There are already a number of institutions and specific schemes meant for the development of handicrafts and agriculture. These institutions and schemes need to be aligned with GI implications. Lack of interest and promotional activities will not only discourage the artisans and dissuade the young generation to pursue skill-based craft, it will also lead to the erosion of knowledge—a social capital of immense value.

The authors have argued well through case studies that while the consumers still recognize the geography and quality link of the products, the producers, given their socio-economic and institutional constraints, are unable to tap the economic potential through brand building. Even when the brand building exists, it is the intermediaries and not the primary producers who benefit from the GI tag (not necessarily in the legal sense since in most of case studies in this book, though the GI registration has already been done, the necessary mandates are yet to be implemented). This has been mainly due to the gaps in horizontal and vertical linkages along the value chain. There are multiplicity of actors but with low levels of networking and coordination, they are unable to ensure protection of authentic rights of the product or brand it. The lack of a collective organization has been highlighted by the authors as one of the reasons for this situation. In products with relatively lower number of producers, authenticity is ensured as the supply is controlled. However, the small holders/enterprises could be helped through collective organization with clear functions and strategies.

The authors have highlighted interesting evidences of GI products from other countries, indicating the way a societal trust based on good will and quality has been built on standards of production. Quality and authenticity guarantee system helps the customer to buy the product repeatedly. As the authors have emphasized, such guarantee system has to collectively evolve, leaving no place for free riding by unscrupulous competitors who tend to take advantage of the reputation that has already been created.

Standards of production here does not mean uniform industrial products but products with innovations where the capacity of producers to innovate and modify their products is not lost and the innate creativeness of the artisans or producers is not compromised. Standards here emphasize quality and authenticity that is guaranteed by the producers. These hold the key to success for both the producer and the consumer. If the consumers' attention is brought towards the products that are locally produced, much-needed revival of the products in agriculture and handicrafts will take place. Such revival will check the erosion of the GI goods from the consumers' memory. Thus, an inclusive consumption may help in retaining the diversity of local ecosystems, culture, artisanal skills, and traditional knowledge system. It may also promote innovation with in the traditionally evolved knowledge and skill base by blending new designs, domain applications, and, wherever needed, new tools. I compliment the authors in drawing our attention to these possibilities by suggesting new policies and institutional initiatives.

Anil K. Gupta
Ahmedabad
19 October 2018

Preface

This book arises out of the two studies sponsored by the Indian Council of Social Science Research (ICSSR) on the broad theme of Geographical Indications. The study titled *Socio-economic Implications of Protecting Handicrafts through Geographical Indications: A Case Study of Selected Products from Southern States* was awarded to N. Lalitha (ICSSR Ref. No. 02/01/2011/RPR) and *Socio-economics of Geographical Indications in the Indian Handloom Sector: A Case Study of Pochampally* (ICSSR Ref No. F. No. 2-021/2010-RP dated 16 March 2011) was awarded to Soumya Vinayan. The seed for this book was sown during a chance meeting at Hyderabad that opened up possibilities of collaborative research leading to compiling our thoughts as a volume on GI.

GI could be used as a tool to achieve development in a specific area, as once the GI registered product achieves market popularity, the producers and other stakeholders strive through collective action to ensure quality and create entry barriers to avoid free riders. This process results in the stakeholders deriving appropriate economic returns and the region receiving greater attention. These do not happen in isolation though: there are a variety of challenges in achieving each of the step mentioned above as strategies designed for agricultural products may not work for handicraft products. One question that often comes up in discussions on GI is: does the GI protect the area or the product? The response is that GI secures the rights of the producers of a product in a specified area. Because, when a product X from an area Y is registered with GI, producers of X from other areas need not stop producing their product, but they may not call themselves as producers of

X from Y. Governance, collective action, and consumer awareness are key aspects for the successful use of GI protection. We do recognize that there are challenges and obstacles and not all the products registered with GI would have market potential. This book discusses the challenges and locates possible areas of targeted measures so that products that are on the verge of extinction get required attention for the same, and producers of products that are already in the market are able to establish measures to safeguard the GI uniqueness. We hope this book raises more debates on GI among the researchers, draws attention of the policymakers as well as curiosity from the readers to understand and use the GI products.

Acknowledgements

Research work in the area of GI began with the support of the ICSSR, New Delhi, which sponsored two studies to be conducted by us at Gujarat Institute for Development Research (GIDR) and Council for Social Development (CSD), respectively. These two projects gave us wonderful opportunities to meet with a few of India's finest craftspersons and a chance to witness the production process. We are thankful to the ICSSR for this opportunity. The artisans generously spent their valuable productive time to discuss with us the nuances of the crafts and answered all our novice questions. Discussion with these artisans also taught us to appreciate the rich culture present in different states and instilled in us a burning desire to learn about all the products registered with GI. Officials from the Tamil Nadu Handicraft Development Corporation and Karnataka State Handicrafts Development Corporation were happy to discuss with us the strategies of the government in promoting handicrafts. The marketing managers of Poompuhar: Premkumar at Chennai, Arumugam at Swamimalai, and Venkata Rao at Lepakshi, Vijayawada, were very helpful in connecting us with the artisans.

We also thank the officials at the Directorate of Handlooms and Textiles, the then Government of Andhra Pradesh, Hyderabad, as well as officials at several handloom cooperative societies and traders/ traders' association in the districts of Nalgonda and Warangal, and the Handloom Park at Gundlapochampally. Most importantly, we are extremely indebted to Tadaka Yadagiri and his team for their assistance in conducting the meticulous fieldwork and their insights about the relevance of GI for the sector in particular and about the issues and challenges faced by the hand-weaving community in general, without which the study on Pochampalli would have been incomplete.

We also express our sincere thanks to S.K. Soam, principal scientist, ICM Division, National Academy Agricultural Research Management (NAARM), Hyderabad, and Bhavin Kothari, senior faculty, National Institute of Design, Ahmedabad, for their insightful comments and suggestions on an earlier draft of two of the chapters. Their critical comments helped us to improvize the chapters considerably. We thank the officials at IPR Cell of Andhra Pradesh Technology and Development and Promotion Centre (APTDC), especially Subhajit Saha and S. Ravi for the several rounds of discussion on facilitating the process of registration of GIs and the relevance of protection under GIs in India. Chinna Raja Naidu, deputy registrar, Trademarks and Geographical Indications, and Prashanth Kumar Bhairappanavar, senior examiner, Trademarks and Geographical Indications, were always available for any query. We are grateful to both of them. Discussions with Ashoke Chatterjee, former director, National Institute of Design, Ahmedabad, were very helpful in focusing on specific issues related to crafts.

Findings of these studies were presented at GIDR, CSD, Gujarat National Law University, Gandhinagar, and other academic forums. We are thankful to our colleagues for their comments and the inspiring academic atmosphere. The library staff at GIDR: Minal Sheth, Vyas and Dinesh, the library staff at GIDR; Satya Nagesh at CSD; Anil Kumar, librarian, Asha Desai and Viral, staff in the library of Indian Institute of Management, Ahmedabad, have been very helpful. Delphine Marie Vivien of CIRAD, France, and Tapan Rout from Textile Committee, Mumbai, helped us with the latest articles on GI at the crucial time.

We thank R. Parthasarathy, director, GIDR, and Kalpana Kannabiran, director, CSD, who supported us wholeheartedly in this endeavour of working on this book. We sincerely thank them for their constant support and encouragement.

We are thankful to Aarti Oza, Gani Memon, Ila Mehta, and Urmi Patel from GIDR for helping us in collecting the information from the GI journals meticulously. Megha Sanghvi provided very useful research support. We also thank Shaji S. from University of Hyderabad who has often helped us in procuring relevant material from the Indira Gandhi Memorial Library at University of Hyderabad.

The administrative staff at GIDR—Nair, Kunal, and Prashant—and P. Sanjiv Rao at CSD, facilitated our travel to the field sites and ensured the smooth conduct of the studies. Sheela Devdas and Girija Balakrishnan helped with word processing and Mr Dixit helped in photocopying the materials at GIDR while we thank P. Kumar, Y.S.S. Prasad, Mahalakshmi and P. Lalitha Kumari from CSD for their assistance with data entry, processing, and formatting during the period of field study. Special thanks to Rukmani Kumar for sharing with us the photograph of a 130-year-old Thanjavur painting.

We are thankful to the OUP team for working with us on this project. Our sincere thanks are also due to the two anonymous referees for their constructive comments on an earlier draft that helped us to revise the manuscript substantially. We are also grateful to Sugeeta Roy Choudhury for her meticulous proofreading, which helped us to improvise the draft.

We continuously draw support and strength from our parents, family members, and respective life partners, and their endless faith encourage us to a great extent. Special thanks to Gargi, Aiyswarya, and Hethal for constantly asking us the question, 'when will you complete the book?'.

While we have benefitted a lot from all the persons mentioned here, any lacuna in the analysis rests with us alone.

An Overview of Geographical Indications

The focus of this book is to understand the development potential of geographical indications (GI) in the Indian context. The term GI is a recent concept, whereas, traditionally, place names have prevailed. Place names, which reflect the cultural identity of the associated places, have been in vogue all over the world. India, with her vast history and biodiversity, has several products known by their place names to boast of—for example, Kancheepuram sari and Darjeeling tea. These place names, known as Geographical Indications (GIs) in the intellectual property rights (IPR) parlance, indicate the link between the geographic location and the product. GIs represent the collective right of the communities engaged in the production of goods within a specific territory. GI bridges the gap of information asymmetry between the consumers and producers, and, thereby increases the demand for the product, while it helps preserve the social, cultural, and environmental resources of the region where the rights are collectively held by all the producers of the product within a defined geographical region. In the realm of trade, GIs are denominations, which signal the origin of the product that is indistinguishable from quality that serves as a 'brand' by itself. This entitlement belongs to only those producers who operate within a specified region and thus it excludes members outside a geographical area. Hence, a few of the sustainable development goals such as reducing poverty, empowerment of women, creating sustainable cities and communities can be achieved by the commercial utilization of GI. Realizing this, different agencies of United Nations have started to include GIs as a development tool to cope with poverty, while development aid for less developed countries has been introduced to support regional branding of goods for food products or handicrafts (UNCTAD, 2015, p. 17).

Though GI has been in vogue for long, particularly in the European countries, it is a relatively recent phenomenon for the developing countries, and the discussion with reference to them is newly emerging in this field. There are arguments for and against the relevance of GI in the context of developing countries. While those in favour of GI argue about its development potential, its role in rural development, protection of biodiversity, and so on, the critics of GI argue that GI is an 'institutional monocropping' mechanism and the cost of implementing GI is more than the gains it would deliver. There are merits in both the arguments. Hence, developing countries might not be able to adopt a 'one size fits all' policy and may have to weigh the merits of different cases.

In this introductory chapter, an attempt has been made to present the relevant issues concerning both the for- and against- standpoints on GIs. In doing so, the section 'International Protection' briefly mentions the evolution of the term GI in international agreements. The rationale and characteristics of GI are presented in the section 'Rationale of GIs'. The section 'Potentials of GI' presents the potentials of GI while the section 'Limitations of GI' highlights its limitations. The evolution of the sui generis system of GI protection in India is discussed in the section 'Evolution of Sui Generis System of GI in India'. The section 'Methodologies Adopted in Understanding the Impact of GI' presents the methodological aspects of measuring the impact of GIs. The focus of the book and the chapter schemes are presented in the sections 'Focus of the Book' and 'Chapter Schemes' respectively, and the limitations of the volume are enumerated in the section 'Limitations of the Volume'.

International Protection

The evolution of the term GI is traced in the discussion on international agreements governing intellectual property by Nair and Kumar (2005).[1] The first multilateral agreement known as the Paris Convention for the

Protection of Industrial Property ('Paris Convention') 1883, provided for the protection of 'indications of source' and 'appellations of origin', yet did not define 'indications of source' or 'appellations of origin' and did not use the term GI.

The Convention broadened the scope of industrial property to include, not only industry and commerce, but, also agricultural and extractive industries and further manufactured or natural products. Thus, the broadened scope extends to manufactured and processed items like wines, grains, tobacco leaf, fruits, cattle, minerals, mineral waters, beer, flowers, and flour. The Madrid Agreement also does not use the term 'geographical indications' and uses only the term 'Indications of Source'. The Lisbon Agreement for the Protection of Appellations of Origin and their International Registration (1958), though was the first of such Agreements to define the term 'appellations of origin', but it did not use the term 'geographical indications'. Article 2(1) of the Agreement defines 'appellations of origin' to mean 'the geographical name of a country, region, or locality, which serves to designate a product originating therein, the quality and characteristics of which are exclusively or essentially due to the geographical environment, including natural and human factors'. Hence, the essential conditions for an appellation of origin to be protected under the Agreement are that it has to have a geographical name and the quality and characteristics of such appellation of origin should be essentially linked to the geographical area.

Article 22.1 of the TRIPS Agreement uses the term GI and defines geographical indications as follows:

Indications which identify a good as originating in the territory of a member, or a region or locality in that territory, where a given quality, reputation or other characteristic of the good is essentially attributable to its geographical origin.

Articles 22 to 24 of Section 3 of the TRIPS Agreement provide the basic principles guiding GI. The TRIPS Agreement is not prescriptive regarding GI. Both the important terms in Article 22.1—reputation and characteristic—are not defined by the Agreement and left to the interpretation of the member countries. Therefore, WTO members are free to determine the right option to implement GI.

At the regional level, the European Council uses the Protected Designation of Origin (PDO) and Protected Geographical Indications

(PGI) to protect the origin-linked agricultural product and food stuffs. A PDO[2] has been defined under Article 2(2)(a) to mean the name of a region, a specific place, or a country used to describe an agricultural product or foodstuff originating in that region, the quality or characteristics of which are essentially or exclusively due to a particular geographical environment with its inherent natural and human factors, and the production, processing, and preparation of which takes place in the defined geographical area. A PGI has been defined under Article 2(2)(b) of the Regulation to mean the name of a region, a specific place, or a country used to describe an agricultural product or a foodstuff originating in that region which possesses a specific quality, reputation, or other characteristics attributable to that geographical origin, and the production and/or processing and/or preparation of which takes place in the defined geographical area. Non-Agricultural products are protected by a community trademark. A PDO/PGI not recognized by the European Union (EU) will lose its protection in the member state. In addition to the geographical names, images of famous mountains, flags, monuments, and folkloric symbols are also used to identify GIs. For instance, Bocksbeutel (a German noun) denotes the specific shape of the bottles used by EU for wines from specified areas in Germany, Greece, Italy, and Portugal (Vandecandelaere et al., 2009–10, p. 31).

Other Forms of Protection

Countries also choose to protect their products through certification/collective/trademark. Certification trademark certifies that the goods conform to certain standards that are laid down and enforced by the proprietor of the mark. Generally, the proprietor does not carry on the business or use the mark, but merely licenses the mark for use to those who want to use it and ensures that the standards are met by all the licensees.

Collective marks are usually understood to be owned by an association and any member of such association may use the collective mark to indicate membership of such association which own the mark.

Using the private law approach, United States, Canada, Australia, Japan, and a few African countries use the trademark laws to protect GIs. The sui generis system is popular among African and Asian countries.

India is one of the countries which has adopted a sui generis system that is discussed later in this chapter.

Rationale of GIs

The economic rationale for GIs is the correction of a market failure caused by the information gap between sellers and buyers. In other words, GI institutionalizes the reputation of a product, where, due to information asymmetries, free riding on reputation of a product happens. In the presence of asymmetry of information, both consumers and producers make use of 'reputation' as a coping device—the former through repeat purchases and the latter through adoption of strategies to create and sustain 'reputation'. Reputation can improve market efficiency only by avoiding the impact of information asymmetries, if it is protected through a process of 'institutionalization of reputation' (Bramley et al., 2013). This institutionalization takes place by way of legal instruments (such as GIs) that formalize the nexus between a product's attributes and its region of origin.

The concept of reputation has been used widely in the analysis of markets with imperfect information (Bramley & Kirsten, 2007; Stiglitz, 1989; Tirole, 1988). Shapiro, in his model on reputation, shows that a firm's choices about production to maximize profit is assumed under perfect competition but imperfect information (OECD, 2000). Reputation signifies expectations on quality to such an extent that consumers tend to use the quality of products offered in the past as a benchmark for future levels of quality (Bramley & Kirsten, 2007) and decide their choice. Thus, a value assessment develops over time, leading to price premiums. As mentioned earlier, GIs reflect the inherent link between quality and region. Territory, in this context, becomes not just a signifier of information but a characteristic of an attribute (Pacciani et al., 2001). This leads to the development of an improved market access for origin-labelled products through the creation of niche markets, monopoly information, and value addition (Bramley & Kirsten, 2007). Globalization and the abundance of substitute products have led to efforts on the part of the producers to create a niche area for themselves based on the geographical origin of their products. The GI tag provides an opportunity to create a niche area that functions well in market places with industrial or uniform bulk products

(Hayes et al., 2003) and have the potential to resist the 'erasure of place' (Rangnekar, 2011).

Characteristics of GI

GIs are defined as a collective good (Arfini, 1999; Belletti, 1999; Moran, 1993) or a club good (Thiedig & Sylvander, 2004, pp. 428–37), where a club is 'a voluntary group of individuals who derive benefits from sharing the production costs, the membership characteristics or a good characterized by excludable benefits' (Thiedig & Sylvander, 2004). The main characteristics of a club good are: (a) only those producers who adhere to the specifications of the GI product are allowed to use the indication; (b) the use of the GI by one does not diminish the same for another. Rangnekar (2004) explains the categorization of GIs as a club good where non-members to the collective are excluded, based on criteria such as specification of production process that institutionalizes eligibility of membership to the club. Further, members of the collective club compete with other producers outside the membership which leads to product differentiation. Thus, GIs belong to the economics of monopolistic competition wherein the market appears to be a network of connected small sub-markets, each with one seller. Differentiation leads generally to an increase of production and sales costs, because differentiation cannot create a preference if information is not provided to the buyer, and, in the case of GI, the exclusion mechanism, which includes labelling and specification, are the extra costs. Thus, GI are aptly considered to be collective monopolies in the neo-classical economics sense (Moran, 1993). This emphasizes the need for collective actions. Collective action requires that all producers along the supply chain adhere to the quality standard which signifies the quality or reputation. Therefore, any 'opportunistic' behaviour on the part of any producers can damage the reputation of the indication (Prisoner's Dilemma).[3] Thus, there exists the problem of 'free riding' wherein producers do not conform to the quality standards of the products but, through various ways and means, 'free ride' on the reputation of the goods.[4] The more the consumers are aware of the GI product, the higher will be the price (Gal, 2017) or the rent received by the territorial region (Belletti et al., 2001). The success of GI is influenced by three factors: (1) higher price paid for the GI product as reflected by the hedonic price index; (2)

higher the GI production area (restricted through entry barriers) compared to the excluded area, higher will be the revenue per hectare for the GI product; and (3) the success of the collective action will be more when the homogeneity among the producers group is high (Gal, 2017). In other words, usurpation of rights of the producer who has built reputation over time linking quality with the origin, has been recognized as unfair and this becomes the core of treating GIs as IPR.

Jena and Grote (2010) emphasize that the uniqueness of the product is intrinsically related to the geo-climatic characteristics and the use of traditional skills. Thus, the focus is on the use of local resources and the non-replicable nature of the produce. Jena and Grote identify four justifications for considering GIs as IPR—equity, conservation concerns, preservation of traditional practices and culture, and prevention of misappropriation. Therefore, GIs, like other IPs, provide a bundle of rights to the proprietors. These are control of the resource, the right to determine the conditions of use and the right to exclude (Dagne, 2012, p. 381). GI also works as a tool to protect the traditional knowledge (TK) and skilled labour of a particular region because, most often, GI is associated with the products that are available in a particular region as well as with human resources which knows the utility value of such products. But to protect the TK in GI, (a) the product should be in tangible form, (b) the knowledge available should be associated with a particular area, and (c) the product must enjoy commercial reputation (Singhal, 2008). Particularly, GI would help in preserving the TK, only if the product's unique qualities depend on local traditional knowledge. The TK will be lost when the TK in the product is abandoned or modified (Hughes, 2009). The neglect of TK or its substantial modification by resource rich producers, who might introduce newer technologies in the production of GI product, would lead to the small producers getting disintegrated from the GI system completely.

Role of Government in GI

Marie-Vivien and Bienabe (2017) talk about the different levels of governance in GI that require the involvement of the state at the (i) international or meta, (ii) national or macro, (iii) product or micro, and (iv) meso level which connects the national and the product levels. At the international level, WTO members adhere to the TRIPS Agreement, while, nations which want protection of their GIs in foreign lands are also party to the Lisbon Agreement. While the EU GI system governs all the EU members, the African Intellectual Property Organization (OAPI) governs East and Central Africa. The GI rules formulated by OAPI are applicable to all the seventeen member countries, as they do not have individual national systems. Therefore, GI registrations done by OAPI are applicable in all the 17 countries. Besides this, the authors observe the prevalence of free trade/bilateral agreements that offer protection to the signatories. At the national level, as mentioned earlier, the trademark system or the sui generis system prevails. China provides an interesting case where trademark as well as two sui generis systems prevail to protect the GIs. The sui generis systems in China are with the Quality Regulatory Authority and the Ministry of Agriculture respectively. The meso level discussed by the authors deals with defining the eligibility to file application, examination of the application, and opposing and checking of the counterfeit GIs.

The role of the state is very important in the design and implementation of a legal framework and in creating a facilitating environment (Quinones-Ruiz et al., 2016). Marie-Vivien (2015) and Marie-Vivien et al. (2017) provide the historical perspective of the role of the state in the protection of the GIs in the context of France where it all began and declined over a period. The year 1905 was the beginning of the law in France that provided for protection against the fraudulent indications of the source and origin of products in the agro-food sector. As the courts had no knowledge of the agro-food products, a new law created the National Committee for Appellations of Origin for Wines and Spirits whose members were producers of wines and spirits. In 1947, this committee came to be known as the National Institute of Appellations of Origin (known as INAO, the French acronym) under the Ministry of Agriculture. This Appellations of Origin (AO) which was originally limited to wines and spirits was extended to the entire agro-food sector in the 1990s. The European community adopted this in 1992 as Protection of Geographical Origin (PGI) and Protection of Designation of Origin (PDO). As a member of the EU, France had to introduce only PGI, as PDO was similar to AO. PGIs required third party certification and used to be directly managed by the Ministry of Agriculture while PDO was managed by INAO. In a policy change, the management of PGI was also changed to INAO in 1999, and the requirement of third party certification was removed in 2006.

In 2005, a major amendment in the EU law was made to comply with the decision of the WTO dispute settlement body. The regulation of 2006 had controls at two levels, macroscopic and microscopic. The macroscopic level focused on controls by a suitable authority of the member state. Controls at the microscopic level concern the monitoring of compliance with the specifications for each PDO/PGI, which may be a suitable expert authority of the member state or a product certification agency or even an independent agency. France also made amendments to its rules following the EU amendment. As per this, INAO became the National Institute of Origin and Quality, with twenty-five branches and five committees. These committees were for appellation of: wines and spirits, wines and ciders, dairy products, food and forestry, organic agriculture and PGI, label rouge, and traditional specialities guaranteed. These committees had the representatives from producers/processors of different products that were benefitting from PDO/PGI. INAO also consists of an approval and control board that enacts control principles for all the products. INAO's governing board decides on the strategy and budget. As the EU shifted from public authority-based controls to controls by private certification bodies, France also followed the same, by shifting from controls by INAO to controls by certification bodies. It also allowed coordination of the different controls and certification mechanisms between PDOs and PGIs. Marie-Vivien et al. (2017) observe that since the reform of 2006, which marginalized local INAO offices in controls, their support in drafting the GI specifications started declining, reflecting the lack of balance in the sharing of responsibilities between the public and private stakeholders. Such changes resulted in: reduced budget of INAO; third party certification leading to the standardization of GIs as the emphasis was on checking the conformity with the predetermined standard checklist which underplays the link with the region and the typicity of the product. The decline in the importance of INAO also meant a lack of transparency in the meetings held. Neither the debates of the committees nor the reports of the enquiry committees were published. As certifications of quality was emphasized over region, the role played by the branches of INAO in different places reduced. As the registration of GIs for non-agricultural products is with the National Institute of Intellectual Property, INAO's role has become very insignificant. This narrative signifies that the adoption of the EU style of regulations in the context of France, has diluted the role of public–private partnership in establishing the link with region, and the emergence of private certifications is now playing an important role.

Marie-Vivien (2015) discusses the significant role of the Indian government in filing GI applications, which is discussed in Chapter 3 of this book.

Potentials of GI

Marie-Vivien and Bienabe (2017) lucidly describe the multidimensional role of GI due to which GIs are not just IPRs but a policy instrument. Citing different studies, in a nutshell, these authors summarize the role of GI as a tool to alleviate poverty and promote biodiversity, marketing of quality-based goods, employment, rural development, sustainable production practices, and tourism. In an ex-ante and ex-post study of the potential GI benefits (Soam & Sastry, 2008), producers believed that GI certification would help them to revive their focus on GI products and leave other livelihood strategies as it would improve their socio-economic status. Improved product demand, brand value, and reduced competition from competing duplicates are some of the benefits of GI registration (Nanda et al., 2013).

GI as a Rural Development Tool

One of the explicit objectives of EUs policy on GI is to promote rural areas (United Nations Industrial Development Organization, 2010). Case studies indicate that such origin-linked products from rural areas generate relatively more positive externalities than negative externalities on the production territory (United Nations Industrial Development Organization, 2010, p. 22). Origin-linked products being a viable tool of rural development depends on the importance of the product to the local economy and the endogenous factors or the amount of local resources that go into the making of the product or the value chain. These factors contribute to the increasing popularity of the product, attracting tourism (Pacciani et al., 2001) and can contribute to the promotion of the other 'place goods' from the region. The contributions of origin-linked products to rural development include not only agricultural growth and agri-business development, but also the development of other local activities, the social aspects and empowerment of local actors (community participation in the definition of objectives, social equity and growth, the local population's confidence, and the role of local resources) (Vandecandelaere et al., 2009–10, p. 19). Belletti et al. (2001) call this extended territorial strategy. Taking the case of agro-foods, they discuss the merits of using the supply chain and the extended territorial strategies in promoting rural development. In the supply chain strategy, when the geographical name of the product per se has value among the consumers, actors in the supply chain create barriers to restrict competition and get involved in collective action to 'increase the rent' due to the geographical name of the product. The pitfall in such a supply chain strategy could be the dilution of the product specification and characteristics arising from the lack of consensus on product specification leading to opening the product to competition from similar products. In the extended territorial strategy, the diversified range of economic activities revolves around the PDO/PGI product within the local economy. The success of the extended territorial strategy however depends on the intensity of the link between the product and the local community. Colombian coffee is an example where promotion of the brand resulted in associated development like setting up of a National Coffee Park. This park, which was developed for the promotion of Colombian coffee traditions and culture, has become an asset for the economic development of the area due to the design of various activities to attract consumers such as coffee museum, botanical path, and other attractions (Vandecandelaere et al., 2009–10).

In the context of the EU, Bramley (2011) notes that more than 70 per cent of all the registered GIs are linked with economically lagging regions and, therefore, GIs are likely to support rural development in such regions. Lagging regions that focus on superior quality goods authenticated by geographical origin and traceability could be linked with the regional and national markets (Libery & Kneafsay, 1998). Libery and Kneafsay also point out that after the 1990 Food Safety Act by the UK, emphasis on standards of production and traceability have become important aspects for the consumers and the producers. A GI certified product with strong emphasis on the use of 'quality and local resources' in the making of the product, can reach a specific and sustainable market, which rewards it with premium price and recognition. Thus, the objectives of GI and rural development converge in realizing the market potential of local resources through sustainable use. Moreover, the major concern of policymakers across the world today is to lessen out-migration from rural to urban areas, especially distress migration, and the production and marketing of 'rural cultural distinction' has become a catchword in local development strategies (Coombe, 2005). Citing Belletti and Marescotti (2006), Vandecandelaere et al. (2009–10) describe the case of Lardo di Colonnata (Italy) which is the maturing of pig fat using marble tub. In this case, production was restricted to small number of producers of Lardo (pig fat) in the village of Colonnata, which acquired notoriety and reputation in the 1990s. This resulted in an increase in the associated economic activities like tourism, attracting the youth who had emigrated earlier to come back and start new economic activities. Similarly, recognition of the quality of the Cotija cheese of Mexico by the consumers resulted in increasing the price and checked the migration of the producers (Vandecandelaere et al., 2009–10).

Sylvander (2004) cautions that the institutionalization of the resource origin alone does not set the conditions for development. Instead, he argues that development depends on how the process is established and on the effectiveness of the strategies built upon it. These strategies could be defining production methods and area, quality standards, implementation, authentication, and traceability enforced by institutions owned by the stakeholders themselves or external agencies (Hayes et al., 2003; Soam & Sastry, 2008). In the EU and Latin American context, GI products have been linked to the rural development strategies and this has resulted in: (a) strengthening the producer associations who have filed the GI applications; (b) specific standards for production of the GI product that are strictly followed by all the identified authorized users; and (c) setting up of quality councils that certify the products resulting in a highly distinguished premium market for the GI products. Depending on the rightful beneficiaries who develop or market the product and the relative reputation of the product (local, national, international), the need and efficacy of the protection is determined (Folkeson, 2005). In other words, the creation of value, based on these regional identities, is dependent on the ability of the producers to coordinate the production process (capacity to form an association and implementing the standards of production), strengthening vertical linkages and fostering trust through an institutional mechanism (Bowen, 2010; Lalitha, 2014; Rich, 2011; Vinayan, 2012).

GI as a Tool to Protect Biodiversity

Lalitha and Vinayan (2017) discuss the potential of registering more GIs using the inventory of People's Biodiversity Register, which may be used to build the local economy. Vandecandelaere et al. (2009–10) present the case of the Neuquen Criollo Goat of Argentina, protected under the FAO inventory of Biological Diversity. The FAO programme led to the identification of the breed, its genetic make-up, and in establishing its relation to the local environment. This programme also brought out the importance of the natural and cultural factors that are linked to geographical origin in giving the meat its specific quality, which subsequently resulted in getting the breed protected under GI.

Positive environmental externalities like protection of biodiversity may not be directly attributed to GIs and the impact could vary from case to case (Bramley, 2011). Because of the reputation of a natural resource coming from a particular region, there is the possibility of increased commercialization of a GI product which could have a chain effect of increase in the harvest value of a product and income to the farmers. In the case of resources concerning the GI product coming from an ecologically fragile region, there are chances of two extreme behaviours by agents who exploit such resources. On the one hand, there is the possibility of rational land use and rational resource use taking into account the fragile nature of the natural resources. On the other hand, the likely increase in demand due to the popularity of the GI product could also lead to the situation of the 'tragedy of commons' and result in pressure on the resource (Lalitha, 2014). But GI recognition of products which are not commercially traded results in documentation of the detailed production process which would be useful for future generations.

Marketing of GI Products to Exploit Price Potentials

The market remuneration of GI products should yield higher than the normal profits as these club goods have to spend on creating, enforcing, and communicating the standards to the consumers which contributes to maintaining the reputation value of the GI product. Indirectly, the market strategies also help in preventing the product disappearing from the production/consumption list due to competition.

For the GI to be successful, it must be backed by a guarantee system as well, particularly with reference to the efforts translated as 'code of practices' followed by different stakeholders in the value chain, to maintain the reputation of the product and traceability of the product to its origin. In the case of Colombian coffee, where the GI denotes the entire country, covering approximately 14,80,000 hectares distributed among 590 municipalities with an average of 1.5 hectare per farmer, the PDO was obtained by the National Federation of Colombian Coffee Growers (FNC). FNC is a non-profit organization. It developed a data base system to trace the following: plots, locations, varieties, and practices; processors and roasters registering and performing technical tests to audit information on equipment, processes, and capacity; certificates for transport agents carrying the coffee to be exported, and registration of exporters with the Ministry for Economy, Industries, and Tourism (cited in Vandecandelaere et al., 2009–10, p. 73). Such a database will help in branding the coffee according to locations or varieties and practices to add more value. Precisely this is what is being done by the FNC, where it is establishing sub-brands under the Colombian and Juan Valdez brands in the export market. These are not based on geographical areas but based on land types: Colina (hill), Sierra (mountain), and Volcan (Volcano) (Hughes, 2009), and also based on characteristics such as sustainability, preservation of biodiversity, origin–sub-regions within Colombia, and special care in the production process. The fact that there is a spurt in trade in Colombian exports of speciality coffee (from 200,000 bags in 2002 to 750,000 bags in 2007 (Vandecandelaere et al., 2009–10, p. 109)) indicate the demand for such products in the world market.

Different types of guarantee or certification systems prevail. Third party verification (such as Fairtrade, Utz, Rainforest Alliance), involving considerable amount of documentation and cost for small holder cultivation is nevertheless popular among international coffee growers. But in GI products, it should be noted that certification by these standard agencies require adhering to their prescribed practices. But the GI producers are standard makers than standard takers (Marie-Vivien & Bienabe, 2017) as GI deals with the producers of local assets. Certifications, in contrast, confirms that the product of regional reputation also conforms to environmental and labour standards, appealing to the section of consumers who pay attention to the environmental and ethical aspects of production at the time of purchase.

Participatory guarantee system (PGS)[5] is popular in the small agricultural landholding systems. PGS is based on the active participation of stakeholders at different levels of GI value chain like producers, traders, or government authorities. Based on trust, social networks and knowledge exchange, PGS is essentially managed by a group of stakeholders (Vandecandelaere et al., 2009–10, p. 74).

When collective organization is involved in the marketing of the product, multiple options could be explored. Depending on the resources, market assessment surveys could be undertaken to find out about the consumers' willingness to pay, preferences and competition. Following the assessment, an appropriate strategy could be made to set up direct marketing outlets, or in collaboration with a local super market to sell in the domestic market, or through exporters to understand the receptivity of the consumers in the export market. The Government of Thailand organizes a GI-week every year in which the GI producer is given space in leading shopping malls to sell their products (Lalitha, 2016). This strategy helps in popularizing the GI label, product, and awareness among the consumers, and it also helps the producer to understand the consumer preferences. Two modes are observed here: First, where the producer organization itself sets up marketing outlets and directly reaches out to the consumers (widely popular); second, the producer organization may also enter into an agreement with a local supermarket or an exporter to sell the products on terms agreed upon by the producer organization, either in the local market or in the export market.

The example of Colombian coffee is very useful since it is a product from a developing country that was launched successfully in the developed country markets. The efforts to internationalize the brand of Colombian coffee began in 1932 when the Colombian President passed an order that all coffee exports from Colombia should be labelled as 'Café de Colombia'. But, a consumer survey in the 1950s showed that only 4 per cent of the surveyed consumers were aware of Colombian coffee, despite the US being Colombia's largest market for coffee. Following this, marketing strategies were aggressively launched and first and foremost important strategy was the creation of an imaginary character 'Juan Valdez', in the 1960s. The character Juan Valdez personified the Colombian coffee farmer and was registered as a trademark in the US. In the late 1970s, a certification mark was also obtained with a few standards like the coffee was (a) grown in Colombia, (b) subject to inspection, and (c) approved for export to the US. By 2008, it was recognized that Juan Valdez was the world's biggest coffee icon. Strengthened by the popularity of the Juan Valdez brand, a chain of Juan Valdez coffee shops, which originally began in Colombia, was set up across the US and the Europe. By 2007, a PGI was also registered in the European Union for Colombian Coffee, the first non-EU product to get PGI in the EU (Hughes, 2009, pp. 82–4).

Price Potentials of GI

One of the purposes of creating entry barriers for the non-GI producers is to create a niche market for the GI products to command a premium price for the GI product. While the gap between the legal protection and the actual enforcement could determine the premium a product would receive, the role played by advertising cannot be undermined and thus it could be a task to quantify the value generated by GI alone (Hughes, 2009). It is also true that the success of GI depends on consumer interest. Thus, more consumers would be willing to buy a GI protected product and pay a premium price for the same if it reduces their search cost. Thus, GI bridges the information asymmetry between the consumers and the producers.

'Ceylon Tea' is the most popular GI of Sri Lanka and is one of the three largest foreign exchange earners for the country. It generated an annual income of around USD 1.5 billion in 2013–14 (Sharma & Kulhari, 2015, p. 47). In the Indian context, looking at the trends in Pochampalli textile products between 2004 and 2009, Rout (2014) points out that the growth rate of production, employment, productivity, and sales turnover increased by 14.09, 8.46, 8.47, and 17.33 per cent respectively. Further, prices of Pochampalli products like silk and cotton saris and cotton fabrics witnessed a growth rate of 17.4, 13, and 12.6 per cent respectively. Similarly, both the Chanderi and Kota Doria weavers had reported earning higher incomes after GI registration (Sharma & Kulhari, 2015).

Consumers' preference for the GI products is also reflected in their willingness to pay premium price. Forty-three and 8 per cent of the consumers in the EU were willing to pay a 10 and 20 per cent premium respectively for a product with GI labelling (Berenguer, 2004). Menapace et al. (2009) conducted a study on the GI impact for extra virgin olive oil. Though this study found that (a) consumers' willingness to pay varies across different countries of origin, (b) within a country, consumers preferred GI labels to non-GI ones. Several other studies such as Bonnet and Simioni (2001) with respect to Camembert cheese from France, Fotopoulos and Krystallis (2003) for apples in Greece, Hassan and Monier-Dilhan (2006) in the case of ham from France, found that origin labelling of either PDO or PGI were fetching higher value. Similar results were also seen for hessian apple wine (Tueber, 2009), wherein the majority of the consumers reported that GI supports local producers by safeguarding their traditional cultural assets and almost half of the consumers were willing to pay more for Hessian apple wine with GI. Reviron et al. (2009) cite examples to show that developing country GI products are in many instances sold at premium prices in the European supermarkets.

Lourerio and McClusky (2000), who used the hedonic price model to calculate consumers' willingness to pay for Spanish meat and Galician veal with PGI label, found that the label applied to high quality cuts of meat increased their value to premium levels of quality. Outside the EU, a study reveals that Thai consumers' willingness to pay is influenced by the origin of the product rather than the GI labels (Seetisarn & Chiaravutthi, 2011). This implies that Thai consumers value the product's origin but do not recognize the importance of the GI label, which could be attributed to the fact that the legislation on GI in Thailand was relatively recent then and hence the label had not yet emerged as a major signifier of quality and origin. In case of Darjeeling Tea from India, Datta (2010) found in a pilot market survey of small group of consumers in Kolkata that 92 per cent of consumers were ready to pay higher prices for Darjeeling Tea. Similar results could also be seen in the case of Darjeeling Tea (in an experimental auction method) (Vinayan, 2015). In their analysis, Soam and Sastry (2008) point out the clear preference of consumers, where, consumers were willing to pay more for GI agricultural products than non-agricultural products.

Limitations of GI

Although there are evidences from the European nations about successful GIs earning price premiums for their farmers, there are hardly evidences of that kind emerging from the developing economies (UNCTAD, 2015).

GI, like any other IPR, provides the bundle of rights to the owner—the right to control the use of the resource, the purpose for which the resource can be put to use, and the right to exclude others. However, unlike the other IPRs, the rights of the GI cannot be sold or transferred to anyone else (Calboli, 2013) because the production is linked to the geography.

Critics describe the concept of GI as 'institutional monocropping'—a system that has been developed over a long time, and functions in a particular kind of economy is then enforced on developing economies which do not have the similar kind of institutionalization. Establishing the institutions is a costly affair for the developing economies and evidences of protected GIs have not yielded much benefits. It is a long process and the involvement of a third party is essential to make the GI work. Thus, adoption of GIs is effective only if there is already an actual or potential market, or at least competition, for the product in foreign countries (quoted in Dagne, 2012, p. 423). The economic success of the GI products depend on the demand for such products in countries where consumers are willing to pay a premium price. GI registration alone would not be helpful in that. But expensive marketing strategies are required. However, such marketing aspects are neglected in the context of GI debates in developing countries (Hughes, 2009, p. 68).

Kolady et al. (2011) raise doubts about the EU inference that GI would benefit the small landholder producers of agricultural products from developing countries. Their analysis shows that the rural development potential of GI in agricultural products exist but is limited. They argue that in cases where there is limited scope for increasing the production area, benefits of GI will accrue to the landowners. Further, if the production is tightly controlled, benefits will be more but to a small group of relatively wealthy landowners. In GI products that are relatively lesser known, GI quality enhancement would not alter the demand beyond the traditional consumers and hence the revenue distributed would be small.

Tregear et al. (2016) examine three of the global value chain strategies which have both positive and negative effects on GI-protected products, which may be applicable in the developing country context. These strategies are: capturing higher margins for existing products, engaging in collective action, and diversifying into new products. Applying these to PDO protected onions from Maco Hungary, the authors find that few consumers were willing to pay a higher price for the protected onion. Importantly as the protected onion variety's yield and resistance were relatively less compared to the modern varieties, farmers considered the PDO as an 'impediment tied to the old varieties'. Second, the formation of a consortium resulted in delimiting the area and code of practices for the producers. However, the power structure within the consortium varied and the small producers did not have bargaining power. Similarly, diversification into new products and markets did not happen on a large scale for Maco onion, as they require investment. The direct involvement of producers was limited. Based on these, the authors conclude that nascent products like Maco onion have limited potential to contribute to the rural development strategy.

Further, only few developing economies will have the infrastructure and governing system that is equivalent to the *then strong* (emphasis added by authors) French INAO system of governance (Hughes, 2009). A valid concern for small producers in developing countries is that emphasizing production standards for GI products could be counterproductive as small and poor farmers might disengage themselves from the GI production totally because of the conditions laid (Hughes, 2009, p. 116). For instance, in the case of Brazil's first registered product, Pampa Gaucho da Campanha Meridional beef, as the code of practices and standards of production specified were far from reality and hard to follow for family breeders, they remained excluded from the larger producer group (Hughes, 2009, p. 116).

Evolution of the Sui Generis System of GI in India

India focused her attention on GI after the bitter battle involving the patents on Basmati rice filed by a US company. The patents sought for Basmati and granted to the US rice development company Rice Tech in 1997 'included a claim to 90 per cent of the rice's germ plasm and traditional varieties cultivated in India' (Mulik & Crespi, 2011, p. 3). This raised serious concerns about the company riding on the reputation of Basmati rice traditionally grown in the Indo-Gangetic plain spread across India and Pakistan and indicated that the superior quality of the Basmati rice cannot be entirely 'due to a combination of cultivated varieties, climate and pedagogical conditions and local cultural practices of North India and Pakistan' (quoted in Marie-Vivien, 2015, p. 18). Based on the volume of evidence provided by the Indian government against the patent as well as various trademarks such as Texmati and Kasmati filed by Rice Tech in the UK and US, Rice Tech eventually withdrew its claims. The use of Indian style Basmati Rice in its product along with the graphic representation of Taj Mahal clearly indicated that Rice Tech was indeed trying to ride on the reputation of Basmati (Marie-Vivien, 2015, p. 19). In fact, the study by Mulik and Crespi (2011) indicate that with the entry of Rice Tech varieties, the distinctiveness of Indian Basmati rice in major export markets of UK and Kuwait fell, while it did not make much difference in other markets such as the US and Canada where there was little premium for Basmati. India, in the aftermath of the Rice Tech controversy, had to engage in bitter legal battles across 351 cases in India and 211 cases abroad (in 2013) to protect the denomination of Basmati at a whopping cost of Rs. 7.62 crores (Mulik & Crespi, 2011, p. 20). These authors further opine that such costs could have been avoided had India registered Basmati as a GI earlier. In fact, one of the main arguments which Rice Tech raised in its favour was the fact that the word Basmati was not protected as a GI for rice cultivated on the Indian sub-continent and hence could be designated for aromatic rice cultivated anywhere in the world (Marie-Vivien, 2015, p. 19).

Realizing that besides Basmati there are several unique rice varieties and that every region in India has unique products to offer—whether agricultural, handicraft, textile, or food stuff—a property regime that would be best suited for the 'regional products', where geography was the core aspect, became the need of the hour. Moreover, as a signatory to WTO, it became clear that under TRIPS, unless protected by national law, GI cannot be granted reciprocal protection in other countries.

India adopted the sui generis legal framework for providing protection to origin labelled products. The sui generis system is preferred where the existing intellectual property regimes are limited to protect the concept of community rights (Wekesa, 2006) such as in the case of the protection of bio-diversity and traditional knowledge. In this context, among other forms of intellectual property rights, GIs stand distinct as a community right.

The Act was introduced and passed in the Parliament of India in 1999 as Geographical Indications of Goods (Registration and Protection) Act, 1999. In the realm of law, protection available for GI at the national level can be broadly categorized under two main approaches—the public law approach and the private law approach.[6] The public law approach involves exclusive protection of GIs through the 'sui generis' legislation, which in Latin means 'special kind' or 'its own kind'. The sui generis systems are based on stronger state intervention (Marie-Vivien & Bienabe, 2017). Section 2(3) of the GI Act defines geographical indication as follows:

> 'Geographical indication', in relation to goods, means an indication which identifies such goods as agricultural goods, natural goods or manufactured goods as originating, or manufactured in the territory of a country, or a region or locality in that territory, where a given quality, reputation or other characteristic of such goods is essentially attributable to its geographical origin and in case where such goods are manufactured goods, one of the activities of either the production or of processing or preparation of the goods concerned takes place in such territory, region or locality, as the case may be.

It may be observed that while the Indian definition is identical to the TRIPS definition, India has defined the term 'goods' to denote any 'agricultural, natural or manufactured goods, handicraft or food stuff'. The definition of 'good' may be compared with the broad industrial property defined by the Paris convention. The rationale for India to give a broad definition of 'goods' in her sui generis system, is multifarious. India is a gold mine of GI (Vinayan, 2012). In fact, the diversity of the country is best reflected in the production of varieties of goods, natural, or manufactured. The know-how, traditional knowledge, bio-diversity, traditional cultural expressions, and the intersections with geography, history, and culture is pronounced in many of these products. Thus, the Indian GI philosophy goes beyond the concept of 'terroir' (which emphasizes the land and soil connection), that is, fundamental for protection in the EU.

It is important to note that the Indian philosophy of protecting the handicrafts which are not based on any natural factors, has influenced the type of protection offered in the EU and France which were entirely 'terroir' based (Marie-Vivien, 2013). Marie-Vivien (2013) argues that when the link with the region is entirely based on human factors, it is weaker than the link which recognizes both the natural and human factors.

The GI Act states that 'any association of persons or producers or any organization or authority established by or under any law for the time being in force in representing the interest of the producers of the concerned goods, who are desirous of registering a GI in relation to such goods shall apply in writing in such form and in such manner and accompanied by such fees as may be prescribed for the registration of GI' (Chapter 3, 11(1)). The Act provides registration in two parts: Part A relates to the registration of GI and Part B relates to the registration of authorized users/proprietors such as names, addresses, and descriptions indicated. Any person, claiming to be the producer of the goods[7] in respect of which a GI has been registered may apply in writing for registering him as an authorized user of such GI. The *sui generis* system of GIs in India provides a fairly detailed definition of the producer, which suggests the role of multiple stakeholders in any GI product. As per the definition, a producer is a person dealing with three categories of goods: agricultural goods including their production, processing, trading, or dealing; natural goods, including exploiting, trading, or dealing; handicrafts or industrial goods including making, manufacturing, trading, or dealing. This broad definition is justified given the informal nature of GI production enterprises, where most of them function as micro entrepreneurial units. Usually, in India, the GI consists of the name of the place of the origin of the good such as Darjeeling Tea. However, non-geographical names like basmati rice also indicates a GI.

The GI applicant will have to detail how the GI serves to indicate goods from a specific region. Further the applicant has to demonstrate that specific quality, reputation, or other characteristics are exclusively or essentially due to geographical environment with its inherent natural and human factors. The production, processing, or preparation of the said good may also take place in such region or locality. The geographical map of the region or locality, in which the goods originate or are being manufactured, is a must. The GI registry is a quasi-judicial authority whose role is limited to accepting and scrutinizing the application and passing the order regarding the acceptance or rejection of the GI application. If there is any opposition to the GI application after the passing of the order by the registry then such cases will be handled by the Intellectual Property Appellate Board.

Infringement of Registered GIs[8]

A registered GI is infringed by a person if he/she (a) uses such GI to indicate that such goods originate in a geographical area other than the true place of origin of such goods in a manner which misleads the persons as to the geographical origin of such goods; or (b) uses any GI in such manner which constitutes an act of unfair competition, including passing off in respect of a registered GI; or (c) uses another GI to the goods, which falsely represents to the persons that the goods originate in the territory or region in respect of such registered GI.

Rectification of a Registered GI

The registrar or the appellate board may cancel or make changes in the registration of GIs or of an authorized user for the contravention or failure to observe the conditions entered on the register. The registrar and the appellate board can take suo moto action after giving notice to the parties concerned and hearing them before passing appropriate orders cancelling, varying, or rectifying the register.

While the TRIPS Agreement provides additional protection only for wines and spirits, the Indian Act prevents the use of expressions such as 'kind', 'like', 'style', and so on, unless they have been notified by the Central Government. However, such additional protections would be granted based only on application by the applicant (form GI-9). Incidentally, the fee for additional protection is Rs. 25,000, which is much higher than the fees for other forms. Additional protection means that a good which is not originating in a geographical region cannot use the GI word in it (like 'Darjeeling Tea' for a tea originating elsewhere).

With this background, in the following section, a few methodologies that are adopted in understanding the impact of GI are presented.

Methodologies Adopted in Understanding the Impact of GI

Belletti et al. (2011) point out that the GI evaluation requires identification of the purpose for which the GI has been filed to help focus on the field of analysis. As pointed out by a number of researchers, analysing the impact of GI is a complex issue as there would be a number of factors that interact in the production of the GI product and hence segregating the impact of GI from other factors becomes a challenge. Despite these challenges, there are a few approaches available to study the impact of GI.

Methodological Approaches to Analysing the Impact of GI

In this section, we briefly examine the various methodological issues in analysing the impact of GI. These issues have been comprehensively documented by several scholars, especially Belletti et al. (2011) and Bramley et al. (2009). We shall summarize the various methods adopted across the world to analyse the impact of GI.

Bramley et al. (2009) review empirical studies on the economics of GI and segregate them into four: assessing reputational effects; supply chain analysis and transaction costs economics; welfare analysis; and measuring the willingness to pay. Reputational effects focus on the collective reputation of the product, while supply chain analysis and transaction cost economics study the governance mechanism to ensure product specification, traceability, consumer awareness, and branding. Welfare analysis focuses on the effect of legal systems such as GI on re-distribution along the supply chain, while willingness of consumers to pay a premium for GI is captured by measuring the willingness to pay (both hedonic and conjoint analysis).

GI scholars also use the Institutional Analysis and Development (IAD) framework in analysing GI. The IAD framework helps in analysing from the perspective of socio cultural, institutional, and the biophysical nature of the resource. The advantage of the IAD framework is that a range of theoretical perceptions including game theory, institutionalism, and social constructism may be used depending on the case in hand. It enables the researcher to focus on unwritten rules that have evolved by the community, analyse the nature of the resource with respect to its ownership, and trust and reciprocal standards prevalent in the community (McGinnis & Ostrom, 2014). Juxtaposing this with the nature of GI, where natural resources and climatic factor of a region or interplay of natural resources of a region and human skills give uniqueness to a product, it is clear that all the three points mentioned above get covered.

Quinones et al. (2016) adopt the IAD framework in their paper. They explain the biophysical characteristics which describe the chosen products' association with the region, attributes of the GI firms which were involved in the process of filing the GI application for the chosen products, the applicable rules, and the informal rules that have evolved due to the prevailing social norms and customs (Quinones et al. 2016).

Paus and Reviron (2009) summarize several studies which have tried to assess the territorial impact of GI use. They point out that before–after and with–without studies might not explain the impact fully since in the former, the differential impact cannot be attributed to the introduction of GI alone (there could be other external factors such as changes in agricultural policy, for example), while in the case of the latter, it is difficult to operationalize such a method in the context of GI wherein the impact is to be analysed with a counterfactual (a strong control group which has similar characteristics) (Paus & Reviron 2009). They in fact refer to the method adopted by Jena and Grote (2010), where the comparison of GI Basmati rice is undertaken against non-rice producers to analyse the welfare effects. Thus, they deduce that there are 'objective' and 'subjective' methods. The with–without approach (synchronic evaluation) and before–after approach (diachronic) fall under the objective methods, while the studies that adopt 'subjective' method are based on 'grading' the perceived impacts of an intervention. In the case of evolving GI systems, as in the case of most developing countries, they point out that it is not possible to 'assess the effective impact' but one can 'identify and assess the factors' that could possibly have an impact (attributable to GI intervention). In this regard, they refer to the typicity of GI products suggested by Barjolle et al. (2009) who typologies GI-in-progress into 'enthusiasts' (focus on market stabilization, value creation, and sustainable local resources), 'socio-environmentalist' (emphasis on social and environmental issues rather than economic ones), and 'undecided' (high scores for economic impacts while social and environmental issues are low priority for local stakeholders). In other words, Paus and Reviron (2009) conclude that the evaluation of GI systems may involve an assessment of the supply chain, analysis of the legal framework, or the institutional mechanism for implementing the GI regulatory framework. Thus, the methods used to analyse these factors would differ. Studies from the EU indicate the presence of collective organization as key to the success of GI whereas evolving a code of practice and certification that guarantee the quality and origin are also crucial. In other words, they conclude that there is no single framework to explore the impact of GI and a combination of methods needs to be assessed given the characteristics of the product especially the size of the territory, survey sample, indicators to be analysed, and so on vary.

Given these complexities, Belletti and Marescotti (2009) have tried to lay out a framework to study the impact of GI systems. While GI is considered as an intervention by the state, it is considered as a project through which stakeholders strategize development goals. In this context, they argue that focusing on a counterfactual, as mentioned earlier, becomes crucial since GI systems are 'small systems' where exogenous factors play an important role. Thus, finding a counterfactual or control group becomes extremely complex and difficult. Moreover, the supply chain of local stakeholders with linkages to exogenous actors makes it very crucial to understand different perspectives on the GI system from the point of view of these stakeholders so that the impact of GI registration can be holistically analysed and captured. Use of quantitative as well as qualitative data is important since the latter would throw light on the processes and causal relationships. Thus, impact analysis covers three important components: Outputs, Outcomes, and Impacts. The first order effects cover four important components: coverage of the GI scheme, potential of GI, real use of GI, and producer awareness (logo, certification). The second order effects are immediate manifestation of the outputs: instances of infringement, consumer awareness and satisfaction; while the third order effects refer to larger impacts encompassing social, environmental, and development issues.

This framework of analysis fits in with the evaluation process set out in the theory of change (TOC) which helps in explaining the interaction of different factors that cause change or result in certain expected outcomes. Thus TOC is useful in the selection of indicators that would guide the impact and data collection is focused on those indicators. The data may be then analysed to see whether the intended outcomes have been realized or not. In a project, TOC helps in understanding the changes caused by the project and the role of other casual factors (Kumar et al., 2015).

Neilson et al. (2018) use the TOC framework to analyse the implementation of GI in the Indonesian coffee sector to present the possible impacts of the GI systems, through assessing and identifying factors which need strengthening to achieve the desired outcomes and impacts. Six different stages, namely institutional establishment, institutional embedding, quality control, market recognition, monitoring of use and violations, and localized value culture have been identified as impact pathways for the TOC. Each of these stages lend themselves to a set of 19 assumptions or indicators (Figure 1.1). These indicators manifest into a process of change. For instance, the quality control indicators, via the assumptions on monitoring farm practices and product quality, would lead to improved farm practices, with an outcome of improvement in environment, product, and quality. The case studies indicate that while the identification of the product and the registration of the GI had taken place, the institutional governance mechanism which is crucial for ensuring distributive justice for the producer community was weak. Membership in the local GI boards (or Masyarakat Perlindung an Indikasi Geografis—MPIG) was low as was the awareness levels among the producer community. The levels of monitoring by the GI board to ensure GI and product quality links was also missing. There was also a low level of recognition of GIs within the mainstream consumer market, that is, the use of the GI tag was limited. Even when it was used, it was a violation of the GI and this was not monitored or reported by the MPIG. Thus, with a low level of institutional embedding, outcomes in the form of higher prices, improved livelihoods were obviously not found. Irrespective of these outcomes, there has been an 'enhanced sense of regional and cultural pride, as expressed particularly by local elites and government representatives' (Nielson et al. 2018).

Given the nascent stage of the GI system in India, in the context of the legal framework which has become operational in 2003, in Chapter 3 of this volume we use the theory of change to analyse the possible impacts of GI registration through select case studies on registered handicrafts and textiles in South India.

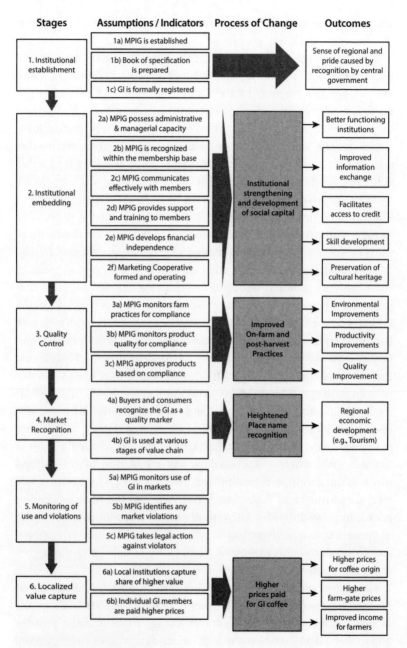

FIGURE 1.1 A Theory of Change for the Rural Development Impacts of GIs in the Indonesian Coffee Sector
Source: Neilson et al. (2018).

Focus of the Book

The discussion presented in the different sections of this chapter leads to a few questions which need to be probed into for the context of India. These are: (1) What type of products have been accorded the GI registration and what type of opportunities do they present? (2) What has been the impact of GI registration on the livelihoods of the producers? (3) What is the role of collective organizations in implementing the collective community intellectual property right GIs in India? These questions are analysed with the help of information collected from GI journals, case studies conducted by the authors, and other published sources. Discussion on these questions form the content of the different chapters that constitute this volume.

Chapter Schemes

Including the introductory chapter in which an overview of GI and the associated aspects were detailed, this book consists of five chapters. The second chapter, 'Status, Opportunities and Challenges before the GI Products of India', details the profile of the GI products registered in India. This chapter also throws light on several issues that are debated in India with respect to GI. Given the fact that handicrafts and textiles (both handmade and machine made) are also popularly recognized by consumers through origin labelling, it becomes crucial to establish the link between the geography/region and the characteristics of the product. Thus, this chapter examines the issues surrounding the defining of the geographical area, establishing uniqueness of the product owing to the importance of institutional governance in ensuring the implementation, and the use of GI in India.

The third chapter presents the impact of GI as evidenced from case studies conducted by the authors. The impacts are analysed through the theory of change framework. This chapter focuses on examining the processes and factors that are important in achieving the potential gains of GI—not only in the realm of economic rewards to the producer, but also in achieving larger social, environmental, and developmental goals. Considering the GI intervention in a project mode, this chapter analyses the process of change—inputs and the resultant outputs—and the outcomes and impact of GI so far.

In the light of the case studies and emerging concerns, Chapter 4 introduces and explores in detail the role of collective organization in the implementation of GI. Governance and institutional mechanisms prevalent in the selected registered products are discussed along with the role of governmental and international agencies in promoting collectivization of institutional mechanism and the specific role played by the GI registry in promoting the establishment of collective bodies.

The fifth chapter presents the broad conclusions and policy suggestions for GIs to serve their development role in the context of India.

Limitations of the Volume

This volume is based on limited primary data and large qualitative information drawn from the GI journals. Primary data are limited to eight GI products (discussed in Chapter 3) and include the following:[9] Thanjavur Painting and Swamimalai Bronze Icon from Tamil Nadu; Machilipatnam Kalamkari, Kondapalli Toys, and Pochampalli Ikat from Andhra Pradesh; Aranmula Mirror from Kerala; and Mysore Agarbathi and Kasuti Embroidery from Karnataka. Of these products except for Mysore Agarbathi which belongs to the manufactured product segment, the rest of the products are categorized into handicraft products by the GI registry.

There is no official data on handicrafts at the individual state level. Similarly, official data on the specific agricultural products are also not available at the state level. Due to the informal nature of the enterprises, quantitative data was not available with the producers to support the qualitative information collected during the interviews. Hence, the information presented for the different crafts vary. Due to lack of adequate data, it was difficult to draw inferences on the impact of the craft/crop on the local economy.

The GI Registry provides rich information on the different products that is available in the public domain. Particularly the statement of case and the reports of the consultative meeting provide an understanding of the product per se and the objections if any. However, as the documentation refer to the historical link between the place and the product, information on the current state of affairs had to be collected from other published sources, such as reports by the government or civil society organizations, newspapers, and other journal articles.

The discussion on the government schemes does not cover the entire gamut of schemes meant for the benefit of the craft and agricultural sector but focuses on a few selected schemes relevant for the promotion of GI.

As the volume focuses on understanding the impact of GI on the livelihood of the producers of registered GIs of India alone and leaves out foreign products registered in India, it also focuses less on 'well known products' and products that are traded in the organized sector.

Notes

1. This section ('International Protection') draws from (Nair & Kumar, 2005).

2. European Council Regulation (EC) No. 510/2006 of 20 March 2006.

3. Prisoner's dilemma is a situation where lack of information or other factors leads to obstruction in cooperative action between different agents (prisoners). Consequently, each agent, acting on limited information, make sub-optimal decision in comparison with an outcome based on cooperative action (Rangnekar, 2004, p. 19).

4. Rangnekar (2004) quotes the example of West Country Farmhouse Cheddar—a PDO cheese where manual cheddaring and a nine-month period of ripening is a key specification. Nonetheless, some firms sell cheese before the nine months of ripening and thereby are not entitled to use the PDO. However, these firms employ a variety of marketing strategies to highlight its association with the protected product (Endnote 26: 38).

5. PGS is recommended by the Ministry of Agriculture, Government of India in the context of promoting organic agriculture. Find more details at http://pgsindia-ncof.gov.in/pgs_india.aspx

6. http://www.fao.org/fileadmin/user_upload/foodquality/fichefiles/en/c6.1.pdf accessed on 11 April 2016.

7. The producer needs to specify in the application the class under which his product could be classified. The products can be categorized into any of the 34 classes which are provided in Appendix 1.

8. Sections 'Infringement of Registered GIs' and 'Rectification of a Registered GI' were compiled from the information available on the GI Registry's website.

9. The primary data has emerged from the projects conducted by N. Lalitha and Soumya Vinayan. The study titled 'Socio Economic Implications of Protecting Handicrafts through Geographical Indications-A Case Study of Selected Products from Southern India' was carried out by N. Lalitha, supported by and submitted to the Indian Council of Social Science Research (ICSSR), New Delhi in 2014 (Lalitha, 2014). Another study titled 'Socio-economics of Geographical Indications in the Indian Handloom Sector: A Case Study of Pochampally' was carried out by Soumya Vinayan, supported by and submitted to the ICSSR, New Delhi in 2013 (Vinayan, 2013).

2

Status, Opportunities, and Challenges before the GI Products of India

At the International Symposium on Geographical Indications (held at Beijing from 26 to 28 June 2007), speakers converged on the fundamental values of GIs, which are: (1) helping producers get a premium price for their products, (2) providing guarantees to consumers on the values of the products, (3) developing the rural economy, and (4) protecting local knowledge and traditions.[1] These fundamental values may be realized over a period of time, with targeted focus on strengthening the opportunities and addressing the challenges that each of the GI products may place before the policymakers. As highlighted in the introductory chapter, the Indian GI system provides protection to agricultural, handicraft, manufactured, and food products. Most of the producers of handicraft/manufactured goods function as micro-entrepreneurial units. Agricultural products are manufactured both for self-consumption and the market. While the ratio of the contribution of nature to that of human contribution to a product, at a given geographical location, confers geographical association to a GI and thus determines its quality (Soam et al., 2007), there are products which are exclusively associated with human skills in a particular region with the skills having been traditionally handed down over generations

(Marie-Vivien, 2013). Based on such characteristics, numerous products have been filed with the GI registry by a variety of organizations. The advantage of being a proprietor of a GI product is that it enables the producers to adopt a Blue Ocean Strategy,[2] where the producers differentiate the product from the rest using the uniqueness derived from the GI factors. The advantage can be utilized to the core if (1) the area of production is defined clearly, (2) there is consensus among the producers to adopt certain strategies to retain and sustain the quality and uniqueness and there is assurance to the consumers of that quality, and (3) the quality of the product and the authenticity are certified by an institution.

In India, the agriculture, handicraft, and handloom sectors support the livelihoods of a sizeable percentage of the population. Hence, by using GI as a development tool, a few of the sustainable development goals could be: '(1) end poverty in all its forms everywhere, (2) end hunger, achieve food security and improved nutrition, and promote sustainable agriculture, (3) achieve gender equality and empower all women and girls, (4) promote sustained, inclusive, and sustainable economic growth, full and productive employment, and decent work for all, (5) reduce inequality within and among countries', which may be achieved by focusing attention on the post registration activities for the GI registered products (UNDP n.d.).

The purpose of this chapter is twofold. First, it provides a status profile of the different GI registered products, which is presented in the section 'GI Registration Details'. Second, it also reviews the registered GIs to understand the prevalence of issues, if any, that require institutional governance intervention to reap the benefits of GI. These are discussed in the section 'Institutional and Governance Aspects' and its different subsections. The conclusion provides the summary.

GI Registration Details

The number of GI applications filed every year ranges widely. Over the 13-year period 2003–04 to 2015–16, an average of 41 applications has been filed every year, with a peak of 148 applications in the year 2011–12 (Figure 2.1).[3] Compared to 2004, when GI registrations began, 2007–08 and 2008–09 have been the two years when there has been a spike in registration, with 31 and 43 applications filed respectively.

Out of 301 registrations with the Indian GI registry as on 31 October 2017, there were 260 products with origin in India, twelve products of foreign origin, and twenty-nine separate applications for logo (products of Indian origin).

Of the 260 registered products in India as of 31 October 2017, agriculture (33 per cent), handicrafts (27 per cent), and textiles (32 per cent) account for more than 90 per cent of the total registered products in India. Manufactured goods and foodstuff constitute 4 and 3 per cent respectively (Table 2.1). Karnataka leads the rest of the states with 35 registrations. Karnataka (13 per cent), Maharashtra (12 per cent), Tamil Nadu and Kerala (9 per cent each), are the four states in the top three ranks. Rajasthan Marble is the only product that has been registered under the category of natural products.

Of the 86 agricultural products registered with the GI Registry, Maharashtra leads the rest of the states in the total number of registered products (23 out of 86),[4] followed closely by Karnataka (16) and Kerala (11). Thus, these three states together account for 59 per cent of the total agricultural products registered in the country. Assam and

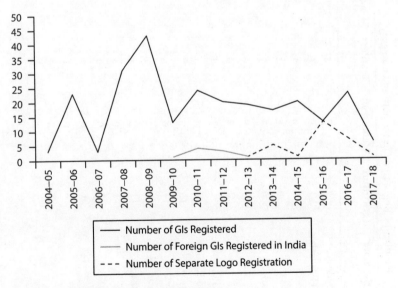

FIGURE 2.1   GI Registration Details, 2004–17
Source: Compiled from http://www.ipindia.nic.in/writereaddata/Portal/Images/pdf/Registered_GI.pdf, accessed on 31 October 2017.

Table 2.1 Number of Registered GIs by State and Category

Name of the State	Agriculture	Handicraft	Textiles	Manufactured	Foodstuff	Natural Good	Total	% to Total Registered GIs
Andhra Pradesh	2	7	7	0	2	0	18	7
Arunachal Pradesh	1	0	0	0	0	0	1	0
Assam	4	0	1	0	0	0	5	2
Bihar	0	2	3	0	0	0	5	2
Chhattisgarh	0	3	1	0	0	0	4	2
Goa	0	0	0	1	0	0	1	0
Gujarat	2	2	6	0	0	0	10	4
Himachal Pradesh	1	1	3	0	0	0	5	2
Jammu and Kashmir	0	4	3	0	0	0	7	3
Karnataka	16	8	7	3	1	0	35	13
Kerala	11	6	6	0	0	0	23	9
Madhya Pradesh	0	2	3	0	1	0	6	2
Maharashtra	23	2	4	1	0	0	30	12
Manipur	1	0	3	0	0	0	4	2
Meghalaya	2	0	0	0	0	0	2	1
Mizoram	1	0	0	0	0	0	1	0
Nagaland	2	0	1	0	0	0	3	1
Odisha	2	2	10	0	0	0	14	5
Puducherry	0	2	0	0	0	0	2	1
Rajasthan	0	4	3	0	1	1	9	3

Sikkim	1	0	0	0	0	0	1	0
Tamil Nadu	5	8	9	2	0	0	24	9
Telangana	0	6	3	0	1	0	10	4
Tripura	1	0	0	0	0	0	1	0
Uttar Pradesh	3	10	5	4	0	0	22	8
Uttarakhand	1	0	0	0	0	0	1	0
West Bengal	6	1	4	0	3	0	14	5
Punjab, Haryana, Delhi, HP, UK	1	0	0	0	0	0	1	0
Punjab/Haryana/Rajasthan	0	0	1	0	0	0	1	0
Total	86	70	83	11	9	1	260	100

Source: Compiled from http://www.ipindia.nic.in/writereaddata/Portal/Images/pdf/Registered_GI.pdf as of 31 October 2017.

Uttar Pradesh (3.6 per cent each), West Bengal (4.8 per cent), and Tamil Nadu (6 per cent) account for an additional 18 per cent of the total agricultural products registered. Punjab, Haryana, Himachal Pradesh, and Jammu and Kashmir together hold the Basmati GI. Among the northeastern states, Meghalaya, Mizoram, and Sikkim have registered GIs only in the agriculture category. Bihar, Chhattisgarh, Goa, Jammu and Kashmir, Madhya Pradesh, Puducherry, Rajasthan, and Telangana are yet to register any agricultural product under GI.

Within handicrafts, Uttar Pradesh (14 per cent), Tamil Nadu, and Karnataka (11 per cent each), account for 36 per cent of the total registrations. Kerala and Telangana account for 9 per cent each, followed by Andhra Pradesh, Bihar, Gujarat, Jammu and Kashmir, and Rajasthan. Arunachal Pradesh, Assam, Goa, Manipur, Mizoram, Meghalaya, Nagaland, and Sikkim do not have any registration in the handicrafts category.

Odisha leads in textile registrations, with ten varieties of textiles, followed by Tamil Nadu, and Karnataka with seven each, and Kerala and Gujarat with six each. Arunachal Pradesh, Goa, Mizoram, Meghalaya, Puducherry, Sikkim, and Tripura are yet to register a GI in the textile category.

Out of the eleven products in the manufactured category, Uttar Pradesh, and Karnataka have four and three products each, the rest are from Tamil Nadu (two), Goa (one), and Maharashtra (one). In the food category, there are nine products, out of which two and three are products from Andhra Pradesh, and West Bengal respectively. Hyderabad Haleem from Telangana is the first processed meat product to get a GI.

There are some states which do not have registrations so far in some of the sectors. This, however, does not mean that these states do not have products that qualify for GI protection. It is perhaps because the filing of the GI application takes a considerable amount of organizational effort to (a) form the producers' group and (b) provide documentary historical evidences of the products' regional association.

Constituents of GI Categories

A quick look at the description of the GI-protected agricultural products indicate that they consist of high value crops like 34 fruits (40 per cent),

13 spices (15 per cent), 15 food grains (17 per cent), six each beverages and vegetables (7 per cent), five flowers (6 per cent), four others (5 per cent), two dry fruits, and one variety of pulses.[5]

Fruit GIs consist of different varieties of oranges (six), banana (five), mango (eight), pineapple (two), grapes (two), lemons (two), and one each of coconut, strawberry, litchi, custard apple, pomegranate, fig, guava, and chickoo. The different constituents of spices are: chilly (five), cardamom (three), ginger (one), pepper (one), kokum (one), bay leaves (one), and turmeric (one). There are eleven rice varieties and one variety of wheat under food grains. Of the five varieties of flowers, four are varieties of jasmine. Four tea and two coffee varieties (GI for processing) constitute the beverages segment. Of the six vegetables that have a GI, two each are onion and eggplant varieties, and one each for tomato and beans (Appendix Table 2.1).

Among registered textile products, five categories can be discerned, and, within each, further categorization can be made based on uniqueness. Thus, out of the 83 textile products, about 70 per cent belong to saris and fabrics, and the rest are shared by embroidery, carpets and rugs, hand block prints and shawls, and furnishing materials. Among fabrics and saris, ikat or tie and dye weaving stands apart for their highly intricate and time-consuming process. The well-known ikat products registered so far are: Pochampalli Ikat, Orissa Ikat, Khandua saris and fabrics, Sambalpuri Banda saris and fabrics, Bomkai saris and fabrics, Berhampur Phoda Kumbhasari, and Joda, and Patan Patola. Madurai Sungundi and Kachchh shawls involve tie and dye in the final processing of the product. The hand block prints involve both vegetable dyes and chemical dyes. Srikalahasti and Machilipatnam Kalamkari use hand block prints and also kalam or pen. Farukkhabad Prints are based on screen printing. Shawls and carpets/rugs make use of both local (desi) and non-local wools, the differentiation between the two being a major feature in their marketing (Appendix Table 2.2).

The 70 Handicraft GIs can be grouped under nine categories. This includes metal crafts (26 per cent), wood (24 per cent), paintings (11 per cent), clay (7 per cent), fibre (17 per cent), leather, stone and glass (10 per cent), and paper (4 per cent). However, for presentation's sake, they have been clubbed in Appendix Table 2.3.

The GI registered manufactured goods range from agarbathi, oil, soap, perfume, wet grinder, scissors, to alcoholic beverages. Eight foreign

TABLE 2.2 Details of Proprietorship of Registered Products

Type of Proprietor	Agricultural	Handicraft	Textile	Manufactured	Foodstuff	Natural Goods	Total
Commodity Board	10	4					14
Central Government	2	17	4				23
FPO	1						1
State Government	22	5	28	3	2		60
Trust			1		2		3
Trust and Cooperatives		1					1
University and Society	5						5
University	3						3
Associations (Farmer/Producer/Trader/Manufacturer)	10	5	9	4	4	1	33
Producer Society	16	8	9	1	1		35
Company	1						1
Foundation/Trust	3	3	6				12
Cooperatives/Apex Society	1	9	16				26
Cooperative and Corporation		1					1
Cooperatives & Associations & State			1				1
Corporation or State Government Enterprise	10	13	4	2			29
State Government & Cooperative/Society			2				2
State Government & Association		2	1				3
Central Institution and Society			1	1			2
State Government & Association & NGO & Cooperative			1				1
University & NGO	1						1
NGO	1	2					3
Total	86	70	83	11	9	1	260

Source: Compiled from the Registration of Certification of each of the Product available at http://ipindiaservices.gov.in/GirPublic/Detail...CP...

alcoholic beverages have also been registered under manufactured goods (Appendix Table 2.4). In the category of foodstuff, there are sweets (eight), savouries (two), and processed meat (one) (Appendix Table 2.5).[6]

A detailed look at the profile of the GI registered products of India suggests that the protection ranges from very regional products like Puneri Pagadi or Kasuti Embroidery to well-known Madhubani paintings and Kashmir walnut carvings in the handicrafts segments; Pokkali rice and Appemidi mangoes to the famous Basmati rice and Darjeeling tea. Such protection informs us that legal protection in India is not always guided by economic returns or by the threat of infringement but is also driven by the need to create an inventory of cultural and heritage products as the GI protects the name associated with a region.

Proprietors of GI

A variety of proprietorship is evident from Table 2.2, where besides the central and state governments, a religious organization also has ownership of a GI. Overall, different state governments have topped the list in registering GIs in the handicrafts and textile categories. This is followed by central government and producer societies in handicrafts and cooperatives and producer associations in the case of textile products (Development Commissioner, Handicrafts, and Handlooms). In agriculture, farmer producer organizations (FPOs) rank first in filing GIs, followed by state (horticulture department), central government [Agricultural and Processed Exports Development Agency (APEDA), and North Eastern Regional Agricultural Marketing Corporation Ltd (NERAMAC)], agricultural universities and commodity boards (tea board, spices board). The involvement of the government has been on the ground that the 'producers are few and unorganized, and would be unable to bear the GI filing expenditures' (Garcia et al., 2007) and the documentation required to file the application. Marie-Vivien (2015) adds that the disadvantaged position of the producers of GI products and the presence of the government in production activity legitimizes the role of the government in filing the application. Thus, out of the 260 products, in 119 cases (46 per cent), the central and state governments have been present either directly or in association with societies or other apex organizations.

Registration in textile goods was pioneered by the Textiles Committee under the Cluster Development Programme of the Government of India,[7] further strengthened by the United Nations Industrial Development Organization's (UNIDO) initiative (under the cluster approach),[8] and is thus more widespread as a pan-India IP policy.

Analysing the legal nature of GI applications, Marie-Vivien (2015) points out that producer associations, apex and village cooperatives, religious organizations, commodity boards, state patent information centres, and state universities do confirm with the definition of the applicant as mentioned in the GI Act of India. The reason is that these categories either belong to the nomenclature of an association or an authority created under law; however, central and state government applicants are not provided for in the law. The status of the government and private enterprise applicants are also doubtful.

Proprietorship matters in issues relating to creating awareness (both before and after GI application), creation of code of practices, marketing, and in matters relating to infringement. Particularly at the time of filing a GI application, (also dealt with in Chapters 3 and 4), it is essential that there needs to be a consultation process to sensitize the producers about GI, and the purpose and benefits of filing a GI application. When this process evolves among the producers, then ideally it is expected that the discussion on GI would lead to awareness and arriving at probable consensus about forming the producers' association. There are greater possibilities of spreading awareness among fellow producers when the system is evolving from within the producers. However, depending on the purpose of the involvement of the third party, like cluster development and so on, the activities concerning the craft could continue for long. On the other hand, if any agency is only involved for the purpose of filing the application, then the consultation process is different and, hence, information percolation could also vary depending on the interest shown by the different stakeholders.

Opportunities for the GI Products

Recognizing the role of differentiated products in creating a niche market, Japan and Thailand have been promoting their products through models such as One Village One Product, One GI One Province, and One Tambon One Product. Both the UK and European Union have adopted the concept of 'the creative economy' based on cultural and creative industries (CCI), where the CCI converge with creative sectors like architecture, media, publishing (Mubayi, 2016). According to the Ministry of Textiles, 60 per cent of the total production of the handicrafts and handlooms are exported while the rest are consumed domestically. According to the Export Promotion Council for Handicrafts (EPCH), export of handicrafts reached INR 21,457.9 crores during 2015–16. The USA is the single largest importer of Indian handicrafts followed by the UK (All India Artisans and Craftsworkers Welfare Association, 2017). The major export segments are: art metal ware, wood wares, hand printed textiles and scarves, embroidered and crocheted goods, shawls, artware, zari and zari goods, imitation jewellery, and miscellaneous handicrafts (AIACA, 2017) and, as discussed in the earlier section, there are GI protected products in each of the segments (Appendix Tables 2.1–2.5). Due to the lack of data by state or by product category, we may not be confident about the size of the exports of GI products but it is highly possible that some of the GI products are exported, perhaps without a mention of GI.

In the agricultural segment, climate changes, monsoon failures, and the low and fluctuating farmer income cause distress to farmers. In India, the census of 2011 has already reported a decline in the number of farmers. Farmers losing interest and leaving farming will have a serious impact on the future of agriculture and food security in the country. In order to address these issues, the Government of India has set a goal to double the farmers' income by 2022–3, and a variety of strategies within and outside the agriculture sector are being discussed. One of the strategies discussed within agriculture includes diversification towards high value crops (HVC) and increasing the area under fruits and vegetables by 5 per cent every year (Chand, 2017). Further, rising income (of at least a section of the society) and changes in lifestyle are contributing to the demand for nutritive and quality products. Importantly, for fruits, vegetables, pulses, and livestock products, the income elasticity has become positive and very high in India (Acharya, 2015). In the earlier section, we pointed out that in the agricultural GIs, there are a variety of HVCs. Theoretically, concentrating on the GI-protected HVCs could achieve the double goal of promoting GI products as well as improving farmers' income. A few GI products like Basmati Rice, Darjeeling Tea, Assam Tea, Nilgiri Tea, coffee, spices, jasmine, and few vegetables have already established a good export market, besides a sizeable domestic market. Here again there is no data available for the export of GI registered products separately except for Basmati rice (Table 2.3).

In the international context, in Thailand, price of the Doi Chang green coffee bean increased from 12 US$/kg to 65 US$/kg after its GI registration.[9] Nakonchaisri Pamelo's (Thailand) quality attributes stem from the specific geographical conditions and the human intervention in farming practices. The fruit from Nakhon Patham, which is a

TABLE 2.3   Export of Select Agri Products and Percentage Share of Top Five Countries in Total Quantity Exported from India (in Metric Tonnes)

Mango Pulp	Basmati Rice	Fresh Grapes	Wheat
Saudi Arabia (32.6)	Saudi Arabia (23.5)	Netherland (32.5)	Bangladesh (55.1)
Netherland (9.3)	Iran (17.2)	United Kingdom (11.5)	Nepal (19.3)
Yemen Republic (8.4)	United Arab Emirates (15.1)	Russia (8.8)	United Arab Emirates (16.1)
Kuwait (6.9)	Iraq (10.4)	United Arab Emirates (8.4)	Taiwan (2.4)
United Arab Emirates (6.6)	Kuwait (4.5)	Saudi Arabia (5.2)	Malaysia (1.2)
Total (128,866)	Total (4,045,796)	Total (156,218)	Total (618,020)
Floriculture	Fresh Vegetables	Mango	Onions
United States (23.0)	Nepal (31.9)	United Arab Emirates (55.0)	Bangladesh (20.9)
Germany (10.1)	Pakistan (17.4)	Nepal (22.8)	Malaysia (20.3)
United Kingdom (9.8)	United Arab Emirates (13.2)	United Kingdom (4.1)	Sri Lanka (16.6)
Netherland (8.4)	Sri Lanka (6.0)	Saudi Arabia (3.9)	United Arab Emirates (14.1)
United Arab Emirates (6.7)	Malaysia (5.0)	Qatar (2.8)	Nepal (5.8)
Total (22,519)	Total (699,600)	Total (36,329)	Total (1,201,245)

Source: http://agriexchange.apeda.gov.in/indexp/reportlist.aspx, accessed on 5 November 2016.

Note: Figures in parentheses indicate the percentages to total.

TABLE 2.4 Comparison of Prices between Origin Differentiated and Non-differentiated Roasted Coffees in International Markets, August–December 2006 (US$/pound)

Average Retail Price	**3.17**
Colombian Supremo	9.92
Guatemala Antigua	10.07
Costa Rican Tarrazu	10.09
Tanzanian Peaberry	11.14
Sumatra Mandheling	11.16
Papua New Guinea	11.22
Ethiopian Harrar	11.28
Java estate	11.36
Ethiopian Yirgacheffe	11.45
Sula Wezi	11.91
Kenya AA	12.00
100% Kona	29.87
Jamaica Blue Mountain	43.44

Source: Cited in Vandecandelaere et al. (2009–10, p. 20).

GI designated area, receives 2 to 4 Baht higher than the price received by fruits from other areas (cited in (Vandecandelaere et al., 2009–10)). Table 2.4 indicates the price difference for GI products in the international markets.

If the opportunities in the domestic and export market are exploited based on the differentiated quality in both the agriculture and other GI products, the benefits could percolate to the producers. However, in order to derive such benefits, a few of the institutional and governance aspects need attention. These have been detailed below.

Institutional and Governance Aspects

Geographical Coverage of Products

Geographical region is the core of GI and very interesting facts emerge when we look at the region specifically. For instance, a variety of products have been registered from the same region, indicating the very rich diversity in livelihood practices that are dependent on the local resources. Mysore is a case in point, with several GI registered products in handicrafts, agriculture, and the manufactured products category like Mysore silk, Mysore sandal soap, and so on (Appendix Table 2.4). In Tamil Nadu, four handicrafts have originated from Thanjavur, namely, doll, paintings, art plate, and veenai (musical instrument). In Telangana, paintings, toys, and craft, and furniture products have been registered from the Nirmal region. Similarly, Varanasi boasts of wooden lacquer toys, gulabi meenakari craft, brocades and rugs, and metal repoussé craft. Kerala's Wayanad has registered two aromatic rice varieties known as Wayanad Jeerakasala rice and Wayanad Gandhakasala rice. Nagaland and Coorg so far have only agricultural products. From Bastar, Dhokra wooden craft and iron craft have GI recognition. From Alleppey, two distinct products namely, coir and cardamom have got GI recognition.

Some of the GI products from Kashmir, Nagaland, and Odisha carry the entire state's name, as they are practised in multiple locations within the state. Three products from Manipur—Shaphee Lanphee, Wangkhei Phee, and Moirang Phee—are practised across the state. In case of Phulkari, an embroidered craft, the coverage extends across several parts of three states, Punjab, Haryana, and Rajasthan. Monsooned Malabar Robusta Coffee, Monsooned Malabar Arabica Coffee, and Malabar Pepper are grown in Kerala, Karnataka, and Tamil Nadu; Alleppey cardamom and Nagpur oranges are grown in a minimum of two states, while Basmati rice is cultivated in Punjab, Haryana, Delhi, Uttarakhand, parts of Western Uttar Pradesh, Jammu and Kashmir, and Himachal Pradesh.

In the case of manufacturing products, though the raw materials could come from different places, production processes are mostly reported to be in one or two clusters in particular districts, confined to numerous micro and small enterprises. The production of Kanpur Saddlery and Kannauj perfume are cases in point. A sizeable percentage of production of Mysore Agarbathi takes place outside Mysore, which creates a potential for controversy in the use of the GI tag. Feni (alcoholic beverage) is produced across the state of Goa; Mysore sandalwood oil, Mysore sandalwood soap, Kanpur saddlery, and Coimbatore wet grinder are spread across at least two districts while that of EI leather is spread across four districts in Tamil Nadu—Trichy, Dindigul, part of North Arcot district, and Pallavaram. The rest of the manufactured goods are produced in single districts—Nashik Valley

Wine (Nashik), Kannauj Perfume (Kannauj), and Meerut Scissors (Meerut). Production of the lone Makrana marble in the natural goods category is restricted to two tehsils—Makrana and Parbatsar.

As many as 23 agricultural products are grown in just one district of different states, while, the bay leaves of Uttarakhand is cultivated in thirteen districts. Naga tree tomato and Navara rice are cultivated in ten and nine districts of Nagaland and Kerala respectively. Arunachal Pradesh oranges, Coorg oranges, Nanjanagud bananas, Byadigi chilli, Coorg green cardamom, Appemidi mango, Bangalore rose onion, Central Travancore jaggery, Pokkali rice, Kaipad rice, Madurai malli, Bhalia wheat, Naga mircha, Sikkim large cardamom, Vazhakulam pineapple are grown in more than three or four districts.

Mirzapur Handmade Dari is spread across ten districts of Uttar Pradesh, Orissa Ikat and the handmade carpet of Bhadohi are manufactured in nine districts each of Orissa and Uttar Pradesh. Sambalpuri Bandha, and Bomkai saris and fabrics are spread across seven and six districts of Odisha respectively. Banaras brocades and saris are woven in five districts of Uttar Pradesh. Kota Doria, Ilkal saris, and Cannanore home furnishings are concentrated in three districts each of Rajasthan, Karnataka, and Kerala respectively.

In the case of foodstuff, the geographical coverage throws up interesting scenarios. It ranges from areas within a 'temple' (in the case of Tirupathi Laddu), the smallest area compared to all other GI products, to specific blocks in a municipality (Joynagar Moa) to districts, namely Dharwad (Dharwad Pedha), Bikaner (Bikaneri Bhujia), Ratlami Sev (Ratlam), and Hyderabad (Hyderabad Haleem, the first product in the processed non-vegetarian food category in India) (Appendix Table 2.5).

Governance Issues Regarding Geographical Areas

The geographical spread indicates the skill and knowledge spread of the craft and its importance for the local economy. It also indicates the vulnerability and coping strategies of the people using the natural resources and craftsmanship, as, according to the season and demand, there could be movement of artisans from one occupation to another. Hence, appropriate ground work needs to be done to define the area for the GI product. GIs have the power to exclude and the power to exclude is the power of property (quoted in Rangnekar, 2011). It could lead to exclusion of producers from enjoying the fruits of GI (Gopalakrishnan et al., 2007). The Madurai malli GI covers the areas of Madurai, Virudhunagar, Theni, Dindigul, and Sivagangai districts. However, the plants raised in the Mandapam and Thangachi madam areas also produced the famous Madurai malli and these farmers were not included in the GI. Farmers from the Mandapam region, who raised the issue at a farmers' grievance meeting, said it was unfortunate that farmers who raised them were left in the lurch.[10]

GI for the Baluchari sari (hand woven) is associated with the village Baluchar in the district of Murshidabad. Though the village does not exist anymore (as it has been swallowed up by a river, which almost resulted in the extinction of Baluchari weaving), weavers from Bishnupur from the district of Bankura took efforts to revive the craft rather than the weavers of Murshidabad. With a distance of 200 km between these two districts, the question is which is the legitimate region for GI. However, as the state agencies took the lead to file the GI, the entire state came to be indicated as the GI region, which may not be very appropriate (Nanda et al., 2013).

In the GI for Konark stone carving, while the mineral composition of the stone is detailed, the geographical origin of the stone is not documented. Similarly, in the case of Kondapalli Bommalu (toys) the GI application indicates that the wood comes from the surrounding region of Kondapalli, but the area identified includes only the area where the toys are made (a village of 1.5 square kilometres) and does not include the nearby forests from where the critical raw material is obtained (Marie-Vivien, 2013, p. 197).

The map submitted for Bagh printing excluded some areas where Bagh printing existed for decades. A major error in the case of Madhubani painting is that it is protected under class 16 (paper) which leads to the Madhubani painting on cloth going unprotected (Kumar & Bahl, 2010).

Uniqueness Due to Geographical Factors

The uniqueness of the product linked to a region is very essential to get GI registration and further to strengthen the post-GI marketing activities. Eighty-five and 80 per cent of French wine exports and EU exported spirits respectively use GIs as a marketing tool for promotions, both in the domestic and export market. In the post TRIPS period, GI has become very crucial for 138,000 farms in France and 300,000 Italian employees (Rout, 2014).

In the Indian context, most of the agricultural GIs are dependent on the climatic and natural resources of a specific region. Among the non-agricultural products including textiles, handicrafts, foodstuff, and man-ufacturing, a few explicitly indicate geographic or natural factors as an exclusive factor for the uniqueness of the product, beside human skills. Human skills, either in the form of designs or drawings or the process of pre-loom activities such as warping, sizing, dyeing and the process of weaving itself or the type of loom used, vary, and, thereby, variations in human skills or creativity in the case of textiles is expressed through several kinds of embroidery or paintings. Kancheepuram and Banaras silk saris are world renowned for their intricate weave and designs. It is also emphasized in both the applications that the GI is for handloom products. In case of ikat or tie & dye saris registered across the country, it is needless to emphasize the role of human skill. Depending on the design, a warp of saris (usually eight in number) takes forty-five to sixty days to complete. The complex process of tying and dyeing as per the intricate designs made of several colours is in itself a marvel of human creativity and skill.

Thus, even within a region, one can find 'diversity within diversity' (Kapur, 2016, p. 142). However, both the natural factors and the human skills are subject to challenges that range from climate change to changes in the consumption preferences of the consumers.

Taking examples from different GI segments, in this section we dis-cuss the types of uniqueness of the GI and the likely issues that could crop up or are already evident, which can dilute the GI uniqueness or affect the production of the GI product.

The GI application for Kotpad Handloom Fabric from Odisha, the vegetable dyed fabric produced by tribal weavers, mentions in detail about the use of the bark of Aul trees for dyeing, providing its unique-ness. With respect to Habaspuri saris and fabrics, natural extracts of barks and fruits from the forest located nearby are used for dyeing. Kota Doria uses the juice of onions found locally in the nearby jungles in sizing, while vegetable dyes are used in the production of Mirzapur handmade dari for handspun wool. Use of rice (starch) and coco-nut oil deserves mention in the case of Kuthampally saris as well as

Kuthampally Set Mundu and Dhoti production process. Oil from raw vegetables and flowers are used in the pre-loom process of handmade carpets of Bhadohi and the combination of the materials used in dyeing is kept as a trade secret.

Across the spectrum, products, especially handwoven textiles, have originated in places which have flourished around a river. This is because dyeing is an important part of weaving and here, invariably, most of the products either use the available river water or other natural resources (such as plant-based dyes) or locally available resources in the making of the machinery of the craft which influences the style and texture of products made. Particularly, the use of the river has been an integral part in the making of Bhavani Jamakkalam, Madurai Sungudi, Kullu Shawl, Kovaikora Cotton, Gopalpur Tussar Silk, Bagh Prints of Madhya Pradesh. However, the drying up of water sources in most places is a cause of concern for tie and dye work in Kutch, Machilipatnam Kalamkari, Bhavani Jamakkalam, and Srikalahasti Kalamkari, to mention a few. Places like Pochampalli suffer from water pollution as the Musi river drains the wastewaters of Hyderabad city and hence the groundwater is laden with salts and other contaminants. This also affects the dyeing quality (Reddy, 2007).

Further, due to the rising cost of materials and time involved in procuring raw materials and processing the same, the use of natural materials in tie and dye is depleting fast and it is increasingly dominated by chemical materials.

Muga silk of Assam is yet another classic example of the uniqueness linked to geographic and natural factors. The special silkworm, Antheraea Assama, produces shimmering golden yellow silk which is native only to the region (Brahmaputra valley). The silkworms are exclusively found only in the state of Assam and feed on 'som' (*Machiliusbombycina*) and 'soalu' (*Litsaeapolyantha*). But, in the recent years there has been a set-back to the quality of muga silk due to the following reasons: Diminishing area in muga cultivation induced by the competing rubber crop, diseases at the cocoon stage, and loses incurred due to the outdoor nature of muga rearing. The price of muga silk has increased but it has nothing to do with GI registration. Apparel with 100 per cent muga yarn has become rare or is only made-to-order. Muga silk is often blended with imported tussar silk from China or other indigenous silk yarn, affecting the quality (Nanda et al., 2013).

Some of the products protected in the Indian context can be differentiated from their conventional counterparts because of their specific and unique value characteristics, yet they are not commercially competitive in terms of productivity, volume, and prices (Vandecandelaere et al., 2009–10, p. 19). One such example is Bhalia wheat, a registered GI product from Gujarat, which is produced in ecologically poor, saline ingressed areas of Gujarat. But the wheat produced in such region has distinct taste and quality which is appreciated by food connoiseurs.

The GI documents of Kannauj perfume, which belongs to the manufactured product category, mention that with time 'there is much erosion of the role the environment has played in the making of Kannauj as the hub of natural perfumes. Therefore, it is human skills, knowledge of perfumery craft, and goodwill earned by the Kannauj perfumery industry that can be classified as the uniqueness of Kannauj natural perfumes (attars)'.[11]

During the discussion on GI for Coorg green cardamom, it was indicated that as

> the area of production extends from Wayanad District in North Kerala to Singampatti in Tirunelveli District in South Tamil Nadu, the soil and climatic conditions as well as the elevation and shade pattern of cardamom plantations are likely to vary in this long stretch. As such, a check can be made, and, if possible, GI may be restricted to one or more contiguous districts of similar soil, environmental conditions, culture and heritage. Based on the possible quality variation in the product, one or two more GIs may be identified later, according to the demand of the situation. (minutes of CGM held on 3 August 2007)

Marie-Vivien (2015) also echoes this view that while vast areas might indicate the production dynamism of a crop, it would erode its GI uniqueness.

Wooden crafts, like the Mysore Rosewood inlay or Mysore Agarbathis or sandal oil or soap manufacturing depend on the government release of the required type of wood and in the required quantity. Due to the degradation of forests and indiscriminate use of resources, there are restrictions on the availability of forest materials. Artisans overcome the difficulties in accessing the original raw materials by resorting to 'look alike' plastic/synthetic material in the case of rosewood or accessing bamboo from distant Assam and other North-Eastern states in the case of agarbathis. Such substitutions could deceive consumers and affect the reputation of the product.

In the enthusiasm to file the maximum number of GI applications, states often tend to file products which show limited uniqueness (Kumar & Bahl, 2010) or products that are widely grown. In the absence of a separate market for the GI products, such products compete with the bulk products of that area. Most often the 'uniqueness' of the product is blurred and does not emerge clearly in the statement of the case, for instance, in the case of pineapples, oranges (Memon Narang is an exception), which calls for more scientific rigour (Soam & Hussain, 2011) in seeking GI registration.

However, erosion in the natural factors, restrictions on availability of raw materials and the lack of remunerative price for the handicrafts, have resulted in crafts-persons slowly withdrawing themselves and finding livelihood opportunities elsewhere.

Code of Practices

Code of practice (CoP) refers to 'a set of measurable voluntary practices for the production of a GI product, which every producer needs to comply with' (Vandecandelaere et al., 2009–10). There are several elements to CoP: (a) defining the specificities of the production, (b) delimiting the geographical area of production, and (c) the guarantee system. Particularly when the geographical production areas are widespread, there could be obvious heterogeneity in the products, be it agriculture or craft or food products, due to differences in the natural resources or human practices/skills. Hence, CoP becomes very essential so that uniqueness to the region is maintained in all the products to target niche markets. Continuous following of the CoP has resulted in the credibility of internationally renowned products like Champagne, Parma Ham, and Tequila.

Mainly CoPs focus on the following elements that give the products their uniqueness: (1) the main physical appearance and scientific composition of the product; (2) core raw materials used in the process of production chemical and biological aspects of the product; (3) process protocols followed in production, harvest, processing packing, and transportation; (4) specification and demonstration of the unique quality linked to the geographic region; (5) demarcation of the production area; (6) labelling rules; and (7) process of verification (Vandecandelaere et al., 2009–10). Aspects (3) and (5) also require the identification of the persons/agencies that will be responsible for the pre and post-production process, packing, and transporting. Thus, drafting the CoP involves the identification of the value chain, with clear responsibilities, laying down quality parameters, and the institution that will monitor and implement the same. Adoption of the CoP by every producer in the group is the core of GI, and when the product is duly inspected and certified by a responsible agency, it increases the authenticity and credibility of the product. Drafting a CoP that is acceptable to all the producers, facilitating adoption and implementation of the same for product quality and uniqueness, requires a collective approach (more on this in the fourth chapter) and the presence of appropriate institutions which will govern the entire process and authenticate it.

In Thailand, the government is actively involved in the promotion of standards for the registered products. The Thai government has established (1) control mechanisms for traceability and (2) certification from the accreditation bodies for the GI product. For each product, a manual is developed for the production and method for tracing the origins. The Department of Intellectual Property (DIP) has a memorandum of understanding with the Department of Thai Industrial Standard Institute (TISI) and National Bureau of Agriculture Commodity and Food Standard (ACFS). The MOU means that these agencies work for the development of control systems in Thailand. Once the systems are developed, the DIP validates the specifications and inspection methods. TISI and ACFS accredit the control body that comprises of both internal and external control (Lalitha, 2016). At the top of the control body is the GI Board. These mechanisms ensure that the GI products of Thailand are of good quality and traceability can be ensured. Such measures adopted in the case of Jasmine rice of Thailand have resulted in producers receiving a premium price.

Another example following a CoP from the beginning (rearing of pigs) to the end (final packing of the product for retail sale) is the case of Parma Ham of Italy.[12] The pig selected for Parma Ham is a 'special' pig, born and reared in only ten regions of central northern

Italy, exclusively of Large White, Landrace, and Duroc breed, and fed on quality food such as maize, barley, and whey from the production of Parmigiano-Reggiano cheese. The Parma Ham consortium which was started in 1963 with twenty-three members, now has 150 members. The consortium undertakes the following activities: checks any illegal activity in the use of the brand Parma Ham; works for creating awareness and market in Italy and elsewhere; lays down quality control measures; and supervises the observance of provisions of quality and rules. The consortium's responsibilities also include the following: identification of the pig starts from the time when the owners of the young pigs put a tattoo on their legs indicating the month of the birth of the ham. In the authorized slaughter house, a permanent branding is done. This identifies the slaughter house. A metal seal made up of a circular sign on the meat indicates the date by which the curing began; and, finally, the ducal crown branding is done which indicates the producer and the quality. The restricted membership allows the same to be withdrawn in case of non-compliance with regulations. The police can carry out a sudden inspection anytime at any stage of the process including packing and transportation. Thus, it is evident from the highlight of the Parma Ham case that the details cover all aspects of institution and governance in maintaining the quality and traceability, which commands a premium price.

Naidu (2014) states that the statement of case provided for each of the product is the CoP. A typical statement of case contains the following: name of the applicant, address, list of association of persons, type of goods, specification, nature of GI, description of goods, GI area and production map, proof of origin, method of production, uniqueness, inspection body, and other related information.

It is observed that a few important aspects like packing and transportation, labelling rules, and control/verification system are lacking and need to be emphasized in the Indian cases. However, when agencies like Spice Boards or APEDA are involved in the filing of GIs, keeping international trade in mind, detailed CoPs are maintained for export purposes.

It is possible that the CoP that is currently followed is different than what is stated in the application (Rangnekar, 2011) (for example for the Thanjavur Painting case discussed in the following chapter).

In Indonesia, while the traditional practices are being followed, modern farming practices are mentioned in the CoP (Durand & Fournier, 2017) with the purpose of modernizing the agriculture sector there.

In textiles, as detailed earlier, the code of practice mentions the use of natural materials or river water in the tie and dye process. Yet due to non-availability of materials and the drying up of rivers, alternatives are being used.

Marie-Vivien (2015) observes that the involvement of the government in filing the GI applications, particularly in handicrafts, can help in assuring the consumer about the authenticity of the products without the need for any control systems.

Authorized Users

Evidence from Europe in the cases of successful GIs indicates that the secret of success lies in effective identification of the value chain, which is equivalent to the term 'authorized users' (AUs) in the GI parlance in India.

In India, GI application is divided into two parts: Part A and Part B. The part relating to the registration, where the GI certification legally recognizes the link between the product and the producer, is Part A of the GI application process. But to use the GI tag for any purpose, the producer/trader needs to get listed as the authorized user by the registered proprietor. This is referred to as Part B of the application. The registration of authorized user becomes important for two reasons. Only an authorized user has the exclusive rights to use the GI in relation to goods in respect of which it is registered. Only a registered proprietor or an authorized user can initiate any action against infringement. But, as the definition of the producer is wide,[13] identifying a trader or a dealer could be another difficult task,[14] unless the producer association has identified all the stakeholders in the value chain. For instance, under the authentication process that is supervised by the Tea Board, 171 companies dealing in Darjeeling tea have registered with the Tea Board, seventy-four of which are producer companies and ninety-seven of which are trader/exporter companies (Pai & Singla, 2016, p. 17).

The number of AUs registered is very less as evident from Table 2.5 and Appendix Table 2.6. An interesting question that arises here is whether this means that those producers who are not registered are unauthorized users? The scenario is a bit complex since majority of the goods registered under GI have been well known in their respective places of origin and continue to be known, and thereby the producers are also 'recognized' in the local areas[15] while the legal protection is relatively less known. However, it may be counter argued that before the enactment of GI trade in place goods happened in good faith and the counterfeit products went unchecked. But, now with the GI Act in vogue, it is possible to take action against counterfeit producers, provided the value chain is sensitized about the original and the duplicate products.

The use of GIs in sui generis systems is not necessarily conditional upon membership in a particular collective entity that may have exclusive rights to use the GI. Rather, it is based upon adherence to the conditions of production in a geographical region (Dagne, 2012). The authorized user is supposed to adhere to the rules and regulations specified by the producer group.

The registration of a GI is for a period of ten years but it may be renewed indefinitely. The registration of an authorized user is also for a period of ten years or for the period till the validity date of the GI. The GI Registry started receiving applications to register AUs since May 2009. Appendix Table 2.6 gives the list of products with authorized users.

There are several reasons for the low levels of registration of authorized users with the GI. The supreme most is the limited

TABLE 2.5 Details of AU Applications Received till 31 March 2016

GI Category	No. of AU Applications Received	No. of AU Applications Registered
Handicraft including textiles	2250	1095
Agricultural	29	24
Manufactured	56	56
Foodstuff	14	9
Total	2349	1184

Source: Government of India (2015, p. 61).

awareness and clarity on eligibility. Second, for most products the producer groups have either not been formed or formed with very few members and a tentative list of producers is not available uniformly in the case of the registered GI products. Hence, in such cases, identifying the different stakeholders in the value chain becomes a Herculean task. In West Bengal, despite the fact that the patent information bureau (which has been the proprietor of GI products) is willing to give a no objection certificate (NOC) to the producers, there have been no takers (Sharma & Kulhari, 2015, p. 91). But in the case of most GI products, the producer deals with the market directly only to a small extent. The rest is done through the 'middlemen', who might have more stakeholders dealing with them. Hence, the identification of the value chain remains an unfinished agenda for the GI products.

The reason why AUs are more in textile products is perhaps due to the fact that the yarn has to be from one particular source and most GIs in textiles have been filed by exporter 'association', 'samitis', and cooperatives—thus, it is relatively easy to establish the value chain to a certain extent. Hence, by identifying an association, all the members become AUs. However, mere registration of AUs is not sufficient. A suitable watchdog mechanism is also required to ensure that the code of practices specified for the different stakeholders identified and AUs are followed diligently as mentioned in the Parma Ham case. At present, there is a lack of clarity about the accountability of the different AUs and their different roles. Under Section 27 of the GI Act, cancellation of registration of the non-complying member from the list of authorized GI producers is possible.

In view of these significant lacunae, in the recent grant of GI, the registry clearly mentions a few post-GI activities to be undertaken by the applicant. One of these activities is to file a certain required number of AUs within a fixed time limit. However, given its quasi-judicial nature, the registry cannot take any action against such applications which have not registered any AU.

GI Infringement

GI infringement is widespread and hence calls for institutional mechanisms to be set up throughout the value chain, as mentioned in the

Parma Ham case, to check the free riding by producers who do not belong to the GI area.

The Darjeeling Tea GI has been an example of the most successful case in fighting infringement in the international scenario because of the serious involvement of the Tea Board in protecting the GI which has also employed an international watchdog agency to report any GI infringement. GI on Mysore Silk is fiercely guarded by the Karnataka state government, where the Mysore silk materials are sold only through the government-owned emporiums and sales franchise is not given to other textile dealers. Tirupathi Devasthanam, as owner of the GI of Tirupathi Laddu, has also effectively controlled the 'Tirupathi Laddu' sales at Tirupathi and other nearby railway and bus stations and different sweet meat shops including in Chennai.[16] After the GI, it is available only to persons who have visited the temple. But in the case of both Mysore silk and Tirupathi Laddu, it is relatively easier as the producer is controlling the distribution channels.

However, for a majority of other products, though it is widely known that look-alike GI products float in the market, causing steady market erosion for the original registered products, only a few cases of GI infringement have been made public. The likely reasons for this are: (1) lack of awareness about GI, (2) lack of institutional mechanisms to monitor the GI product, (3) lack of identification of the value chain involved in the sales, and (4) lack of teeth about infringement in the GI Act itself. But the problem with the GI Act of India is that while the situations leading to infringement is defined but it does not mention anything about the ways of fighting against the infringement and this a larger governance issue (Kumar & Bahl, 2010, p. 8). 'Craft producers, when asked about the possibility of obtaining redress from the courts for infringement of ownership rights on their products, will generally respond with a hearty laugh. Of the many dealers, manufacturers, and exporters we interviewed, not one expressed any optimism regarding the possibilities for legal enforcement of ownership rights' (Liebl & Roy, 2003), which explains that the producers have reconciled to the fact that they have to simply cope with the duplicate products.

Infringement is more pronounced particularly in cases involving handlooms in a scenario where the invasion of powerlooms is killing the handlooms. The case of Banaras saree has been particularly discussed by many scholars (Basole, 2015; Das, 2010; Pai & Singla, 2016). In the context of the uncontrolled imitated Banaras saris circulating in the market, which has led to lot of weavers leaving the profession, an important expectation from the GI status of Banaras sari is whether it will curb the sale of duplicates so that the weavers are back on their job. The expectation from the legal status of the registration is also due to the fact that the majority of the weavers do not have the wherewithal to fight the infringement on their own (Kumar & Bahl, 2010, p. 8). This is despite the fact that a clear mention of five inspection bodies for the Banaras saris for quality-check has been made in the GI application clearly showing the lack of enforcement of the inspection mechanism. It is reported that the downfall of Banaras saris began when the Surat powerlooms developed the technique to replicate the traditional designs woven in handlooms and also lured away the best weavers of Banaras (Dikshit, 2014). Unable to fight the infringement, the Banaras weavers have also started producing cheaper imitation saris to reduce their production cost and meet the challenges posed by the powerlooms (Pai & Singla, 2016).

In the case of Ajrakh printing of Gujarat (the GI was later filed but is yet to be granted), a fashion designer from India wanted to replicate it in his designs using the design of a skull. None of the block makers agreed to do so with the skull but still this designer created digital designs of Ajrakh with skull[17] although Ajrakh printing involves depicting life in the form of nature, flowers, trees, and creepers. Such controversy could have been avoided if Ajrakh printing had been protected under GI.

An effort to register the GI name Bikaneri Bhujia, which is produced by hundreds of small producers as a trademark by Pepsi Snacks, was stopped and the applicant had to withdraw the application (Maheshwari, 2014).

Inspection Body

As mentioned elsewhere, GIs, as opposed to the industrialized products, are produced in a rural and village environment. There has to be an inspection mechanism to authenticate the quality and traceability of the product to the region to ensure credibility of the product and to create a niche market. In the case of internationally traded commodities like Basmati rice, Darjeeling tea, and spices, the respective commodity boards and APEDA have drawn quality standards which also take care of the regional authenticity. For instance, though Darjeeling tea got its GI status in 2004, the inspection structure was readied in the year 2000 itself (Das, 2010).

Due to the strict licensing by the tea board, only 100 per cent Darjeeling tea can be identified with the Darjeeling tea GI and all other tea mixtures have to be identified as blends. In a huge victory for Darjeeling tea, the EU norm which allowed the EU importers to blend 51 per cent of Darjeeling tea with any other tea to the extent of 49 per cent and still can be called as Darjeeling tea was revoked in 2016. This should give a boost to the Darjeeling tea exports as only 100 per cent Darjeeling tea will be available to the EU consumers (Pai & Singla, 2016).

The Basmati.net drawn by the APEDA requires all the stakeholders in the value chain like the farmers of Basmati paddy in GI area, commission agents, agriculture produce markets, paddy traders, Basmati rice millers and processors, and Basmati rice exporters and suppliers in the domestic market to register themselves at Basmati. net. With separate logins and passwords, these different stakeholders have to register the area sown under paddy, quantity bought and sold, and so on. As all the stakeholders are required to adhere to the rules and regulations set by the APEDA, quality and traceability are ensured.

Nair (2016) observes that products like Champagne, Cognac, and Parma Ham have become GI icons due to the consistent emphasis on quality. EU law necessitates that effective verification and controls exists at multiple levels in the supply chain, ensuring compliance with product specification before placing it in the market and market monitoring of the use of the names to ensure legal compliance, which safeguards that consumers get authentic product and thereby build on consumers' trust (Nair, 2016). In the EU, the quality standards are enforced through Competent Authorities (CAs) designated by member states who are responsible for verifying compliance with the legal requirements relating to quality schemes. Reports of the audit activities of these CAs must be included in the annual national control plans submitted by every member state to the EU. Further, at the time of the registration of the PDO or PGI, the applicant group is required to identify one or more accredited certification bodies which will confirm that the product specifications associated with the GI products are met before the goods are placed on the market. The operation of the accredited certification bodies is subject to the scrutiny of the CA (Pai & Singla, 2016). Such an integrated system builds reputation and helps the products to command a premium price. In the context of the GI Act of India, such emphasis on quality is lacking (Nair, 2016; Pai & Singla, 2016). In the GI Act of India, the word 'inspection' occurs only in the context of requiring an applicant to list the particulars of the inspection structure and in asking for the details of the inspection mechanism but does not specify the actual responsibilities. Though a functioning inspection mechanism is a must and boost consumers interest in the GI product, under the GI Act of India, failure to set up an inspection structure is not considered as a sufficient ground for demonstrating the inadequacy of an application to register a GI (Pai & Singla, 2016).

From the information available in the GI journal on inspection body regarding registered GI products, five categories may be identified. The first category refers to those where the inspection body has been proposed to be set up. The second relates to those applications where the process to set up an inspection body has been initiated. In the third, information provided states that an inspection body has been set up and then enumerates the details of the officials designated for the purpose. This type does not give the specific job description of the inspection body. The fourth category refers to those applications where the role of the inspection body is to check the quality of the product, which is spelt out in detail. The recent applications from Maharashtra filed by the farmer producer organizations are a case in point. The fifth category is where the purpose of the inspection body is specifically stated in the application as 'the GI Inspection body has been constituted to regulate the use of GI in the territory to which it relates and to maintain the quality of the GI produce'. For example, the applications filed by NERAMAC fall under category five. For the purpose of enforcing the GI and authenticating the product, the inspection body should be of the nature of Type 5 and should actually be engaged in doing so.

It is evident from Table 2.6 that 34 per cent belong to category 3, which means that the inspection body is set up with officials designated for the job, but the job description is not mentioned clearly. A majority of agricultural and textile products belong to category 3. Twenty-one and 11 per cent of the GI products belong to category 4 and 5, with specific roles delineated to take care of the quality of the product and GI implementation respectively. Interestingly, sizeable numbers of agricultural products fall under category 5. For 22 per cent of the products, an inspection body does not exist and for 11 per cent, the process had been initiated at the time of submission. Implicitly, nearly 33 per cent of the GI registered products are sold based on mutual faith and trust between the buyer and seller and there is no guarantee of quality. Traceability of the product is not vouched for by the one associated with the product. Much of the handicraft and textile registrations belong to this category.

TABLE 2.6   Categories of Inspection Body Available for Registered Products

GI Category	1	2	3	4	5	Total
Agriculture	15	6	28	13	24	86
Metal Products	5	2	10	0	0	17
Wood Crafts	5	4	5	3	0	17
Clay/Pottery	3	0	2	1	0	6
Leather/Stone/Glass	3	1	4	1	0	9
Paintings	2	3	3	0	0	8
Paper	1	0	1	1	0	3
Other	4	0	6	1	1	12
Textile	16	11	24	30	1	82
Manufacturing	2	1	2	3	2	10
Foodstuffs	2	1	4	2	0	9
Natural Goods	0	0	0	0	1	1
Total	58	29	89	55	29	260
% to total	22	11	34	21	11	100

Source: Compiled from GI journals and GI registry http://ipindia.nic.in/girindia/, updated up to 31 October 2017.

Note: Details of the categories are mentioned in the above paragraph.

The involvement of agricultural universities as co-applicants in the agricultural applications has been useful as they serve as information providers for quality and technical inputs for the growers.

The scope of the inspection body mentioned in the application[18] in the case of Kullu Shawl provides a road map to check the authenticity and regulate the GI, and it could probably serve as an ideal case for products which have not yet formulated the roles for the inspection body. Here the role of the inspection body has been defined to work on (1) issues related to quality control, (2) legal issues related to GI, (3) random checking at the production/sales counters for violation of GI, and (4) awareness about GIs, IPR issues, and technology upgradation. Accordingly, the Central Wool Development Board at Kullu is authorized to issue the quality control certification to Kullu shawl weavers. The Kullu Shawl Weavers Association (KSWA) will also set up its own testing laboratories and Research and Development facilities. The General Manager of District Industries Centre, KSWA, will deal with the legal issues regarding infringement of GI, particularly at production and sales counters, by undertaking random checking. The KSWA will also evolve marketing strategies for Kullu shawls while the Himachal Pradesh Patent Information Centre, the State Council for Science, Technology, and Environment in collaboration with the Technology Information Forecasting and Assessment Council will organize training programmes on GI and IPR related issues.

The association, in the case of Chettinad Kottan,[19] has initiated multiple efforts to authenticate the quality. For instance, Chettinad Kottan has received the Craftmart certification for palm leaf craft. It has been recognized with the 'UNESCO seal of excellence in handicrafts products in South Asia in 2004, 2006, 2008, and 2009. The seal is awarded in recognition of demonstrated excellence and standard setting in high quality craftsmanship, creative and successful alliance of traditional skills and innovative application of indigenous material, traditional technique and endogenous design, expression of cultural identity and traditional aesthetic value, and respect for the environment' (Government of India, 2012).

Sharma and Kulhari (2015) note that while the master weavers check for the quality of their products done at their instance, in other cases, only 40 per cent of the respondents indicated that their products were inspected for quality before they were sent out for sales to the customers.

Lack of adherence and monitoring also costs dearly when the product is sold in the export market. The Malda mango of West Bengal, which is much sought after in the export markets of Europe and UAE, faced a threat due to the relatively high pesticide residue content in the mangoes. The Ministry of Climate Change and Environment, UAE, had expressed its concern and as a result required that each consignment be accompanied by the phyto-sanitary certificate regarding the levels of pesticide residue and that these tests be carried out by any APEDA certified laboratory. The UAE tops the list of mango exports from India with 55 per cent share in total quantity[20] that is exported. Hence, India cannot afford to ignore the concerns of the UAE. In 2014, the EU countries placed a ban on mango exports from India. This ban was withdrawn in 2015 after satisfactory corrective measures were undertaken. Despite that the export of Malda mangoes reduced from 63,500 tonnes in 2011–12 to 43 thousand tonnes in 2014–15 (Sarkar, 2016).

As mentioned elsewhere in this chapter, authentic raw materials are no longer freely available. While the government is making efforts to provide the same through setting up of raw material banks (Government of India, 2011), procedural delays and competition may lead to substitution of materials with cheaper alternatives leading to the consumers being deceived. Hence, it is essential that there is an inspection body which vouches for quality control.

The Odisha government is initiating a raw material bank to help the stone sculptors (Panda, 2015). The sculptors were left in the lurch when the state cooperative 'Utkalika', which used to provide the stones to the sculptors, could not renew their lease of the quarry. The quarry was located in the land belonging to the Puri temple administration (PTA) and the PTA had refused to renew the lease. For large orders, the sculptors would get the stones illegally from elsewhere and when such consignments were caught the craftsmen had a tough time. Now the government is intervening to set up a raw material bank in Narangarh in Kurdah, which will also function as a testing centre. In the absence of any agreed upon number of crafts-persons or agencies (which work on behalf of the artisans) which are allowed to draw on the natural resources, any uncontrolled exploitation of the natural resources, or unapproved area developmental programmes, would leave the artisans high and dry.

Issues in GI Protection for Non-Agricultural Products from EU

Europe has been the torchbearer of GIs, particularly for agricultural products which are protected either by the PDO or PGI. The reputation of Champagne has been built over a period of 150 years. 'If the GI of Champagne is dismantled, they believe, the champagne flute will soon contain an inferior sparkling wine. This devotion to quality control is a foundation for the designation of champagne as an appellation of origin, as opposed to a mere indication of source' (Jay & Taylor, 2013).

In a study (Insight Consulting, OriGIn, REDD, 2013) that was undertaken with an idea of providing legal and economic information on GI-protected and potential non-agricultural products (NAP) of the member states of the EU, the experts found that many of the GI-protected products were not produced any longer in Germany, and, in other countries, such protected products could not be identified. There was no harmonized protection system across countries. An analysis of these legal instruments showed that they deal with collective strategies to promote or protect the local craft industry and do not go much further than consumer deception laws. Further, the experts involved in the study also found that the non-agricultural sectors were poorly documented, and the quantity and the quality of the data varied according to the cultural background and understanding of the GI concept. Out of the 127 products studied, the number of products with data varied on the chosen indicators like employment, profit, and market. To the extent the data were available on NAP, employment provided was significant. Twenty-five products had access to European and international export markets and faced stiff competition. For 66 products, 50 per cent of the sales were in the domestic market; 57 per cent of 94 products faced infringements. Products which faced infringements or imitation issues were in the ceramics/pottery, glass, stone/marble, and traditional clay category, and the loss of market affected sales and employment. Forty-seven per cent of the products spent no money on promotion of products and used their own labels rather than the geographical name. Producers of products which faced competition were favourable towards uniform GI protection across the EU. All the producers of the NAP converged on the fact that there is a need for a uniform legal framework for NAP all throughout the EU. The authors recommend that as and when such legal framework is established, there is a need for creating strong awareness across all stakeholders as there was a general lack of GI awareness. They also emphasize on the training for those officials who are in charge of the day-to-day management of the GI system. This summary of the EU system highlights that the situation in the EU countries, which have a variety of famous GI agricultural products, is no different than India when it comes to the issues related to the crafts sector.

Pending GIs

While the discussion so far revolved around the registered GIs, mention may be made here about the applications for GIs from both Indian and foreign applicants that are pending approval from the GI Registry. A total of 125 applications from foreign countries are awaiting decision by the GI Registry. France (33), Spain (28), Italy (22), Greece (13), and Germany (11) account for 86 per cent of the total applications pending decision. Fifty-four per cent of the applications belong to wines, 27 and 17 per cent are applications for food products and spirits. The presence of Indian producers in these segment of products is very less in the GI arena. Compared to the 12 foreign applications granted so far, this is a significant increase in the number of foreign applications. As compared to this, there are 139 applications from Indian nationals waiting for the decision. Forty-one per cent of the applications are for handicrafts. The applications for agriculture, textiles, and foodstuff account for 24, 15, and 12 per cent respectively. It would be interesting to see how many of these products have a link with the region in terms of natural or climatic factors. If the human skill factor is the only link factor with the region, chances are that there could be similar products existing in other parts of India. As of 31 October 2017, the number of agricultural GI applications are more than handicraft applications, which could change with GI recognition for the products mentioned in the pending applications. With 31 applications, Tamil Nadu is leading the rest of the states in the number of applications pending approval, followed by 13, 11, and 10 applications from West Bengal, Uttar Pradesh, and Maharashtra. There could be a healthy competition among the states to secure GIs for the products of their states. But in that competition, the GI uniqueness should not be lost. The GI registry will have to carefully assess the applications with the help of technical experts that form the members of the committee to examine the applications. While filing applications, care should be taken to include all the eligible producers as stakeholders and ensure that the production area is contiguous and not widespread. When the GI areas are too spread out, there could be wide heterogeneity in the product, leading to less uniqueness and more challenges in clearly defining CoPs, which could reduce the 'unique selling point' of the product.

★★★

This chapter provided a profile status of the GI registered products and also highlighted the institutional issues where strong governance needs to be brought in to correct the gaps and promote the GI products.

The recent National Handicrafts Policy Report notes that 'the six states of West Bengal, Uttar Pradesh, Odisha, Andhra Pradesh, Rajasthan, and Assam, together account for 65 per cent of all rural handloom and handicraft establishments in India' (AIACA, 2017). While Uttar Pradesh, Andhra Pradesh, and Rajasthan have registered fourteen, ten, and six products, Assam is yet to register any handicraft product. In textiles, Odisha, Andhra Pradesh, and Uttar Pradesh have ten, seven, and five products each. Evidently, there exists a huge potential for registering more GI products from these states, given their strength in handicrafts and handlooms. Similarly, in the agricultural sector, while a few states have fielded several products, some states are yet to file any GI application. This does not mean that there are no products worth GI registration. What the status implies is that an intervention needs to be made by the government to create awareness regarding GI and to take efforts to identify crafts or handlooms that could be registered with GI.

The discussion in the chapter also shows that there is a scope for a lot of improvement in the pillars of GI, namely the geographical coverage, uniqueness, and CoPs. Producers should be made aware about the importance of CoP, and the scientific body in that particular craft/crop of the region should help the concerned producer association to develop CoPs. CoPs are essential to ensure that all the products produced in the region have the uniqueness and the same is also certified either by a participatory guarantee scheme or by other suitable third-party agency. However, the emphasis is that the certification by the third party agency does not guarantee uniform products that are similar to the industrially produced products, but guarantee the consumers that standards of quality production were followed by the producers.

Evidence from elsewhere shows that the producers' collective is supported by government quality control and enforcement. In India too, there needs to be a separate government agency that should work along with the producers of the GI registered products. States, when they compete to file more GI applications, should remember that uniqueness is clearly identified.

In the following chapter, using the theory of change framework and the evidence from the empirical research carried out by the authors, an attempt is made to understand the possible impact on select products due to GI registration.

Appendix

APPENDIX TABLE 2.1 Details of Agricultural Products Registered with GI

Name of the State	Total No. of Agricultural Products	Total No. of GI Products from Each State	% of Agricultural to Total	Details of Agricultural Products
Andhra Pradesh	2	18	11.1	Guntur Sannam Chilli, Banaganapalle Mangoes
Arunachal Pradesh	1	1	100	Arunachal Orange
Assam	4	5	80	Assam Tea (Orthodox) Logo, Assam Karbi Anglong Ginger, Tezpur Litchi, Joha Rice of Assam
Gujarat	2	10	20	Gir Kesar Mango, Bhalia Wheat
Himachal Pradesh	1	5	20	Kangra Tea
Karnataka	16	35	45.7	Coorg Orange, Mysore Betel leaf, Nanjanagud Banana, Mysore Jasmine, Udupi Jasmine, Hadagali Jasmine,

				Coorg Green Cardamom, Devanahalli Pomello, Appemidi Mango, Kamalapur Red Banana, Byadagi Chilli, Udupi Mattu Gulla Brinjal, Bangalore Blue Grapes, Bangalore Rose Onion, Monsooned Malabar Arabica Coffee, Monsooned Malabar Robusta Coffee
Kerala	11	23	47.8	Navara Rice, Palakkadan Matta Rice, Malabar Pepper, Spices—Alleppey Green Cardamom, Pokkali Rice, Vazhakulam Pineapple, Central Travancore Jaggery, Wayanad Jeerakasala Rice, Wayanad Gandhakasala Rice, Kaipad Rice, Chengalikodan Nendran Banana
Maharashtra	23	30	76.6	Mahabaleshwar Strawberry, Nashik Grapes, Kolhapur Jaggery, Nagpur Orange, Ajara Ghansal Rice, Mangalwedha Jowar, Sindhudurg & Ratnagiri Kokum, Waghya Ghevada, Navapur Tur Dal, Vengurla Cashew, Lasalgaon Onion, Sangli Raisins, Beed Custard Apple, Jalna Sweet Orange, Waigaon Turmeric, Purandar Fig, Jalgaon Brinjal, Solapur Pomegranate, Bhiwapur Chilli, Ambemohar Rice, Dahanu Gholvad Chikoo, Jalgaon Banana, Marathwada Kesar Mango
Manipur	1	4	25	Kachai Lemon
Meghalaya	2	2	100	Khasi Mandarin, Memong Narang

(continued)

APPENDIX TABLE 2.1 *(Continued)*

Name of the State	Total No. of Agricultural Products	Total No. of GI Products from Each State	% of Agricultural to Total	Details of Agricultural Products
Mizoram	1	1	100	Mizo Chilli
Nagaland	2	3	66.6	Naga Mircha, Naga Tree Tomato
Odisha	2	14	14.3	Ganjam Kewda Rooh, Ganjam Kewda Flower
Sikkim	1	1	100	Sikkim Large Cardamom
Tamil Nadu	5	24	21	Eathomozhy Tall Coconut, Nilgiri (Orthodox) Logo, Virupakshi Hill Banana, Sirumalai Hill Banana, Madurai Malli
Tripura	1	1	100	Tripura Queen Pineapple
Uttar Pradesh	3	22	13.6	Mango Malihabadi Dusseheri, Kalanamak Rice
Uttarakhand	1	1	100	Allahabad Surkha, Uttarakhand Tejpat
West Bengal	6	14	42.8	Darjeeling Tea, Laxman Bhog Mango, Khirsapati (Himsagar) Mango, Fazli Mango grown in the district of Malda, Tulapanji Rice, Gobindabhog Rice
Punjab, Haryana, Delhi, HP, UK, parts of western UP and J & K	1	1	100	Basmati
Total	86	260	33.1	

Source: Compiled from GI journals and GI registry http://ipindia.nic.in/girindia/, updated up to 31 October 2017.

APPENDIX TABLE 2.2 Details of Textile Products Registered with GI

Name of the State	Total No. of Textile Products	Total No. of GI Products from Each State	% of textile in Total	Products in the Textiles Category
Andhra Pradesh	7	18	39	Pochampalli Ikat, Srikalahasthi Kalamkari, Machilipatnam Kalamkari, Uppada Jamdani Saris, Venkatagiri Saris, Mangalagiri Saris and Fabrics, Dharmavaram Handloom Pattu Saris and Paavadas
Assam	1	5	20	Muga Silk
Bihar	3	5	60	Applique—Khatwa Patch Work of Bihar, Sujini Embroidery Work of Bihar, Bhagalpur Silk
Chhattisgarh	1	4	25	Champa Silk Saree and Fabrics
Gujarat	6	10	60	Kutch Embroidery, Tangaliya Shawl, Surat Zari Craft, Kachchh Shawls, Patan Patola, Jamnagari Bandhani
Himachal Pradesh	3	5	60	Kullu Shawl, Chamba Rumal, Kinnauri Shawl
J & K	3	7	43	Kani Shawl, Kashmir Pashmina, Kashmir Sozani Craft
Karnataka	7	35	20	Mysore Silk, Ilkal Saris, Molakalmuru Saris, Udupi Saris, Kasuti Embroidery, Sandur Lambani Embroidery, Guledgudd Khana

(continued)

APPENDIX TABLE 2.2 *(Continued)*

Name of the State	Total No. of Textile Products	Total No. of GI Products from Each State	% of Textile in Total	Products in the Textiles Category
Kerala	6	23	26	Balaramapuram Saris and Fine Cotton Fabrics, Kasaragod Saris, Kuthampully Saris, Chendamangalam Dhoties & Set Mundu, Kuthampally Dhoties & Set Mundu, Cannanore Home Furnishings
Madhya Pradesh	3	6	50	Chanderi Fabric, Bagh Prints of Madhya Pradesh, Maheshwar Saris & Fabrics
Maharashtra	4	30	13	Solapur Chaddar, Solapur Terry Towel, Paithani Saris and Fabrics, Karvath Kati Saris & Fabrics
Manipur	3	4	75	Shaphee Lanphee, Wangkhei Phee, Moirang Phee
Nagaland	1	3	33	Chakshesang Shawls
Odisha	10	14	71	Kotpad Handloom Fabric, Orissa Ikat, Pipli Applique Work, Khandua Saree and Fabrics, Gopalpur Tussar Fabrics, Dhalapathar Parda & Fabrics, Sambalpuri Bandha Saree & Fabrics, Bomkai Saree & Fabrics, Habaspuri Saree & Fabrics, Berhampur Patta (Phoda Kumbha) Saree & Joda

Rajasthan	3	9	33	Kota Doria, Sanganeri Hand Block Printing, Bagru Hand Block Print
Tamil Nadu	9	24	38	Salem Fabric, Kancheepuram Silk, Salem Silk known as Salem Venpattu, Kovai Cora Cotton, Arani Silk, Chettinad Kottan, Toda Embroidery, Bhavani Jamakkalam, Madurai Sungudi
Telangana	3	10	30	Gadwal Saris, Narayanpet Handloom Saris, Siddipet Gollabama
Uttar Pradesh	5	22	23	Lucknow Chikan Craft, Banaras Brocades and Saris, Handmade Carpet of Bhadohi, Farrukhabad Prints, Lucknow Zardozi
West Bengal	4	14	29	Santipore Saree, Baluchari Saree, Dhaniakhali Saree, Nakshi Kantha
Punjab/ Haryana/ Rajasthan	1	1	100	Phulkari
Total	83	260	32	

Source: Compiled from GI journals and GI registry http://ipindia.nic.in/girindia/, updated up to 31 October 2017.

APPENDIX TABLE 2.3   Details of Handicrafts Registered with GI

Name of the State	Products in the handicrafts Category	Total No. of Handi- craft Products	Total No. of GI Products from Each State	% of Handi- Craft to Total
Andhra Pradesh	Budiiti Bell & Brass Craft, Kondapalli Bommalu, Bobbile Veena, Udayagiri Wooden Cutlery, Etikoppaka Toys, Andhra Pradesh Leather Puppetry, Durgi Stone Carvings	7	18	39
Bihar	Sikki Grass Work of Bihar, Madhubani paintings	2	5	40
Chhattisgarh	Bastar Iron Craft, Bastar Dhokra, Bastar Wooden Craft	3	4	75
Gujarat	Sankheda Furniture, Agates of Cambay	2	10	20
Himachal Pradesh	Kangra Paintings	1	5	20
J & K	Kashmir Walnut Wood Carving, Khatamband, Kashmir Paper Mache, Kashmiri Hand Knotted Carpet	4	7	57
Karnataka	Bidriware, Karnataka Bronze Ware, Mysore Rosewood Inlay, Channapatna Toys & Dolls, Kinhal Toys, Mysore Traditional Paintings, Ganjifa Cards of Mysore, Navalgund Durries	8	35	23
Kerala	Aranmula Kannadi, Payyannur Pavithra Ring, Maddalam of Palakkad, Alleppey Coir, Screw Pine Craft of Kerala, Brass Broidered Coconut Shell Crafts of Kerala	6	23	26

Madhya Pradesh	Bell Metal Ware of Datia and Tikamgarh, Leather Toys of Indore	2	6	33
Maharashtra	Puneri Pagadi, Warli Painting	2	30	7
Odisha	Konark Stone Carving, Orissa Pattachitra	2	14	14
Puducherry	Villianur Terracotta Works, Tirukanur Papier Mache Craft	2	2	100
Rajasthan	Thewa Art Work, Kathputlis of Rajasthan, Blue Pottery of Jaipur, Molela Clay Work	4	9	44
Tamil Nadu	Temple Jewellery of Nagercoil, Thanjavur Art Plate, Swamimalai Bronze Icons, Nachiarkoil Kuthuvilakku, Thanjavur Veenai, Thanjavur Doll, Thanjavur Paintings, Pattamadai Pai	8	24	33
Telangana	Silver Filigree of Karimnagar, Pembarthi Metal Craft, Nirmal Toys and Craft, Nirmal Furniture, Cheriyal Paintings, Nirmal Paintings	6	10	60
Uttar Pradesh	Moradabad Metal Craft, Banaras Metal Repousse Craft, Banaras Gulabi Meenakari Craft, Saharanpur Wood Craft, Varanasi Wooden Lacquerware & Toys, Nizamabad Black Pottery, Varanasi Glass beads, Firozabad Glass, Agra Durrie, Mirzapur Handmade Dari	10	22	45
West Bengal	Santiniketan Leather Goods	1	14	7
Grand total		70	260	27

Source: Compiled from GI journals and GI registry http://ipindia.nic.in/girindia/, updated up to 31 October 2017.

APPENDIX TABLE 2.4   Details of Manufactured Products Registered with GI

Name of the State	Total No. of Manufacture Products	Total No. of GI Products from Each State	% of Manufactured Products to Total Number of Products	Manufactures
Goa	1	1	100	Feni
Karnataka	3	35	9	Mysore Agarbathi, Mysore Sandalwood Oil, Mysore Sandal Soap
Maharashtra	1	30	3	Nashik Valley Wine
Tamil Nadu	2	24	8	Coimbatore Wet Grinder, EI Leather
Uttar Pradesh	4	22	18	Kannauj Perfume, Kanpur Saddlery, Meerut Scissors, Khurja Pottery
Total	11	260	4	

Source: Compiled from GI journals and GI registry http://ipindia.nic.in/girindia/, updated up to 31 October 2017.

APPENDIX TABLE 2.5   Details of Foodstuff Registered with GI

Name of the State	Foodstuff	Total	Total GI Registration from Each State	% of Foodstuff to Total
Andhra Pradesh	Tirupathi Laddu, Bandar Laddu	2	18	11
Karnataka	Dharwad Pedha	1	35	3
Madhya Pradesh	Ratlami Sev	1	6	17
Rajasthan	Bikaneri Bhujia	1	9	11
Telangana	Hyderabad Haleem	1	9	11
West Bengal	Joynagar Moa, Bardhaman Sitabhog, Bardhaman Mihidana	3	14	21
Total		9	91	10

Source: Compiled from GI journals and GI registry http://ipindia.nic.in/girindia/, updated up to 31 October 2017.

APPENDIX TABLE 2.6   Products with Authorized Users

Name of the Product	Category	State
Machilipatnam Kalamkari	Textiles/Handicrafts	Andhra Pradesh
Pochampalli Ikat	Textiles/Handicrafts	Andhra Pradesh
Muga Silk of Assam	Textiles/Handicrafts	Assam
Bastar Dhokra	Handicrafts	Chhattisgarh
Patan Patola	Textiles/Handicrafts	Gujarat
Surat Zari Craft	Textiles/Handicrafts	Gujarat
Kangra Rice	Agriculture	Himachal Pradesh
Kinnuri Shawl	Textiles/Handicrafts	Himachal Pradesh
Kullu Shawl	Textiles/Handicrafts	Himachal Pradesh
Kashmir Paper Mache	Handicrafts	Jammu and Kashmir
Kashmir Walnut Wood Carving	Handicrafts	Jammu and Kashmir
Khatamband	Handicrafts	Jammu and Kashmir
Kani Shawl	Textiles/Handicrafts	Jammu and Kashmir
Kashmir Pashmina	Textiles/Handicrafts	Jammu and Kashmir
Kashmir Sozani Craft	Textiles/Handicrafts	Jammu and Kashmir
Byadagi Chilli	Agriculture	Karnataka
Dharwad Pedha	Foodstuff	Karnataka
Ganjifa Cards of Mysore	Handicrafts	Karnataka
Karnataka Bronzeware	Handicrafts	Karnataka
Navalgund Durries	Handicrafts	Karnataka
Molakalmuru Saris	Textiles/Handicrafts	Karnataka
Central Travancore Jaggery	Agriculture	Kerala
Navara Rice	Agriculture	Kerala
Palakkad Matta Rice	Agriculture	Kerala
Pokkali Rice	Agriculture	Kerala
Vazhakulam Pineapple	Agriculture	Kerala
Bell Metalware of Datia and Tikamgarh	Foodstuff	Madhya Pradesh
Leather Toys of Indore	Manufactured	Madhya Pradesh
Ajara Ghansal Rice	Agriculture	Maharashtra
Mangalwedha Jowar	Agriculture	Maharashtra
Navapur Tur Dal	Agriculture	Maharashtra

(continued)

APPENDIX TABLE 2.6 *(Continued)*

Name of the Product	Category	State
Sangli Raisins	Agriculture	Maharashtra
Sindhudurg and Ratnagiri Kokum	Agriculture	Maharashtra
Vengurla Cashew	Agriculture	Maharashtra
Warli Painting	Handicrafts	Maharashtra
Naga Mircha	Agriculture	Nagaland
Orissa Pattachitra	Handicrafts	Orissa
Bomkai Saree and Fabrics	Textiles/Handicrafts	Orissa
Sambalpuri Bandha Saree and Fabrics	Textiles/Handicrafts	Orissa
Phulkari	Textiles/Handicrafts	Punjab, Haryana, Rajasthan
Bikaneri Bhujia	Foodstuff	Rajasthan
Blue Pottery of Jaipur	Handicrafts	Rajasthan
Kota Doria	Textiles/Handicrafts	Rajasthan
Kamalapur Red Banana	Agriculture	Tamil Nadu
Thanjavur Paper Plate	Handicrafts	Tamil Nadu
EI Leather	Manufactured	Tamil Nadu
Bhavani Jamakkalam	Textiles/Handicrafts	Tamil Nadu
Kancheepuram Silk	Textiles/Handicrafts	Tamil Nadu
Koval Kora Cotton Saris	Textiles/Handicrafts	Tamil Nadu
Salem Silk	Textiles/Handicrafts	Tamil Nadu
Hyderabad Haleem	Foodstuff	Telangana
Karimnagar Silver Filigree	Handicrafts	Telangana
Varanasi Wooden Lacquerware Toys	Handicrafts	Uttar Pradesh
Banaras Brocades & Saris	Textiles/Handicrafts	Uttar Pradesh
Handmade Carpet of Bhadohi	Textiles/Handicrafts	Uttar Pradesh
Lucknow Chikan Craft	Textiles/Handicrafts	Uttar Pradesh

Source: Compiled from GI journals and GI registry http://ipindia.nic.in/girindia/, updated up to 31 October 2017.

Notes

1. http://www.wipo.int/wipo_magazine/en/2007/04/article_0003.html, accessed on 27 October 2017.

2. It is a marketing strategy to create a differentiated market, such that the market and the profits are bigger.

3. Calculated from the information available in Government of India (2015, p. 57).

4. The spurt has been provided by the World Bank funded Maharashtra Agricultural Competitiveness Project (MACP). The World Bank has provided US$100 million to implement the project. MACP which began on 20 September 2010 ended on December 2016. It aimed to enhance the productivity in agriculture and improvement of quality production through capacity building of producers with the help of extension programmes. It also aimed to enable the farmer to fetch a competitive price for agriculture produce, through various alternative channels of marketing that were proposed to be developed. It mentioned in passing of GI indicators in the section on agri-business promotion facility (Government of Maharashtra, 2010, p. 42).

5. Percentage of each category to total agricultural products.

6. In this category too, two foreign goods were registered—cheese products from Italy—Prosciutto di Parma and Parmigiano Reggiano.

7. http://textilescommittee.nic.in/services/geographical-indications accessed on 2 August 2016. The list of products facilitated by Textiles Committee, Government of India include Pochampalli Ikat, Gadwal Saris, Uppada Jamdani Saris, Banaras Brocades and Saris, Lucknow Chikan Craft, Paithani Saris and Fabric, Khandua Saris and Fabric, Pippli Applique Work, Balaramapuram Saris & Fine Cotton Fabrics, Kasaragod Saris, Kuthampully Saris, Chennamangalam Set Mundu and Dhoties.

8. Chanderi silk and Kota Doria registration of GI were spearheaded by the Cluster and Business Linkages Division of UNIDO (See http://indiatogether. org/gi-economy and http://www.cuts-citee.org/pdf/Briefing_Paper10-Geographical_Indications_in_India-A_Case_Study_of_Kota_Doria.pdf accessed on 2 August 2016).

9. Communication with a BEDO Officer from Thailand in January 2016.

10. See http://agritech.tnau.ac.in/daily_events/2013/english/dec/21_dec_13_eng.pdf, accessed on 25 June 2016.

11. For details, see http://ipindiaservices.gov.in/GI_DOC/157/157%20-%20 Reply%20to%20FCR%20by%20Applicant%20-%2003-08-2009.pdf, accessed on 17 August 2016.

12. Draws from Sharma & Kulhari, 2015.

13. In the Payyanur Pavithra Ring case, the IPAB clarified that the persons 'who really need the protection are the artisans and the actual craftsmen and the growers. The object of the Act is to protect those who are directly engaged in exploiting, creating or making or manufacturing the goods' (Marie-Vivien, 2015, p. 203).

14. Discussion with the officials of the GI Registry on this yielded that a dealer or a trader may be identified as an authorized user, if he deals with the registered proprietor directly.

15. It was observed during the field work, the local transport and community would effortlessly direct us to the artisans' home or workplace.

16. Discussions with officials of the GI Registry on 26 December 2016. It was also the experience of the first author when she enquired about the 'laddu' at the famous sweetmeat shop at the Chennai airport, and the salesman responded, 'it is *like* Tirupathi Laddu, but it is not Tirupathi Laddu'.

17. http://www.vam.ac.uk/blog/fabric-of-india/fashionable-fabric, accessed on 31 October 2017.

18. http://ipindiaservices.gov.in/GI_DOC/19/19%20-%20GI%20-%20 Revised%20Application%20-%2006-07-2005.pdf.

19. Basket made of palm leaves.

20. See http://agriexchange.apeda.gov.in/indexp/reportlist.aspx, accessed on 5 November 2016.

3

Impact of GI Registration
Evidence from Case Studies

In India, the handicrafts and handloom sector is the second largest source of livelihood after agriculture, and can remain a strategy for ensuring the prosperity and dignity of the artisans and workers engaged in it (Chatterjee, 2003; Vinayan, 2007). The goods from the sector were known by their place of origin and, thus, origin labelling in India predates the legal framework by several centuries. Handicraft GIs symbolize the intersection of culture, heritage, and human skills. Nonetheless, it is important that these GI-protected crafts do not remain as just a reminder of a glorious past but also serve as a tool to address sustainable development goals by providing livelihoods, whereby producers could earn adequate returns.

As mentioned elsewhere in the volume, statistical data pertaining to the handicraft sector is hardly available. In the absence of appropriate data from any source, the case study method serves the purpose as it helps the researchers understand a stated problem from different perspectives. However, as the case studies pertain to informal enterprises where entrepreneurship is thriving in the form of own account micro and small enterprises, the systematic maintenance of quantitative information regarding the craft was found to be notably absent and the information shared was mostly qualitative in nature. There are certain known limitations of the case study approach: (1) results of the case studies are typical to a particular situation and cannot be generalized; (2) certain issues related to non-GI handicrafts are applicable to the GI registered products as well, and hence, it is difficult to separate the issues specific to the GI products.

In this chapter, we use the framework of the theory of change (ToC) outlined in the first chapter to analyse the impact pathways of GI registration, using several indicators that reflect the institutional, governance, and livelihood aspects. Ideally, the changes could have been better captured with an understanding of the initial position at the time of GI registration, followed by a survey after GI registration. However, due to various constraints, such repeated visits to the study areas were not possible for the authors. Hence, keeping the information obtained from the GI journals as the baseline for every product, the changes and impact of the GI in the post-GI scenario have been discussed with the help of the data collected during the survey for the chosen products using the case study approach. It needs to be mentioned at the outset that there are data constraints at the baseline as well as in the case study approach. The information in the GI journal does not provide details about employment or market status of the craft at the time of filing the application. Further, because of the informal nature of the sectors, the cases also present limited quantitative data.

Selection of Products and GI Registration

The products for the case studies in this chapter were chosen from the four southern states[1] of India as these states were leading the rest of the country in filing GI applications, with a share of 48 per cent of the total registered GIs in 2014 (44 per cent in 2017). These products were: Thanjavur Painting (TP) and Swamimalai Bronze Icons (SBI) from Tamil Nadu; Machilipatnam Kalamkari (MK), Kondapalli Toys (KT), and Pochampalli Ikat (PI) from Andhra Pradesh; Mysore Agarbathis (MA) and Kasuti Embroidery (KE) from Karnataka; and Aranmula Mirror (AM) from Kerala (Table 3.1). Except the TP and MA producers where a few individuals/units are in the urban areas, the rest of the crafts are located in the rural areas. The chosen products were also the early entrants in their respective craft segments, and the GI for these products were obtained between 2004 and 2007. However, each of the crafts has been associated with the region traditionally and known by

TABLE 5.1 Products Chosen for the Study

State	Product	Year of GI Application	Year of GI Status	Registration Validity	Registered Proprietor
Andhra Pradesh	Kondapalli Toys	10 November 2005	12 January 2006	9 November 2025	LANCO Institute of General Humanitarian Trust and Kondapalli Wooden Toys Manufacturers Association
	Machilipatnam Kalamkari	16 April 2007	10 July 2008	15 April 2027	Vegetable Handblock Kalamkari Printers Association
Telangana	Pochampalli Ikat	15 December 2003	31 December 2004	14 December 2023	Pochampalli Handloom Weavers Cooperative Society and Pochampalli Handloom Tie & Dye Silk Saris Manufacturers Association
Karnataka	Kasuti Embroidery	31 March 2005	30 January 2006	30 March 2025	Karnataka State Handicraft Development Corporation
	Mysore Agarbathis	11 August 2004	2 June 2005	10 August 2024	All India Agarbathi Manufacturers Association
Kerala	Aranmula Kannadi (mirror)	8 December 2003	19 September 2005	7 December 2023	Vishwabrahmana Aranmula Metal Mirror Society, later name changed to Parthasarathy Handicraft Centre
Tamil Nadu	Thanjavur Paintings	4 January 2006	16 May 2007	3 January 2026	Thanjavur Oviya Padukappu Sangam
	Swamimalai Bronze Icons	26 July 2006	22 April 2008	25 July 2026	Development Commissioner, Ministry of Textiles, Government of India, New Delhi

Source: Compiled from http://ipindia.nic.in/girindia/.

that name. Except MK, PI, and MA, which were being operated as small and medium enterprises with hired workers, the rest of the crafts were functioning as household (HH) enterprises operating in the informal sector. In the HH enterprises, while family labour was fully involved, the use of hired labour varied according to the size of the operation. Further, each craft involves a very specific human skill and the techniques are widely known.[2] While interviews were conducted with key informants using a semi-structured questionnaire for all the products, only in the case of Pochampalli, a primary survey with a sample of 354 weavers was conducted in the districts of Nalgonda and Warangal in the year 2011–12 (Table 3.2).

TABLE 3.2 Sample for the Case Studies

Name of the Product	Production Units	Male	Female	Details of the Respondents
Thanjavur Painting		8	–	Six craftsmen (including the master craftsman cum teacher and the Vice-President of the Thanjavur Oviya Padukappu Sangam), managers of Poompuhar at Chennai and Thanjavur.
Swamimalai Bronze Icon		6	–	Secretary of the Co-op society, sculptor with Poompuhar, Manager of Poompuhar, one craftsman/cum direct exporter and the rest, craftsmen.
Aranmula Mirror		6	2	President and Secretary of Parthasarathy Handicraft Centre and the rest, craftspersons.
Kondapalli Toys		6	1	A social worker, President and Secretary of Kondapalli Toy Manufacturers Association and the rest, craftsmen.
Machilipatnam Kalamkari	6 production units	–	–	Secretary, Vegetable Handblock Kalamkari Printers Welfare Association; one direct exporter;

			one merchandise exporter; one block producer; and, the rest, small scale units.
Pochampalli Ikat		330	24	Weavers
Kasuti Embroidery		1	20	All embroidery workers.
Mysore Agarbathi	8 production units			Six units (belonging to large, medium, and small-size based on the capital invested) were members of the All India Agarbathi Manufacturers Association (AIAMA) and the other two were informal sector units. All located in Mysore. Telephonic interview conducted with the then president of the AIAMA in 2014.

Source: Field survey.

Indicators of Change Due to GI Protection and Implementation

Figure 3.1 identifies certain indicators based on the literature on GI from India and elsewhere, and observations from the field. The figure consists of four boxes starting with the inputs or the principal intervention mechanism at the bottom. We assume that these interventions lead to the process of change that may be identified as direct output of the intervention process. These outputs tend to cause certain outcomes, leading to the setting up of institutions and governance mechanisms. Such outcomes may have a wider impact on society, the producers and the consumers. The sections 'Inputs: GI Registration', 'Outputs/Process of Change', 'Outcomes Due to GI Registration and Implementation', and 'Societal Impact', in this chapter analyse the inputs, outputs, outcomes, and the wider impact due to GI registration, and the last section presents the discussion and conclusion.

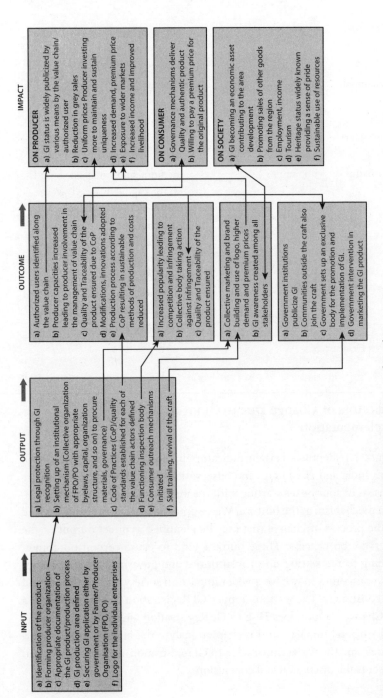

INPUT

a) Identification of the product
b) Forming producer organization
c) Appropriate documentation of the GI product/production process
d) GI production area defined
e) Securing GI application either by government or by Farmer/Producer Organisation (FPO, PO)
f) Logo for the individual enterprises

OUTPUT

a) Legal protection through GI recognition
b) Setting up of an institutional mechanism (Collective organization of FPO/PO with appropriate byelaws, capital, organization structure, and so on) to procure materials, governance)
c) Code of Practices (CoP)/quality standards established for each of the value chain actors defined
d) Functioning inspection body
e) Consumer outreach mechanisms initiated
f) Skill training, revival of the craft

OUTCOME

a) Authorized users identified along the value chain
b) Producer capacities increased leading to producer involvement in the management of value chain
c) Quality and Traceability of the product ensured due to CoP
d) Modifications, innovations adopted to CoP
e) Production process according to CoP resulting in sustainable methods of production and costs reduced

a) Increased popularity leading to competition and infringement
b) Collective body taking action against infringement
c) Quality and Traceability of the product ensured

a) Collective marketing and brand building and use of logo, higher demand and premium prices
b) GI awareness created among all stakeholders

a) Government institutions publicize GI
b) Communities outside the craft also join the craft
c) Government sets up an exclusive body for the promotion and implementation of GI.
d) Government intervention in marketing the GI product

IMPACT

ON PRODUCER

a) GI status is widely publicized by various means by the value chain/authorized user
b) Reduction in grey sales
c) Uniform prices Producer investing more to maintain and sustain uniqueness
d) Increased demand, premium price
e) Exposure to wider markets
f) Increased income and improved livelihood

ON CONSUMER

a) Governance mechanisms deliver Quality and authentic product
b) Willing to pay a premium price for the original product

ON SOCIETY

a) GI becoming an economic asset contributing to the area development
b) Promoting sales of other goods from the region
c) Employment, income
d) Tourism
e) Heritage status widely known providing a sense of pride
f) Sustainable use of resources

FIGURE 3.1 Key Indicators of Change Due to GI Protection and Implementation
Source: Developed by the authors.

Inputs: GI Registration

The first and foremost step in GI filing is to identify a product with uniqueness that is linked to the region (Table 3.1). The uniqueness could be human skills, natural factors, or a combination of both. These are detailed in this section.

Thanjavur Paintings

The art of Thanjavur Paintings, also known as Tanjore Paintings (TP), was first introduced by the Maratha king, Raja Sarfoji. He and his descendants who ruled from the seventeenth to the nineteenth century, with Thanjavur as capital, have contributed significantly to the different art forms that have taken roots in Thanjavur. TP is completely handmade. A typical TP consists of one main figure, a deity, with a well-rounded body and almond shaped eyes. This figure is then housed in an enclosure created by means of an arch, curtains, and so on. The painting is made by the gilded and gem-set technique—a technique where gold leaves and sparkling stones are used to highlight certain aspects of the painting like ornaments, dresses, and so on. The rounded body, almond shaped eyes, and the gold and gem set technique distinguishes the TP from the Mysore Traditional Painting, which uses relief work with gold but does not use stone embellishments.

The GI application for TP, Thanjavur Wall Paintings, and Thanjavur Glass Painting was made by the Thanjavur Oviya Padhkappu Sangam (TOPS), Thanjavur, represented by an advocate based in Chennai in January 2006, and it was certified on 16 May 2007. The certificate, which was valid till 3 January 2016, has been extended up to 2026. The vice president of TOPS, who is also the son of one of the senior-most artists who was interviewed, indicated that the association started with eleven members and has now grown to eighty members. The scope of TOPS is not only for Thanjavur Painting but also for other crafts. TOPS provides training in the making of Thanjavur dolls too. As per the GI journal information, the craft is located in the district of Thanjavur.

Swamimalai Bronze Icons

The Swamimalai Bronze Icon (SBI) is completely handmade. It is made with a special alluvial soil which is available only on the river bed of the Cauvery, within a kilometre range from Alavanthipuram to Thimmakudi in Thanjavur, which is an important factor for the location of the craft in Swamimalai.

SBI artisans shared that the special binding quality of the soil has been scientifically proven by earlier research carried out by the Shastra University located in Thanjavur. A couple of artisans practising this craft in Coimbatore are also dependent on this soil. Presently, this soil is available free of cost. Generally, artisans collect the required soil in summer, mix it with water, make balls and save it for the rest of the season because when the river is in full flow, the collection of sand is not possible. The production of SBI as per the details mentioned in the 'shilpa shastras'[3] requires a high standard of skills to create the required minute details of the body parts, ornaments, apparels, and the designs on the crown/headgear and so on. Hence, along with the GI factor, human skill plays a crucial role in the making of the SBI.

SBI respondents reported that a sum of Rs 1.5 crores was earmarked by the government for the project to acquire a heritage town status for Thanjavur and a part of this fund was used for the documentation required for GI. The GI application for SBI was filed in the year 2006 by the Development Commissioner, Handicrafts (Ministry of Textiles, New Delhi), as belonging to Class 6 (common metals and their alloys). The Part A registration came through in the year 2008, which was valid till 2016 and has been extended up to 2026. Artists in the region of Swamimalai are engaged in the making of the craft.

Aranmula Kannadi (Mirror)

Natural resources, namely, the clay from the paddy fields of Aranmula that is used in the making of the disk as well as the human skill in mixing the metals and polishing the metal disk meticulously to get the reflection like a glass mirror, contribute to the GI uniqueness of the Aranmula mirror. These are the reasons for the location of the craft in Aranmula. The art has been traditionally passed on from one generation to another.

The GI application for Aranmula Mirror was filed in the year 2004 by the Vishwabrahmana Aranmula Metal Mirror Society in December 2003. The name of the society was later changed to Parthasarathy Handicraft Centre, which is the name of the presiding deity of the Aranmula temple. The GI certificate was obtained in the year 2005 and the mirror is classified under Class 20. As the initial GI certification expired in December 2013, the association renewed the GI which is now valid till December 2023.

Kondapalli Bommalu (Toys)

Kondapalli Toys are delightful expressions of the rich traditional art made from the wood 'Tellaponiki', which is also known as 'White Sander' (*Jiuotia Rotteri Fromis*). The trees are found in the forests and hills adjoining Kondapalli village. The specialty of this particular wood is that it is light in weight and when heated mildly at low temperature, it is amenable to being carved minutely. Yet another uniqueness of the craft is that it is handmade and the locally made instrument 'bahudara' is used to carve the desired shapes from the wood. All the artisans live in Kondapalli and the art is not being practised anywhere else. Thus, both the natural resource and the human skills are located in the Kondapalli region, contributing to the GI uniqueness.

The GI application for Kondapalli Bommalu (toys) was filed by the LANCO Institute of General Humanitarian Trust, Hyderabad, and the Kondapalli Wooden Toys Manufacturers Association (KTMA) in November 2005 under Class 16 (collectibles, souvenirs, and so on), 20 (goods of wood), 27 (wall hangings), and 28 (playthings and decorations). The registration was obtained in September 2006 and the GI certification, which was valid till November 2015, has now been extended up to 2025. LANCO officials were the first ones to recognize the potential of GI protection for the craft. All the craftsmen in Kondapalli formed a society and, jointly with LANCO, filed the GI application. According to the secretary of KTMA, the Association was historically established in 1936 as an industrial co-operative society, but it did not have funds for any activity. After the LANCO power project was initiated, a former Member of Parliament, Lakdapatti Rajagopal, undertook certain initiatives in the artisans' favour and the government gave land for the society's building free of cost. LANCO contributed Rs. 17 lakhs to build the building, of which Rs. 5 lakhs came from the MP Development Fund, Rs. 6 lakhs were used for documentation, and the rest was utilized for meetings in Chennai. The secretary and his brother demonstrated the entire process of making the toy before the GI officials at Chennai.

Machilipatnam Kalamkari

The GI uniqueness of this craft is the use of (a) vegetable dyes, (b) intricate block designs, (c) hand block printing, and (d) special characteristics of the water quality in Machilipatnam which gives brightness to the colours. The Kalamkari cloth undergoes ten different processes such as bleaching, applications of *myrobalan*, block printing, washing, dyeing, bleaching, starching, application of alum and yellow colour, and, finally, bleaching with soap. The entire process takes several weeks and is dependent on nature, as the process requires bright sun to dry the cloth, flowing river water to wash the cloth, and raw materials from a variety of plants that grow in the nearby forests. According to the GI Registry's authorized user no. AU/396/GI/19/12, the production of MK is geographically limited only to Pedana town, with 90 per cent of the units operating there and in its neighbouring villages of Machilipatnam, Polavaram, and Kappaladoddi in Gudurumandal of the Krishna district (Naidu, 2013a).

The GI application for Kalamkari was filed by the Vegetable Handblock Kalamkari Printers Association in April 2007. The GI certification was obtained in July 2008 and its validity has now been extended till April 2027. The GI classification of MK belongs to Classes 24 (textiles), 25 (clothing), and 27 (furnishing). According to the secretary of the association, the Handicrafts Department of the state government of erstwhile Andhra Pradesh and the National Institute of Fashion Technology helped in the documentation of the Kalamkari craft for GI certification. The entire cost was borne by the government. There was no opposition of any kind for this application.

Pochampalli Ikat

Pochampalli Ikat was the first GI to be registered in the textiles segment. Ikat weaving has been in vogue in Nalgonda for more than a century. Even though there exist ambiguities about the origin of tie and dye weaving in

Nalgonda, the craft's origin is linked to Nalgonda and Warangal. It does not appear to be indigenous to the region but is a learnt one (Dharmaraju, 2006). The technique of tie and dye is believed to have been brought to Pochampalli from the coastal town of Chirala (in the present district of Prakasham) (Buhler et al., 1980) as early as 1915. Ikat weaving as prevalent in Pochampalli is different from Bandhini and Sungudi in Gujarat and Tamil Nadu respectively. In Pochampalli style, the yarn is tied and dyed (as in the case of Patan Patola and Orissa Ikat), while in Bandhini and Sungudi, the cloth is tied and dyed. The Pochampalli designs are laboriously worked upon from the graph. For every colour to be dyed, other colours marked in the yarn (weft or warp) are intricately wrapped, usually with rubber strips from the tyres of bicycles so that these do not stain during the dyeing process. In order to dye the rest of the yarn with colours as per the design, the dyed parts are tied while the undyed parts are untied to be dyed, and the process is repeated depending on the intricate designs. This is followed by putting the warp and weft on the loom and weaving. The natural movement of the weaving results in a feathered touch to the designs, which is a unique feature of this technique. The uniqueness of the craft is its single or double ikat in several variations like use of diamond designs, geometrical or floral figurative motifs, stripes or other variations produced in cotton or silk or a combination of both.

The entire process of registration was facilitated under the Cluster Development Programme (CDP) of the Textiles Committee, Government of India. The Regional Office of the CDP took the lead to sensitize the stakeholders about the GI Act. To facilitate the process of registration, the Textiles Committee roped in the services of the Andhra Pradesh Technology Development and Promotion Corporation (APTDC), which houses the IPR Cell of the Confederation of Indian Industry (CII). In fact, the major role played by the APTDC was to translate the technical information about Pochampalli Ikat weaving into legal language. M/S Anand & Anand (located in New Delhi) served as legal consultants to facilitate the legal process of registration. The APTDC also succeeded in involving the National Bank for Agriculture and Rural Development (NABARD), which bore the costs of filing the application (around Rs. 1.5 lakhs). In fact, to cultivate a sense of ownership among the weavers, NABARD had suggested a part of the costs to be borne by the weavers. Nonetheless, since this was a pioneering initiative and the first product to apply for registration from the textiles sector, NABARD funded the entire cost including the expenses of workshops, meeting of the GI consultative group from the Registry, legal fees, and other miscellaneous expenditure. The Textiles Committee had identified the Pochampalli Handloom Weavers Cooperative Society (PHWCS) and the Pochampalli Handloom Tie and Dye Manufacturers' Association (PHTDA) as applicants for the registration and this was conveyed to the APTDC. There have been a series of workshops conducted for the weavers on sensitizing them about the relevance of GI. The application was filed in December 2003 and granted in 2004.

Kasuti Embroidery

Kasuti Embroidery is practised in the Hubli, in the Dharwar region of Karnataka, by a limited number of skilled artisans. The special feature of Kasuti is that the embroidery, once completed, is identical on both sides of the cloth. There is no knot used, neither at the beginning nor at the end of the thread. Kasuti is done by counting the warp and weft of the cloth. The GI journal (No. 11) notes that there are four types of Kasuti, namely Neyge Kasuti (darning stitches), Muragi Kasuti (zigzag stitches), Menthaye Kasuti (forked or cross stitches), and Gavanthi Kasuti (double running stitches). There are over 700 designs under categories like Gandole Kamala, Gopi Kamala, Chittu Kamala, Dagabhagigopura, Kalee, peacock, Neyge Godambi, elephant, lion, Venkipatti, Kayapatti, and so on.

The GI application for KE was filed by the Karnataka State Handicrafts Development Corporation in March 2005 and the registration was obtained in October 2005. The registration, which was valid till March 2015, has now been extended up to 2025.

Mysore Agarbathi

Various roots, herbs, petals, barks, natural essential oils, resins, and charcoal are used for making Mysore Agarbathi. The GI journal Number 4 lists fourteen names of roots, five kinds of wood, five varieties of bark, eight different kinds of leaves, eight kinds of buds and flowers, nine kinds of fruits and nuts, thirteen varieties of resins, six different oils, and five other miscellaneous items that are used in the process of agarbathi-making. Though agarbathi-making bears the name of Mysore, it is not restricted to Mysore alone but has spread to other parts of Karnataka as well. However, the GI is known as Mysore Agarbathi, perhaps due to the status of the erstwhile State of Mysore.

A few of the strong factors for GI of this product in favour of Karnataka is that *Mattipal* or *Halmadi* (in Kannada), an important ingredient in the making of the agarbathi, was sourced from the tree Ailanthus Malabarica, which was originally found only in Karnataka.[4] Further, the bamboo available in Shimoga, Karnataka, possesses unique characteristics that are suitable for agarbathis. Also, the sandalwood oil from the sandal wood, Santalum Album, is mainly found in Karnataka.

The GI application for Mysore Agarbathi was filed by the All India Agarbathi Manufacturers Association (AIAMA), Bengaluru, under Class 3 (agarbathi, oodupatti, or incense sticks) in August 2004 (now renewed up to 2024) and the logo was registered in November 2004. There are close to 570 manufacturers who are members of the AIAMA, of which 369 (68 per cent) are from Karnataka alone.

Thus, different products were chosen for GI registration and their uniqueness was appropriately documented, with a demarcation of area facilitating the GI registration, which has also been renewed in all the cases (Table 3.1).

Outputs/Process of Change

Setting up a Collective Organization

Social capital/cohesion in the form of collectivizing the artisans has been built in all the products except KE and SBI. However, the by-laws for the collective organization have been created in the case of MK, PI, KT, and MA. But none of them is engaged in pooled procurement of materials to benefit the GI producers. In the case of SBI, the industrial cooperative society which was set up to help the producers has framed the by-laws, but this society was not party to GI filing and now it only facilitates the selling of SBI. The society charges an entrance fee of Rs. 25 for the membership. Shares are priced at Rs. 500 a share. The government also provides capital and the society has an elected body, elected according to the society by-law.

In Aranmula, the Parthasarathy Handicraft Centre was started with five members for the purpose of filing the GI application. Membership fee for the association is Rs. 50. Other than this, the society has not built any share capital among the members. In the case of Kondapalli toys and TP, there are no common funds.

An important post-Pochampalli GI development was the setting up of the Pochampalli Handloom Park under the CDP, using the public private partnership model, involving local entrepreneurs, the state and central government and Textiles Committee.[5] The objective was to build and support the art of ikat weaving. Given the networking during the GI registration, several entrepreneurial weavers in Pochampalli formed an association and registered a company called Pochampalli Ikat Weavers Private Limited, located in Kanumukkala village, about ten kilometres from Pochampalli Village in Nalgonda, popularly known as the Pochampalli Handloom Park. The Park is situated in twenty-four acres of land, with an outlay of Rs. 47 crores. The capital for the project was raised by the entrepreneurs through short and long-term loans, and later, from the Infrastructure Finance & Lending Services Limited (IF & LS) that was hired to execute the project. The state government contributed Rs. 1 crore and the central government contributed Rs. 13.5 crores for infrastructure development under the Scheme for Integrated Textile Park (SITP). The mobilized funds were used for purchasing land, dyeing units, and equipment. The Park started its operation in 2008 and has the capacity to run 2000 looms, of which 550 have been installed and 150 were operational. The park has elaborate infrastructural facilities for the pre-loom work preceding the weaving such as dyeing, warping, and winding machines, and it can undertake bulk orders. The park caters to both the export and domestic market. The product range has been widened to include designer saris and home furnishing (wall art, table linen, furnishing cloth) aimed at the high-end market.

According to the CEO of the Handloom Park, the first four years, 2008–12, were spent in technological upgradation, research and development, and training, and, only in 2012–13, did the project became commercially viable.

Logo for the GI Products

Except for PI and SBI, which filed separate applications for logos, logos have been filed along with the GI application.[6]

Code-of-Practice

Code-of-Practice (CoP): The statement of cases of all the products mention in detail the production process followed. But CoPs are not mentioned for procuring raw material (except Kondapalli Toys), packing, and marketing. As the authorized users are not identified at different levels, the CoP for the different value chain players is yet to be done.

Setting Up of the Inspection Body

The GI Registry requires that a suitable inspection body, with external members, be set up for each product that would be responsible for the quality of the GI products produced. While going through the applications carefully, it was realized that the GI filing associations of AM, KT, and KE had only assured the Registry that a suitable inspection body would be set up.

The SBI application mentions the setting up of an inspection body consisting of (1) the Regional Director Southern Region, Office of the Development Commissioner (Handicrafts), Chennai, (2) the Chairperson, Crafts Council of India, Chennai, (3) a representative from a handicrafts Non-Governmental Organization, (4) a representative from the National Institute of Design, (5) a non-official member associated with arts and craft. For Machilipatnam Kalamkari, besides the president and the secretary who were the immediate inspection authorities for the goods produced at Pedana, the officials of the Craft Council Andhra Pradesh, National Institute of Fashion Technology, and Andhra Pradesh Handicraft Development Corporation were inducted into the inspection body to provide inputs on product quality, development, and quality assurance of the goods.

The application of Pochampalli Ikat mentions the availability of about 100 master weavers with expert knowledge in aspects relating to visualization of design, who would do the inspection and approve the materials for the market. In addition, consultations for the establishment of an inspection structure were being negotiated with the Textiles Committee, under the Ministry of Textiles, Government of India; WSC, Hyderabad, Government of India; and DHT, Government of Andhra Pradesh (GI Journal No. 2, September 2004). The PHTDA was not satisfied with the implementation of the inspection structure. In May 2005, as per GO Rt. No. 310, the Commissioner, DHT and Development Commissioner for Apparel Export Parks constituted a State-Level and a District-Level committee which would meet at least once a month/quarter to look into the implementation of GI in Pochampalli. The terms of reference were: to leverage on the registered GI for the benefit of the weavers and use it as a competitive tool for socio-economic prosperity; to facilitate coordinated action and combat counterfeit products of Pochampalli Ikat; to strive for revitalization and emancipation of Pochampalli's brand image, both domestically and internationally; to create awareness among the stakeholders and end-users about the tangible benefits of the GI and motivate them to use it; to facilitate a mechanism to uphold the qualitative aspects of Pochampalli through technical interference; to create a niche in the country about Pochampalli Ikat among policymakers, bureaucrats, and stakeholders of the GI to evolve similar efforts in other products; to develop a database of possible infringes of Pochampalli Ikat. The period of both the committees was for two years from the date of issue of the GO. Though several SLC meetings were conducted, nothing concrete emerged. The Assistant Director clearly stated that due to inadequate staff in the day-to-day functioning of his office, he did not have enough human resource to conduct the DLC.

The Fame R and D centre, founded jointly by the Government of Karnataka and the AIAMA, was named as the inspection structure for Mysore Agarbathi, which would take care of the periodic testing of fragrance, spread of fragrance, and the time taken for burning.

In KE, the NGOs or middlemen serve as the inspection body as the job orders are placed by them.

Interviews with the officials of the producer associations in the case of textiles did not yield much insight into the role and function of the inspection body. It was found that independent weavers took care of the quality in their individual capacity whereas in case of weavers working under master weavers, the supervisors or the master weavers themselves were responsible for quality check.

Consumer Outreach Mechanism

Three common modes of marketing were observed in all the crafts: (1) direct marketing by the craftspersons; (2) sales through the state government sales emporiums; and (3) sales through private traders. Because of the TP artists' reputation, each of the craftspersons had work orders (at the time of interview in 2014) that would keep them busy for at least a year and a half. Further, each reported a fixed clientele who would buy the TP from their doorstep. Some of them were also selling it abroad through intermediaries. Thanjavur being a place for religious tours and cultural events, these artists were using pamphlets to advertise their art in such events.

In the case of products from Tamil Nadu, sales through Poompuhar, the Tamil Nadu state government-owned handicrafts sales emporium, is possible only if the artisan fulfils certain quality criteria set by the government. These include: originality of the materials used in the craft; the reputation of the artists and his/her mentor; and the technical specifications of the products, for example, the size of the painting and the kind of frame that is used in the case of TP and rates of metals, to mention a few. However, Poompuhar does not pay the artist immediately on acquiring the painting and hence the artist has to wait till sales takes place. Institutional sales only complement the income for TP for some of the producers as not all are dependent on institutional sales. Hence, a few artists, who are willing to wait, avail this facility of marketing the craft through Poompuhar. SBI makers have the option of going through the society, which is availed by many artisans. For immediate cash needs, SBI artisans also sell their products through shops which sell metal utensils.

The use of the e-channel for marketing was observed in one or two enterprising units engaged in the craft of Kalamkari and SBI. In other crafts, it was notably absent. For KT makers, the sales of the toys could be in the ratio of 20:60:20 per cent in the form of direct sales, through Lepakshi, the Andhra Pradesh sales emporium,[7] and the private traders respectively.

Except the secretary of the KTMA, who had set up a shop which is air conditioned with toys well displayed, most Kondapalli artisans were using the front portion of their house as a shop. Lack of appropriate packaging is a serious issue, particularly in Kondapalli Toys, especially if the purchases were made at the doorstep of the artisans.[8] The craftspersons did not have an idea about the importance of packaging. In contrast, even at the artisan level, the Aranmula mirror was packed in an attractive jewellery box.

All the Aranmula Mirror craftspersons have their own sales outlets and also sell through Kairali, which is the state handicrafts sales emporium. Kerala being one of the states which has been very effectively promoting tourism, combined with the fact that Aranmula is located on the way to the famous Sabarimala temple which attracts lakhs of devotees from the month of November to January, implies that there is a good demand for the mirror. Kairali places orders with the individual artists, depending on the type of frame that is most preferred by the buyers.

Like other craft forms, Kalamkari printing is also sold both directly to the consumers at Pedana and through traders at Hyderabad and Mumbai. These traders buy the material in bulk from producers at Pedana and sell the same as a value-added item—either ready to wear or ready to stitch. Each unit has an informal arrangement with traders from Mumbai or other places who pick up the consignment. Two of the units had tie-ups with producers in Europe and the US. Both the units allow the importers to affix their label and sell the product. Both the units operate on a higher scale of production and market compared to other units in Pedana.

Marketing of MAs take place through wholesalers, retailers, and the state government emporium.

While cooperatives marketed the products produced by the weavers affiliated to them through own sales depots, exhibitions, and to APCO (Andhra Pradesh State Handloom Weavers Cooperative Society Ltd.), the master weavers, under the PHTDA, had their own sales depots at Pochampalli and were also tied to retail houses in Hyderabad and Secunderabad. Weavers who procured raw materials on their own also sold their produce to the master weavers. This distinguishes them from other weavers who procure raw materials from the master weavers and return the finished product for marketing. Hence, these weavers consider themselves 'independent' though the produce is marketed through master weavers under the PHTDA. The master weavers under the PHTDA also take part in local, national, and international exhibitions. However, there were no changes in the marketing channels between the GI and the post GI periods (Vinayan, 2013). The cotton weaving societies used to have flourishing exports which have now declined due to rising costs leading to loss of competitive markets. The Pochampalli Ikat Weavers Private Limited developed two brands registered with

Box 3.1   Brand Building under Pochampalli Handloom Park Initiative

Source: Pochampalli Handloom Park. Reproduced with permission.

trademarks titled CHIKAT for domestic market (Pochampalli Ikat Weavers Private Limited) and IKAT ART (Ikat Art Private Limited) for the high-end export market (see Box 3.1).

It was evident across crafts that an unwritten code of price level for different products prevailed, below which the producers would refuse to sell, especially when they were dealing with the consumers and wholesalers directly. However, it was particularly reported by TP, AM, and KT craftspersons that producers who use cheap materials would lower the price than what an authentic producer would sell at, and thereby make a quick profit.

Government/NGO Intervention in Skill Training

The Working Group on Handicrafts (Government of India, 2011) observes all the GI registered crafts are languishing in India. A languishing craft is defined as the one which is still being practised by the artists even though the popularity of the craft is declining. Further, it emerged from all the case studies that the interest of the younger generation in the craft is dwindling. Hence, in order to sustain the crafts, differ-ent state governments have been imparting skill training. For instance, there is a state sponsored training programme on TP which was initi-ated after the GI, that takes place in Srirangam, Trichy, in Tamil Nadu.

In order to promote sculpture-making and to attract the younger generation into the craft, the Tamil Nadu government, through Poompuhar, conducts a three-year course on idol making that has been going on for many years. Earlier, fifteen students per batch were admit-ted, which in the recent years has reduced to mere eight students. The selected students get a stipend of Rs 3000 per month. During the three-year course, students are taught drawing, the theory of idol-making (shilpa shastras), and its practical aspects. Knowledge of drawing and interest in the craft are the main factors required to learn it, according to the officials of Poompuhar. A high level of skills is required, par-ticularly in giving shape to the idol and executing minute details on the ornaments and apparel worn by the idol. It also involves occupational hazards for those who are involved in preparing the metal alloy and pouring it into the clay structure through the small opening especially made for the purpose. Those who were trained in the Poompuhar idol making course, started their career as a trainee with established artisans to acquire the required skills in giving fine shape to the idols.

There have been interventions by the government and NGOs to revive Kasuti craft which is also languishing. NGOs like CHINYARD (Chaitanya Institute for Youth and Rural Development) and RUDSET (Rural Development and Self Employment Training Institute) have been providing vocational training and helping the artisans in marketing by ruling out the middlemen (Vattam, 2003). Training by these NGOs in the mid-2000s expanded the profile of KE, as the artisans started embroi-dering on home furnishings, women's accessories besides dress materi-als compared to the earlier situation when the embroidery was done mainly on Lambani dresses (tribal dresses worn by the Lambani women, made of colourful bold designs). These NGOs started numerous self-help groups (SHGs) by involving these artisans to buy materials or saris through SHG funds to do KE—a loan which they paid back through the sale proceeds. NABARD adopted Kasuti work in the Kalghatagi taluka under the NPRI (National Programme for Rural Industries) for various programmes like skill upgradation, technology upgradation, and mar-keting, in addition to other social requirements. Further, the NGOs also helped the artisans to get loans from the Malaprabha Grameena Bank (MGB). The MGB, being a leading regional rural bank at that point of time, took up the cause of the preservation of the traditional Kasuti art and chalked out the programmes to instil confidence among the artisans.

At the time of the study at Kondapalli village, the state government- owned packaging institute conducted a training programme on wrapping the toys with plastic wrappers to prevent damage while transportation, which is very essential to increase the marketability of the products from the doorsteps of the artisans. Artisans also mentioned participating in various training programmes on the use of colours, carving, and so on held by the Government of Andhra Pradesh and Government of India.

It is clear from the discussion in this section that there have been efforts by various stakeholders which triggered collective action in the respective sectors due to GI registration. Moreover, the initiatives of the GI Registry as well as the stakeholders led to each of the crafts acquiring a registered logo. Collective organizations set up for the purpose of filing the GI application, have remained inactive in a few cases. While efforts to reach out to newer consumers, by creating separate brands for the domestic and export markets, are seen in the case of Pochampalli, other crafts have continued with their traditional channels of marketing.

Outcomes Due to GI Registration and Implementation

GI Awareness

GI awareness among the different craftspersons varied. Respondents from TP, PI, and KT mentioned about attending the meetings organized at the pre-registration stage of applying for the GI. However, post registration, except for a senior artist and his son, none of the other artists were aware that TP had got the GI.

SBI craft respondents were aware that SBI has the GI certification, but were clueless about its use and registration under Part B. One of the respondents, who is also a large-scale idol maker (LSI), indicated that the government should take the initiative to organize all the idol makers and educate them about GI and its usefulness. He also added that the awarding of UNESCO heritage site status to the Thanjavur

Mariyamman temple, and the Tarasuram temple helped in popularizing the GI status of the craft. Different opinions prevailed among the artists about the GI certificate. While the Poompuhar officials felt that the GI certificate would increase the sales worldwide, another respondent, who is a sculptor-cum-researcher, told us that he is indifferent to the GI certificate as it has not made any difference to the artisans. According to the LSI, there are master craftsmen in places other than Swamimalai who make idols and call it Swamimalai idols. But he added that such activities have not been checked. Until our visit the cooperative society had not engaged in any GI awareness spreading activity among its members.

GI awareness in the case of AM[9] was relatively better than in other crafts. All the artisans whom the researcher met with were aware of the GI application filing and the outcome. Both the president and the secretary of the association said that the GI had increased the demand for the product as more people were now aware of the authenticity of the product. A few television channels had produced a documentary on mirror making after the GI. It gets re-telecasted from time to time across channels, which spreads awareness regarding the GI and adds to the demand according to the respondents. The GI certificate is prominently displayed in the workshop of the president of the association. One of the respondents indicated that new trader enquirers/visitors are shown the GI certificate, and even the pamphlet of the individual artists prominently displays the GI protection for the mirror. A few respondents said that they inform the buyers about the GI certification at the time of sales. One of the Aranmula artisans has clearly mentioned that the product has got the GI certification in the pamphlets printed for marketing purposes (Figure 3.2). In Kairali showrooms too, the mirrors were sold along with the pamphlets providing information to the consumer about the artisan. The respondents also felt that because of the GI registration, the mirror work continues to remain within Aranmula.

In the case of Pochampalli, a series of workshops were conducted to sensitize the weavers about the relevance of the GI throughout the filing period. Simultaneously, the application for GI was filed on 11 December 2003. A meeting was organized and attended by the officials from the DHT, Weavers Service Centre (WSC), Textiles Committee, APTDC, and weavers from Pochampalli in March 2004 to discuss in detail the GI application for Pochampalli Ikat. Weavers were informed about

REFLECTING A TRADITION

Late. M S Janardhanan Achary
(Master Craftsman, State Award & National Merit Award Winner)

Sudhammal J

Sudhammal J has taken after the ancestral way and specializes in the traditional craft of Aranmula mirror. Sudhammal holds a Craftsman Identity card issued by Development Commissioner of Handicrafts, Ministry of Textiles, Government of India. She is the daughter of late Shri Janardhanan Achary and Ponammal. Taking after her father, Sudhammal keeps the family tradition alive and strong with her skilled craftsmanship, making her one of the most sought after Aranmula mirror craftsperson. She has played a significant role in cultural societies and in Nehru Youth Centres. After her father's demise, she has been completely focused on the mirror, actively carrying out the manufacturing of the mirror under the enterprise Sree Parthasarathy Handicraft Mirror Centre. Sudhammal holds many Government exhibitions nationally and internationally like IITF (India International Trade Fair-Delhi) and caters to a whole range of national and international clients. She has two sons- Niranjan and Govardhan.

SREE PARTHASARATHY
HANDICRAFT MIRROR CENTRE

(A unit of Vishwakarmana Aranmula Metal Mirror Nirman Society)

Sudhammal J
D/o. Late M S Janardhanan Achary
(Master Craftsman, State Award & National Merit Award Winner)

Mangalathu House,
Malakkara P.O., Edayaranmula,
Aranmula,
Pathanamthitta District,
Kerala 689 532

9605450518, 0468 2317948

aranmulakannadikerala@gmail.com

www.aranmulakannadikerala.com
www.aranmulamirror.in
www.sparanmulakannadi.com

ARANMULA
KANNADI
(ARANMULA METAL MIRROR)

www.aranmulakannadikerala.com

ARANMULA

Aranmula is a small village and ancient pilgrim centre situated on the bank of holy river Pampa, it lies in the district of Pathanamthitta, which is well known for its ancient temple "Sree Parthasarathy". The presiding deity of the temple Lord Krishna the charioteer of Arjuna the famous warrior who led and won the Maha Bharath Yudh (the battle between the Kauravas and Pandavas depicted in the epic "Maha Bharath") Another important attraction of Aranmula is the world famous Aranmula Vallamkali and Aranmula Kannadi (Aranmula Metal Mirror). Aranmula Boat race is celebrated on Uthrittathi day in the Malayalam month of Chingam during the Onam festival every year on the holy river Pampa. People come from all over the country as well as the world to witness the magnificent race. The whole river is filled with snake boats from different villages and the banks are charged with the thrill of the event. Aranmula is a global heritage site enlisted by the United Nations. The nearest town is Kozhencherry. The nearest railway station is Chengannur railway station which is located around 10 km from Aranmula.

ARANMULA KANNADI

Cryptic in its creation. This metal mirror is a medieval Dravidian marvel in the annals of metallurgy. Aranmula Kannadi manufacturing was started in the early 17th century. It represents a fascinating area of culture and technological curiosity. Aranmula Kannadi is a unique object. Exclusive to Aranmula, this mirror is made of metal, not glass! There lies its uniqueness and its creation, a closely guarded secret, known to any few Vishwakarma families, has been handed down from generation to generations. Aranmula Kannadi is made by cooling a mixture of molten tin and copper. Every piece of Kannadi is the outcome of hours of hardwork and dedication. Extra ordinary traditional handmade metal mirror, is famous for bringing prosperity, luck and wealth in to life. Aranmula Kannadi is one among the eight auspicious items included famous Ashtamangalya set, which usually used for very auspicious events like marriage. Aranmula Kannadi has received patent, protected with a Geographical indication (GI) tag. The word 'Kannadi' in Malayalam, being "Mirror".

OUR TRADITION

The history of the Aranmula Kannadi lies across centuries, and its making is deeply rooted in the transcendence of tradition, the strength of devotion and purity of dedication. The Mangalathu family claims their rights in the making of the Aranmula Metal Mirror due to their expertise and tradition that has been passed down generations. The intricate and difficult secret to the creation of the Aranmula mirror was passed down from Shri Subrahmanian Achary to his son Shri Janardhanan Achary. Struck down by illness, when Shri Subrahmanian Achary lay bedridden, his son took the family vocation at a young age and excelled in the art, only to become an unparelled master craftsman. He spent most of his life engrossed in his craft, which he loved dearly and held close to his heart. He participated government exhibitions nationally, which led to find the market opportunity for these special mirrors. These exhibitions helped greatly to propagate the artistic value of the Aranmula mirror, making its presence admired all over the world. He got State Award and National Merit Award.

Layout: Govardhan
Mbjanardhan@gmail.com

FIGURE 3.2   Artisans' Details of Aranmula Mirror
Source: Pamphlet provided by one of the respondents, February 2014.

the importance of protecting a traditional livelihood activity like ikat weaving and how the GI could prove to be a powerful marketing and legal tool to counter the competition from powerlooms. Some officials from the DHT opined that the GI ownership should have been with the DHT and not with the PHWCS or PHTDC because they are ill-equipped to find and fight the cases of infringement. Nonetheless, it was pointed out that the ownership needs to be in the hands of the producer, since the GI is a collective monopoly. The weavers though were aware of the pre-GI meetings (Vinayan, 2013),[10] but only 21 per cent were aware about the GI registration and its use. This is disturbing given the fact that the survey took place almost a decade after the GI registration, with less than two years left for initiating the process of renewal of the registration at the time of the primary survey.

All the SBI craftspersons have printed pamphlets about the craft and themselves, but there is no mention of the GI certificate. Poompuhar showrooms in Chennai, Thanjavur, and Swamimalai do not display any information about the GI nature of the craft in the section where the GI-protected crafts were sold. In the case of SBI, the respondents were aware of the award of GI for the SBI craft, but certification was not being used actively on the artisan's letterheads or sales invoices, including that of the cooperative.

In the case of Kondapalli Toys, the office-bearers of the KTMA are aware of the usefulness of the GI but due to the lack of funds, no promotional activity has taken place. Other craftsmen indicated that they were neither aware of the certification nor of the benefits of such protection.

The small-scale units in kalamkari and agarbathi-making mentioned that the domestic buyers were not interested in the GI, but that GI would be more profitable for the units if they have more exposure to the export market. However, the couple of units that do export, do not mention the GI status of the craft in the supporting documents. Amongst the MK producers, there has been no misuse of GI, because none of the producers use synthetic colours and stick to the vegetable colours as mentioned in the application, which is their uniqueness too. But the age-old craft form is facing threat from units which use chemical dyes and screen printers in Pedana, who reproduce the design within a very short time, which the MK units painstakingly develop (Naidu, 2013b).

Most Kasuti artisans have little or no knowledge about the GI certification. Out of the 21 craftspersons that participated in the survey, only two who got training and started the association of KE, had heard about GI. In the case of Mysore Agarbathi, a discussion with the officials of the AIAMA revealed that efforts were not taken to implement the GI, and the rules and regulations remained only on paper. The main issue is the use of 'Mysore' for the registered agarbathis, as there are a number of units located in Bangalore which do not want their products to be known as Mysore Agarbathis. Amid all this, the GI registration was renewed and is valid till 2024. GI awareness varied among the units. While two each of the exporters and medium units were aware of the fact that the GI had been obtained for Mysore Agarbathi, they were completely unaware about the usefulness or benefits of the certification. Medium units also mentioned that the AIAMA had not issued the authorized user certification to the members. The small and informal units were neither aware of the GI concept nor of the GI status of Mysore Agarbathis. None of the workers were aware of the GI certification.

Identification of Authorized Users in the Value Chain

Identifying the authorized users is helpful in implementing the GI. In TP, SBI, AM, KT, and MK, the producers are also direct sellers in the domestic market, with a few who also sell in the export market. As some portion of the product is directly sold to the institutions or traders with whom the artisans have regular contacts, it should be relatively easier to identify the value chain and inform about the GI. But, so far, it has not been done. The geographical spread of the TP artists is wide and beyond the GI map provided by TOPS at the time of filing the application. As reported by the TP artists, the practising artists are now spread in different parts of TN and some even outside TN.

In the handloom sector in general and Pochampalli in particular, there are various levels of vertical linkages involved in the value chain. The production chain is relatively long where weavers form the basic unit of production. The purchase of yarn for weaving (yarn merchant), colour and chemicals for dyeing (traders), dyeing of the yarn (dyers), warping, starching, sizing, bobbin winding of yarn (warpers, sizers, winders), designing of the product (designer), loom staging and weaving (weaver and his family), and marketing (cloth merchants, cooperative, retail, and wholesale outlets) are some of the important stages involved. Moreover, the suppliers of machinery involved in all these stages, such as that of the warping/sizing machines, the loom and its accessories (such as jacquard, dobby) are also important stakeholders within the value chain. Weavers generally work under three institutional arrangements within the clusters—co-operatives, master weavers, and independent weavers. Synchronization along this complex value chain is vital for the fair distribution of rent arising out of the GI. Nevertheless, today there exists virtually no institutional mechanism which brings all these stakeholders in the handloom sector under one umbrella. However, a discussion on defining the authorized users in this craft could identify the crucial players. Absence of such an institutional structure for strengthening backward and forward linkages at all levels to ensure distribution of economic returns poses immense challenge to the operation of GI in the sector. The authorized user certificate has been issued to the PHTDA (comprising of master weavers and traders) and not to the individual members or the weavers working under them. Out of the fourteen members, twelve members have also been certified as authorized users of the GI certificate in the MK craft. However, no logo has been designed by the authorized users and GI is not mentioned in the letterheads or invoices.

Popularity, Competition, and Infringement

Across products, one could discern fierce competition from similar products and instances of infringement. Almost all the TP artists interviewed told us about the craft being practised in different parts of Tamil Nadu and even perhaps outside Tamil Nadu. The style is followed by all the artists, though there could be variations in the materials used in the preparation of the board and so on. In the case of SBI, all the artists noted with concern the increasing competition from the idols made in Moradabad, Uttar Pradesh (which is also a GI product), in the past two decades. It was mentioned by the artisans that the competitors from the idols made in Moradabad make the idols on a large scale, faster and cheaper than SBI, using mould technology, and these are widely available in Tamil Nadu. The SBI artisans reported that unlike them, the Moradabad artisans do not follow the shilpa shastra standards in the making of the idols, and, hence, unconventional depiction of deities is not very uncommon with Moradabad idols. For persons who are familiar with the Cholamandalam tradition of bronze idols, it is easy to distinguish between the SBI and Moradabad idols. However, as these are not sold as SBI, there is no infringement of the GI at present.

According to the MK respondents, demand is good both in the domestic and export market. The production is low in volume because of hand block printing and use of vegetable colours, which provide a niche market. The MK units face tough competition from other states and allege copying of designs by the screen printing units in other states, importantly Gujarat. The difference in the printing cost between machine printing (Rs. 5 per metre) and vegetable printing (Rs. 30 per metre) speaks a lot for the Kalamkari work. According to the office-bearers of the Kalamkari Association, copying of the Machilipatnam designs and replicating the same in machine printing is a gross violation of the GI. Though they brought the infringement to the notice of the textile ministry, no punitive action has been taken thus far.

Interestingly, the metal mirror craftspersons were aware of the two individuals who produce the mirror outside the designated GI area and sell the same in the name of Aranmula Mirror. However, no action has been taken as most of the mirror making craftspersons are related to each other. Besides, the 'infringers' also belong to the same Viswakarma caste which is engaged in the production of mirrors. Similarly, the members alleged the sale of ordinary mirrors as metal mirrors by some persons in the Aranmula panchayat area, but, again, no action had been taken regarding the same.

In the case of agarbathi-making, fragrance infringement is fierce. This deprives the manufacturers of exclusivity. In the case of Kondapalli Toys, though this craft is unique and different from the Channapatna and Nirmal toys, there is competition between the crafts due to the similar price range.

The curious case of the infringement of Pochampalli Ikat is discussed in Box 3.2. The out-of-court settlement of the case is considered by artisans concerned as a classic case of a loss of a golden opportunity to have set precedence for infringement and punitive action.

Box 3.2   Infringement of the Pochampalli GI

In 2005, it was brought to the notice of one of the registered proprietors of GI—PHTDA—that a large retail chain in Andhra Pradesh was marketing machine-made saris as Pochampalli Ikat. Upon investigation, it was revealed that a Mumbai-based businessman was manufacturing the saris and selling them at wholesale rates. The officials at the PHTDA contacted the APTDC who in turn got in touch with M/S Anand and Anand, a legal firm, to argue the case. They agreed to take up the litigation of infringement under the GI Act at a reduced cost for the weavers. However, during the Focus Group Discussion (FGDs)

with the PHTDA and the PHWCS, it was revealed that an out-of-court settlement had taken place and the manufacturer had agreed to destroy the existing stock as well as given assurance not to sell tie and dye printed saris in the name of Pochampalli. The office bearers and members of both the registered proprietors were unhappy about the out-of-court settlement. They also indicated that the infringement was due to a lack of implementation of the inspection structure. They lamented that they were not aware of the terms and conditions and the reasons for the settlement (Vinayan, 2013).

Taking Responsibility of GI

In all the states of India, there are state government-owned emporiums for the promotion of handicrafts and handlooms and the main role played by them is to assist the artisans in marketing their products. However, their role in promoting GI awareness is very less. In the government emporium at Vijayawada, a small tag was attached to each piece of the Kondapalli Toys mentioning the GI feature (Figure 3.3) though the artisans were not aware of such a practice. The craftspersons did not find any increase in sales after the GI certification.

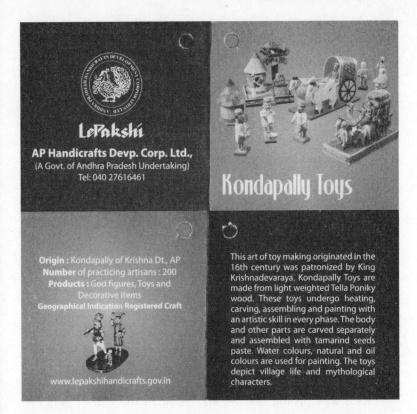

FIGURE 3.3   Details of Kondapalli Craft Provided by the Government
Emporium
Source: Collected from the Lepakshi showroom, Vijayawada, February 2014.
Reproduced with permission.

Except in the case of Aranmula Mirror and Kondapalli Toys, there
were no details of the product in the official showrooms of the different
state governments. Further, it has been observed by the first author that
in the exhibitions organized by the Development Commissioner in different states, though the GI products are displayed, there are no details
about the uniqueness, speciality, and art of the making the product. Such
details encourage the customer to know more about the product and
invest in the same. So far none of the state governments have set up an
exclusive authority to deal with the promotion of the GI craft of the state.

All the craftspersons indicated that while the sales emporiums sell the
crafts at a higher percentage than the price at which they were bought
from the artisans, the artisans are paid a fixed yet fair price. While such

activities have been going on even before the GI registration, the role of emporiums in the post-GI days should be to create awareness about the specific uniqueness about the craft by putting up billboards, appropriate maps, and write-ups about the craft on display in the emporiums. But such things have not happened except in the case of KT, where a brief write-up about the craft and the artist was found in Lepakshi, Vijayawada.

Innovations and Modifications

While critics point out that GIs do not encourage any innovations but promote continuing with the traditional practices and methods of production (Calboli, 2013), in reality, innovations do occur. With the changes in time, artists have started adopting innovations that will help roll out products faster. These are deviations from the traditional way of producing the GI product that has been mentioned in the GI journal, caused due to the lack of availability of the core raw material, or prohibitive cost of the material, and so on. While availability of raw material is a genuine issue, modifications in the production process may move the craft further away from the GI region. Importantly, the traditional knowledge associated with the craft would be lost. It also implies that the skilled employment that the craft generated is also slowly reducing.

For instance, in the case of TP, similar to the case of Feni discussed by Rangnekar (2011), differences are observed between the production process mentioned in the GI journal and the current practice adopted by a few artisans. While some artisans do stick to the original practices mentioned in the journal, changes are happening. The jackfruit wood plank that forms the basic frame, on which the entire painting rests, has been replaced by treated plywood. Plywood is cheaper than a wooden plank and therefore reduces the cost during transportation, either within India or abroad. Chemicals have replaced the tamarind seed paste that was used to protect the painting from termite and other insects. A paste of turmeric and camphor is applied on the back of the plywood and then covered with the thickest binding cloth to prevent the entry of the insects into the frame. In addition, instead of drawing a sketch, trace papers and photocopies are used to imprint the design on the cloth. Instead of natural colours, branded pastel colours are used. Precious and semi-precious stones used to be polished by hand and were then fixed on the cloth using the adhesive called 'vajram'. Now both these practices have been replaced with readymade cut glass which is obtained from Jaipur while Fevicol is the commonly used adhesive.

In SBI, moulds made of plaster of Paris are being used for making idols of political leaders and popular personalities. For agarbathis, the status of the availability of the raw material has changed in recent times. According to the AIAMA, *jigat* is scarce, which has resulted in 40 per cent of the raw bathis being sourced from Vietnam and China. Getting bamboo is also proving to be an issue due to forest regulations. States from North-East India are another viable source, which is becoming difficult due to rising transport cost and forest regulations. To cut costs, some of the manufacturers have brought raw bathi manufacturing machines which can roll out 8000 bathis an hour, compared to 5000 bathis by hand. All these modifications help the artisans in reducing the labour intensity involved in production and cut down costs. But they do have implications on labour and employment.

Traceability of the Product

In some of the crafts like TP, SBI, AM, KT, when the products are sold through the state emporiums, the emporiums assign a code number to each of the items bought from different artisans. This is helpful in assessing the market standing of the producer and in case of any defects, it is possible to trace it back to the producer. Similarly, in MK, where a couple of producers export the textiles to European countries under voluntary production standards, traceability is possible because the producer is also the trader. In Pochampalli too, because the products pass through several hands, traceability is possible only at the producer/master weaver level. Both in MK and PI, sales up to the level of the wholesaler can be traced back to the producer. But once it reaches the retailer, it depends on the type of system followed by the wholesaler.

Quality Checking

Quality-checking is done only at the producer level and there is no regulatory body supervising the craft. State emporiums are responsible only for those paintings and idols which they have acquired for sale. In addition, since each of the artists has his/her own clientele, the quality parameters are those specified by the artist only. Hence, as one of the respondents said, those who stick to the traditional method of production, with emphasis on detailing, would continue to have demands that would be reflected in the repeat orders, thus perpetuating reputation. TP artists allege that there is a compromise of reputation underway, especially the use of gold leaves being replaced by golden coloured papers and other low-quality materials in the painting. Since it is difficult to make out the kind of duplicate products used in the painting in the short run, the low-quality TPs created with such materials are sold through the souvenir shops that are scattered across the main street in Thanjavur. However, in the long run, such practices would erode the confidence of the buyers and affect the reputation of the product.

Communities Outside the Craft

With the efforts of the government in skill training programme, it is expected that people outside a particular community could be involved in the craft. While participants from different communities are involved in TP, in a few crafts, a specific community is involved. Aranmula Mirror and Swamimalai Bronze are dominated by artisans from the Vishwakarma caste while the Padmashali caste is dominant in making Pochampalli Ikat. While kinship can be a binding force promoting cooperation (facilitating terms of credit, supply of raw materials, marketing), it can also lead to conflict of interests. The artisans in the case of Aranmula mirror categorically pointed out that they would oppose if the craftsmanship is taken up by other caste groups. Similarly, the fact that Handloom Park imparts training to others outside the specific caste is a major bone of contention among those in the weaving community.

However, it may be noted here that training in crafts (which are only dependent on human skills) to persons outside the artisan community could lead to spreading of the craft to new places through migration and could be a source of competition from outside the 'geographical area'.

Exclusive Body to Promote IPR

In order to take forward the National IPR Policy of 2016, the central government has set up a Cell for IPR Promotion and Management (CIPAM) vide Order No. 12(09)/2016-IPR-III (Pt.-2)[11] dated 9 August 2016, as a professional body under the aegis of the Department of Industrial Policy and Promotion. The duration of the project is three years, beginning from April 2017 to March 2020, and would cover all major states, cities, and rural areas. One of its objectives is to conduct awareness workshops for the promotion of GIs and on the ill effects of piracy and counterfeiting. Such programs should be held not only for the artisans but also for the general public, students, and concerned government departments. Though this scheme talks about creating awareness, it is hoped that it will link up with the state governments in the implementation of GIs.

Other Issues

Though collective organizations have been formed for the sake of filing the GI application, no constructive role has been played by the associations so far. Collective promotion of the craft, setting up the CoP, collective procurement and so on, to reduce the cost of procurement of materials, are yet to take place. For instance, non-availability of black jaggery to produce the black and coffee brown colour is often an issue for the Machilipatnam units and has even led to the closure of the Pedana units, affecting the livelihood of thousands of workers for a while because this important ingredient was getting diverted to the alcohol producing units (Naidu, 2013c). The state government, acting on the representation by the Kalamkari Artisan Union, lifted the ban on transportation of black jaggery and also advised the union to procure the permanent trade license number. This license would facilitate the union to buy, sell, and transport black jaggery for the purpose of producing kalamkari textiles (Naidu, 2013d).

Societal Impact

Employment and Livelihood Potential

It should be mentioned at the outset that the employment incidence in general, and women's, in particular, in the crafts discussed, is not because of GI, but which has been traditionally associated with it. The discussion here is to suggest that the prevailing wage and the nature of the involvement of the local economy in the craft could be impacted by the different trends in the craft. Also, it was difficult to get any estimate of the profit that would accrue from the craft. Estimates of the craft materials, wherever available, are provided to give a crude idea of the likely profit made by the self-employed. There is a clear division of labour in each of the crafts mentioned here. Women dominate in agarbathi-making, from rolling agarbathis to the finished sticks stage. They are also fully involved in Kasuti Embroidery. In other crafts, their roles are limited, mostly to the pre-production processes which are nevertheless vital—block printing in Kalamkari work, pre-loom processing in Pochampalli Ikat, and post-production painting the toys in Kondapalli. TP was completely male-dominated, with the role of the women limited to fixing the precious stones (discontinued since 2000). But, in recent years, there have been a few women who have made a mark in the field. Two women have taken up SBI after the demise of their husbands although they operate on a low scale, making smaller idols and utensils. Two enterprising women have taken up metal mirror making and operate in the Aranmula panchayat area. They keep the formulae of metal mixing a trade secret and handle the marketing on their own. The rest of the process is handled by the men working in the women's home-based unit. In Pochampalli, as in most of the handloom weaving enterprises, the pre-loom processes—from bobbin winding to sizing to warping—are undertaken by the women in the household, and during the busy season, more women are hired. Though weaving by women is not widespread, it is not unheard of either.[12]

Interviews with the leading craftspersons of TP revealed that there could be around 200 to 250 artists practising TP in the whole of Tamil Nadu, with more than fifteen members in Thanjavur and Kumbakonam[13] alone. Each of the artists indicated that once ten or fifteen of these practising artists pass into oblivion, then the traditional nature of the craft might be difficult to maintain and sustain. The practising craftspersons of TP were well-established, well-known, and, except for three of the artisans who had other sources of income, others were entirely dependent on the craft for their livelihood. According to a senior artisan, to be known in the field requires consistent quality of work and materials. However, it was evident that an emerging craftsperson in this field cannot rely entirely on TP for his/her livelihood. TP is a kind of a cultural asset/showpiece item which is not routinely bought. As the government efforts to teach this craft have been received well by women, in a few years, TP could emerge as an additional income earning activity for these trained women. It is also a possibility that the craft could migrate with these women to other places.

Indirect employment potential in TP exists in the form of workers who prepare the (1) wooden slab on which the TP is drawn, (2) the outer frames, and (3) the back cover of the wooden slab. Each artist keeps a minimum number of forty to fifty wooden slabs of different sizes ready with the cloth finely polished. However, it was difficult to get a clear estimate of the number of artisans engaged in this sector.

Preparation of the jackwood board with cloth and polishing is outsourced, and the same would earn a person Rs. 500–600 per day. Though none of the artists employ anyone with a formal job contract, a person who is trained in the making, polishing, and drawing of the sketch on the wooden plank is paid between Rs. 10,000 to 15,000 a month. This person works for more than one artist. Depending on the size, the cost of the plank starts from a minimum of Rs. 500 and can be in multiples of 1000. Women labourers are paid Rs. 250 a day for fixing the coloured stones. The golden foil comes in a bunch of 160 leaves and costs around Rs. 20,000, which could increase according to the price of gold.

There are about 200 families engaged in the making of SBI, who live in and around Swamimalai, according to the officials of Poompuhar there. Many of them carry on the trade as a household enterprise while a handful of artisans who are engaged in direct exports, have workshops of their own which provides employment to thirty or more skilled workers and are widely known.[14] All the craftspersons were dependent on SBI for their livelihood.

A minimum investment of Rs. 1 lakh is required for starting the idol-making business, and it is inclusive of the tools, metals, and setting up of the furnace. In the case of SBI, all the materials, such as wax, riverbed soil, and metals, are available perennially and there is no issue about their availability. The price per kilogram of the different materials used in the idol-making[15] is as follows: wax Rs. 450; copper Rs. 550; brass Rs. 450; lead Rs. 250; cost of daily labour Rs. 300–500. The majority of the demand for SBI comes from the Hindu temples and devotees, five-star hotels, museums in India and abroad, art galleries, commercial establishments like jewellery and textile showrooms, corporate houses, cultural academies, conference halls, and art collectors.[16]

Basically, the bronze idols are heavy, and the price varies according to the size of the idol, weight, workmanship, and the kind of metal that has been used in the making of the idol. A one-foot idol of Lord Ganesh made of five metals would cost approximately Rs. 15,000. Idols with the antique finish[17] are costlier than the metal finished idols, and these are preferred in the foreign markets. From the several accounts it appears that 15 to 20 per cent of the cost of the idol would be the net income of the craftspersons.

According to the President and Secretary of the Parthasarathy Handicraft Centre, there are fifteen artisans who are engaged in the making and selling of the Aranmula Mirror. The making of the metal mirror craft is limited only to the two panchayats of Aranmula and Mannupuzhachery, where nine and eight producers are located respectively. Out of these seventeen, only fifteen craftspersons are active. Eight of them, of which two are women, are members of the association. One of the female respondents' spouse was employed in a bank. All the artisans whom we met have made mirror-making craft as their source of livelihood. With the mechanization of jewellery-making, goldsmiths have turned to metal mirror-making and work with these fifteen craftspersons. A minimum of Rs. 2 lakhs investment is required to enter the business of mirror-making. All the natural materials in the making of the mirror are obtained at a very low price or at nearly no cost, as most houses in the rural areas of Kerala have these materials. The reported costs of tin, copper, and brass per kilogram were Rs. 2000, Rs. 400, and Rs. 450 respectively. The buffing machinery costs Rs. 10,000 and has a life of six to seven years after which it has to be replaced. The blower machine costs Rs. 2000. The grinding machine used for making the frame of the mirror costs Rs. 2800, and can be used to make up to two hundred pieces. A small 2.5-inch mirror costs between Rs. 1500 to Rs. 2000 while a bigger oval-shaped mirror, measuring more than twenty inches, is priced at Rs. 1.5 lakh although such big sized mirrors are made on order only.

In the process of mirror-making, an average of eight to nine workers are engaged with each of the eight artisans in the Aranmula panchayat. Indirect employment potential exists for those workers who (1) bring the clay from the paddy fields of Aranmula, (2) prepare the clay mixture, (3) make the outer frame and stand,[18] and (4) make the small jewellery carry case for the mirrors that are stitched in velvet and attractive boxes. However, it was difficult to gauge the income accruals to the artisans from the craft. Hired workers are employed on daily wages which range from Rs. 600 to 1000, depending on the level of skill displayed. Payment for working overtime is mostly based on piece rate as this works out to be profitable for both the employer and the employee.

Approximately 200 families are engaged in the making of Kondapalli Toys. Kondapalli toy-making depends entirely on the availability of white sanders wood. The cost of a head load of white sanders ranges between Rs. 400 and Rs. 450, and the wood is cut at a cost of Rs. 200. On an average, wood worth Rs. 3000 is bought per month by the crafts-persons. Enamel, gum, and so on, would cost another Rs. 1000. Though the materials to make natural colours are available regularly, they are not preferred as the preparation is laborious and such colours are bright only in summer. Hence, the artisans use chemical enamel colours that appeal to the customers, which is an innovation of recent times. Except where the artisans get the wood sawed, there is no use of any machin-ery. While the activity goes on round the year, the artisans acquire the wood before the monsoon.

Except for one artisan who owns an SSI unit that provides employ-ment to about twenty-five people, the rest of the units are all household enterprises, mainly assisted by the women of the house. Daily wages for the wood carvers is Rs. 150 and the painters get Rs. 80. The monthly salary for an experienced person engaged in colouring would be Rs. 4500 while an inexperienced wood worker would get around Rs. 2500–3000. An experienced wood carver would get up to Rs. 10,000 per month. Skilled workers who make items like bullock cart or the *dasavatharam* (ten dif-ferent incarnations of Lord Vishnu) set would get closer to Rs. 500 per set, depending on the size. Festivals like *Dussehra, Sankaranthi,* and the marriage season generate lots of demand for these toys, besides being purchased as a collector's item. However, as the number of workers is low, the demand exceeds supply at times. Further, as the toys are very fragile, repeat purchases do happen. In the initial years after the GI reg-istration, the craft of Kondapalli Toys thrived because of the bulk orders given by LANCO, the co-applicant in the case of KT, for social events like celebration of New Year and birthdays. These bulk orders generated good income for the artisans. A gift pack order of six Kondapalli toy items amounted to 4000 pieces and all the craftsmen benefitted by this order.

Fourteen units operating in Pedana are members of the Vegetable Handblock Printers Association that is engaged in MK. The estimate of workers engaged in Kalamkari ranges between 800 to 1200. Including the family members of these workers, it was estimated that around 3000 people were dependent on Kalamkari printing in Pedana alone. Under block printing, a single worker can print up to four metres of cloth per day, which indicates the high skilled employment potential whereas in mechanized printing, thousands of metres can be produced in a day.

However, units resorting to mechanization and synthetic colours will lead to the loss of the GI and the handicraft status.

The owners of the Kalamkari units are entirely dependent on production and trading in Kalamkari textiles. Overall, the distribution of the cost and profit from the sale of Kalamkari cloth is as follows: 40 per cent of the sales value is used for the purchase of the basic grey cloth, 30 per cent for labour, 20 per cent for raw material, and 10 per cent profit. Bigger units buy a minimum of 50,000 metres of cloth which will help them to meet orders for three months while small scale units, depending on their resources, buy 5000 or 10,000 metres of cloth; a twenty-kilo sack of *jajoo* leaves cost Rs. 2000, which is available from the forests of Bhadrachalam and Visakhapatnam (three kilos of leaves are required for boiling fifty metres of cloth, which is essential for obtaining lasting colours). The printing workers are paid between Rs. 120–50 a day and the average income of a worker does not exceed Rs. 4000 a month.

All the units are dependent on the Krishna River, a crucial element in the production process, and the work suffers both when there is inadequate availability of water and when there is excess rain. In 2012–13, when there was no water in the canal, the workers had to travel ninety to hundred kms to wash the clothes in the river, and the cost of transportation increased by Rs. 1000 a day. During such adversities, work suffers and the cost of production increases. Most units have work for eight months a year. During the off season, workers work in the employment guarantee schemes, or as casual farm labourers. Units often face a shortage of skilled workers. It is a common practice among the workers to take an interest-free loan from the owner of the unit and continue repaying it in small amounts over a period. If the requirement for additional amount rises, their strategy, most often, is to approach the owner of another unit who would give them a larger amount which the workers would use for repaying the existing loan and to meet additional needs and join the unit of the new lender. This is one of the reasons why the workers who are on loan, continue to work with the units. But the low level of wages keeps the younger generation away.

The price of the Kalamkari blocks varies according to the intricacy of the design. Recent innovations, like classical dance forms of India and the Warli tribal designs in blocks, have generated huge interest among the Kalamkari producers and buyers.

An estimated 56,00 looms[19] are in use in the villages in and around Pochampalli (spread across Nalgonda and neighbouring Warangal districts). With at least two workers at each loom, there could be a minimum of 11,000 people working in and dependent on the Pochampalli craft for their livelihood.

There was a difference in the operational cost reported by the weavers under the Pochampally Handloom Weavers Cooperative Society (PHWCS) and the Pochampally Handloom Tie and Dye Manufacturers Association (PHTDA).[20] In the case of the PHWCS, for every Rs. 1000 worth of output of Pochampalli Ikat, raw material cost accounted for Rs. 674, wages Rs. 276, and maintenance cost Rs. 50, while in the case of weavers under the PHTDA, raw material cost accounted for Rs. 747, wages stood at Rs. 207, and maintenance cost was Rs. 50. In the case of non-GI producers, the raw material cost stood at Rs. 661, followed by wages at Rs. 273, and maintenance cost at Rs. 66.[21]

One loom requires four kilos of yarn per month. One kilo produces three saris and it requires around 3.5 kilos to produce eight saris (1 kg for warp and 2.5 kilos for weft). The chemicals for dyeing cost around Rs. 1000 per warp and additional Rs. 1000 for pre-loom processes. The cost of yarn (silk) per kilo was Rs. 1100 in 2004 but rose to Rs. 2900 per kilo by 2011–12. Thus, the cost of weaving saris more than doubled and the master weavers who could not afford the rise in input process, reduced the number of looms they operated, resulting in the loss of production. The employment potential for the craft is very high given the long value chain, starting with the yarn merchant to the trader. Given the intricate work that is involved in ikat weaving, weaving remains the major source of income and 95 per cent of the income for the household is derived from only weaving (Vinayan, 2006). Moreover, the pre-loom activities which involve winding, sizing, warping, are mostly done by women in the household and, thus, they are not engaged in any other income generation activity. Of late, the younger generations have diversified into other professions, but, by and large, handloom weaving remains the major activity in the selected cluster of Pochampalli. The majority of the weavers produce saris and they belong to the GI category (weavers working with either the PHWCS or PHTDA). This was closely followed by home furnishings (bed sheets, curtains, pillow covers, table linen).[22] Silk saris are of five to six metres in length and take 45 days to weave.

According to the GI Registry, the number of KE practising artisans could be in the range of five hundred to seven hundred in the Dharwad and Hubli districts of Karnataka. In the Kalghatagi taluka, however, we could trace only 21 craftspersons from different villages and hence the actual number of persons working in the entire craft could vary. In Kasuti, work, cloth, and embroidery materials are provided to the artisans by traders or NGOs. Only the labour charges are paid to the artisans.

The main reason for a few women continuing with the Kasuti work is the flexibility in the hours of work. A highly skilled woman (who also has an artisan identity card) earns an average of Rs. 180 to 220 per day from this work and close to Rs. 70,000 per annum. The piece rate offered for Kasuti work is abysmally low, which is paid according to the 'tab of embroidery' done. One tab refers to two inches of height and four inches of width, which fetches Rs. 40. As orders are not regular, women have shifted to agricultural labour work.

Though KE has been around for ages, it came to be known only in recent years after the KE work on salwar-kameez sets, saris, and other dress materials became popular in large markets like Bengaluru due to the intervention of NGOs after the GI. While the sale of these embroidered dresses and dress materials is slowly picking up, the condition of Kasuti workers is dismal and the number of artisans is dwindling by the day, thanks to the role of middlemen and the absence of direct marketing facilities.

As mentioned in the statement of case for Mysore Agarbathi, more than 90 per cent of agarbathi-making is in the unorganized sector. There are closer to five hundred and seventy manufacturers who are members of the All India Agarbathi Manufacturers Association (AIAMA) of which three hundred and sixty-nine (68 per cent) are from Karnataka alone. According to AIAMA estimates, there were over twenty lakh people all over India working in the industry and, in Karnataka alone, there would be over twelve lakh people in the agarbathi industry. Out of this, 65–75 per cent is permanently employed as packers and hand rollers with different units, while 25–30 per cent work as seasonal workers, during the peak seasons of Dussehra and Diwali. There is no specific skill involved in rolling agarbathis. Many units outsource the rolling of the bathis to the workers, who are paid on a piece rate basis of Rs. 30 for 1000 sticks. A worker working for eight hours a day would earn Rs. 150 to Rs. 250 a day.

An investment ranging from Rs. 4000 to Rs. 10,000 is sufficient to start an agarbathi manufacturing unit. Presently, *jigat* of good quality costs Rs. 100 a kilogram and *jigat* of second-best quality costs Rs. 80

a kilo. Perfumes are manufactured locally, and the price starts from Rs. 200 and vary upwards, depending on the quality and type. Due to fierce competition, price of different raw materials that go into making *jigat* were not disclosed by the units.

Sustainable Use of Resources

Almost all the products which are dependent on the natural resources are using them in a sustainable fashion. For instance, only the thick branches of white sanders are cut for use in KE. Further, the use of machinery is extremely limited, hence the carbon footprint generated is likely to be very less. However, in the case of PI, weavers use chemical dyes which have environmental and health implications (the use of vegetable dyes increases the cost of production, hence, are not prevalent).

Impact on the Producer and Consumer

It was difficult to get any estimate on income or profit for the producer. At best we could get the price estimate of the products from where we had to estimate the likely income/profit for the producer. Price of a piece is fixed according to the intricate design used in the craft, the workmanship, and the quality of materials. The price of the TP depends on the size of the painting and the workmanship. The price quoted by the producer is final in all the crafts, except for KE, where the worker does the embroidery on a piece of cloth. But when the craft is sold through the state emporiums, the emporiums follow fixed criteria to set the price (discussed in the section 'Taking Responsibility of GI'). Producers have also borne the cost of filing the application for GI except for SBI, KE, and Pochampalli Ikat.

A few instances of GI products being promoted as a heritage product could be discerned. Aranmula craftspersons said that after the GI and the documentary shows, some real estate owners started gifting their customers with an Aranmula mirror as an auspicious gift at the time of providing possession of the house. This has created steady work orders for the artists. Similarly, some of the professional associations in Kerala have started honouring their important guests with a gift of AM. The government of Andhra Pradesh usually gifts the famous KT bullock cart to their dignitaries.

Table 3.3 summarizes the entire discussion on TOC.

TABLE 3.3 Impact of GI Registration

Stages	Impact Indicators	TP	SBI	AM	KT	MK	PI	KE	MA
INPUTS									
Identification of the product	Is the product identified?	Yes	Yes	Yes	Yes	Yes	Yes	Yes	Yes
Filing of application	Has the application be filed?	Yes	Yes	Yes	Yes	Yes	Yes	Yes	Yes
Identification of the producers	Has producers of the product identified for registration?	Yes	Yes	Yes	Yes	Yes	Yes	Yes	Yes
	Are primary producers aware of registration?	No	Yes	Yes	Yes	No	No	No	No
Defining the production area	Is the production area clearly defined?	Yes	Yes	Yes	Yes	Yes	Yes	Yes	Yes
GI formally registered	Is the GI name officially registered and available on the IP website?	Yes	Yes	Yes	Yes	Yes	Yes	Yes	Yes
	Has the registration been renewed?	Yes	Yes	Yes	Yes	Yes	Yes	Yes	Yes
OUTPUTS									
Forming of producers' organization	Has any new form of association formed for the purpose of GI registration?	Yes	No	Yes	Yes	Yes	No	No	No
Registration of logo	Has there been registration of logos for individual products?	Yes	Yes	Yes	Yes	Yes	Yes	Yes	Yes
Code of practices established	Is the method of production, as indicated in statement of case filed at the Registry, followed?	Yes#	Yes	Yes	Yes	Yes	Yes**	Yes	Yes

Stages	Impact Indicators	TP	SBI	AM	KT	MK	PI	KE	MA
	Have there been any efforts to establish code of practices for standardization after GI registration?	No	No	No	No	No	No	No	Yes$
Establishing value chain	Are authorized users registered?	No	No	No	No	Yes	Yes	No	No
	Does the identification of value chain reflect all stakeholders?	No	No	No	No	Yes*	No	No	No
Establishment of monitoring/ inspection body	Is there a monitoring inspection mechanism for the use of GI?	No	No	No	No	No	Yes	No	Yes $
Skill Training	Has there been specialized training imparted to artisans?	Yes	Yes	No	Yes	No	No	Yes	No
OUTCOMES									
Awareness	Are producers aware of registered GI?	No	Yes	Yes	Yes	No	No	No	Partial
	Are consumers aware of registered GI?	No	No	No	No	No	No	No	No
Establishing value chain	Are authorized users spreading GI	No	No	No	No	No	No	No	No
Infringement	Have there been instances of infringement of GI registration reported?	No	No	Yes	No	Yes	Yes	No	No
Traceability	Has there been mechanism evolved for traceability of the product?	Yes&	Yes&	Yes&	Yes&	Yes&	Yes&	No	No

(continued)

TABLE 3.3 (Continued)

Stages	Impact Indicators	TP	SBI	AM	KT	MK	PI	KE	MA
Quality compliance before marketing	Given the production structure, is it possible to ensure traceability?	NA	NA	NA	NA	Yes	Yes	Yes	NA
	Is there a separate body involved in inspection before marketing?	No	No	No	No	No	No	No	No
IMPACTS									
Sustainable use of resources	Low carbon print due to low levels of machinery used	Yes	Yes	Yes	Yes	Yes	Yes/ No@	Yes	Yes
GI recognition in the society	GI registration has led to improved income and livelihood			Maybe					
GI and Tourism	Has the GI tag been used in promoting tourism?	No	No	Yes	No	No	No	No	No

Notes: # Variations were reported.

& During direct sales to institutions and at master weaver level respectively and not at the retailer level.

@ Denotes that while no machinery is used indicating green energy, PI craft does involve the use of chemical dyes which may cause environmental pollution and health hazards.

* Authorized users include both primary producers and traders.

** Production of Telia Rumal mentioned in the statement of case is no longer produced in the region though tie & dye rumal had international acclaim in earlier times.

$ Detailed Code of Practices ad monitoring system is clearly spelt out, but remains only in paper.

Source: Developed by authors using the information from the primary survey.

Can GI Registration Change the Market Scenario for the Chosen Products and Impact the Livelihoods of the Producers?

Barjolle and Sylvander (1999) classifies GI products as (1) horizontal or *typicity 1* meaning that the good is *both specific (different) and unique* and therefore relates to a given region, and (2) vertical or *typicity 2* which emphasizes the determinants, that is, the combination of natural and human production factors that go into the making of it. In other words, the ratio of nature's and human contribution at a geographical location confers geographical association to a GI and thus determines its quality (Soam et al., 2007). The involvement of human skill alone as a major contributor to the GI factor could lead to situations contesting the claim to GI because the same craft could be practiced in different places (Tyabji, 2008) and the possibilities of similar products riding on the reputation value of the GI product are high.

Except TP, which we were told is being practised in other parts of Tamil Nadu but is known as TP only, in the case of MK and PI, similar traditions prevail in other states and they have also been protected with GI. In the case of KE, it is not clear whether similar style of embroidery is being practised in other parts of Karnataka or India. From the description of the products, human skills coupled with geographical specificities play an important role in the creation of reputation and uniqueness of all products, except TP, PI, and KE where the reputation is based on human skills alone. So, while TP, PI, and KE can be classified as typicity 1 products, the rest of the crafts may be categorized as typicity 2 products.

All the crafts mentioned here are handmade, with very minimal use of machinery and are thus environment-friendly, a factor that will have trade appeal particularly in the developed country markets. But, in order to retain the typicity 2 status, the sustainable use of resources needs to be ensured in the long run, through appropriate governance mechanism, as the enthusiasm to meet a higher demand should not lead to depletion of resources.

GI protection in the case of TP and KE is purely from the heritage point of view and to prevent the loss of knowledge rather than issues of market and infringement due to competition. As Neilson et al. (2018) says, GI here has more symbolic value and in such cases,

TABLE 3.4 GI Features of the Chosen Products

GI Product	No. of Artisans (Approximate)	Employment Potential	Use of Capital Intensive Machinery	Volume of Production	Export Potential	Distribution Practice	Presence of the GI factor	Use of the GI Registration	Use of the GI logo	Promotion of the Product	Competition
Pochampalli Ikat	10,000	High	Low	Low	High	Self/Government	Human skill	No	No	Self/Government	High
Thanjavur Painting	200–250	Limited	None	Low	High	Self/Government	Human skill	No	No	Self	Low
Swamimalai Bronze Icons	200–250	High	None	Low	High	Self/Government	Human skill & GI	No	No	Self	High
Aranmula Mirror	15	Limited	None	Low	High	Self/Government	Human skill & GI	Yes	No	Self	High
Kondapalli Toys	200	Limited	None	Low	High	Self/Government	Human skill & GI	Yes	No	Self	High
Machilipatnam Kalamkari	14/800*	High	None	Low	High	Self/Trader	Human skill & GI	No	No	Self	High
Kasuti Embroidery	500–700	Limited	None	Low	Medium	Self/Trader	Human skill	No	No	Self	High
Mysore Agarbathis	Many	High	Low	Varies	High	Self/Trader	Limited	No	No	Self	High

Note: * 800 workers employed in 14 units.
Source: Compiled by the authors from the case studies.

it is difficult to estimate the economic benefit and 'the GI does not actually need to be properly functioning, replete with complicated quality control mechanisms, for these outcomes to be realized' (p. 21). TP however may be said has become generic as the raw materials are sourced from different places and the human skill is also spreading to other places.

However, we should also realize that 'GI offers remarkable opportunity to resist the erasure of place and join the social movements of place' (Rangnekar, 2011). In each of the product, the approach to the market has been both direct sales to the consumers, through the state-owned emporiums and traders as well. The channels of market have not changed after the GI certification. As most products are also sold by the producers directly, the producer decides the CoP and inspects the quality that will help retain the reputation and bring in repeated purchases. These are based on mutual faith and the guarantee provided by the producer. But some producers might want to make a quick profit and might make products that are of inferior quality. Such practices would erode the reputation. This is because of the small number of artisans involved in the work. Institutional buyers have their own indicators of quality, based on which orders are placed. The case studies also brought out the fact that the producers with better resource endowment like the SBI artisan or the Kalamkari producers with the export market, have better market reach than other producers.

The state emporiums have ample scope to innovate with their display strategies and create a GI pavilion in their showroom, which would attract domestic and foreign tourists. This is essential as the state emporiums serve as the end-point of the organized value chain, to carry the message to the customers. Similarly, several of the domestic and international airports in India sell their unique crafts. But they do not carry a write-up or a map of the region to attract the attention of the buyers. The origin and uniqueness of the craft should be spelt out in a manner that reaches the consumers so as to generate more demand from them. Because, after reading the information the consumer's decision to buy a craft would not be based on price but based on the appreciation for the craft. The consumers will also be satisfied that they would be paying for an authentic product.

Each product discussed here has its own uniqueness and utility value. TP, SBI, AM, KT, have more artistic values. The demand for KT goes up during certain religious festivals. The rest of the crafts have more functional value. GI awareness could create more market and price difference from consumers who value regional authenticity. In case of Pochampalli Ikat, given the unique technique of tie and dye method of production and the diversity of products, there exists high potential for market differentiation. Kasuti Embroidery, with over seven hundred designs, could create a very special niche market in the ready-to-wear clothes segment, if it is appropriately publicized by fashion designers and apparel houses. If such interventions are planned, then this languishing craft could be revived.

There is a clear binary between registered proprietors and the Handloom Park over the registration and use of the GI. While the GI registration was significant, given the flourishing trade both in the domestic and international market, the inherent problems of the handloom sector—availability of raw material, fluctuations in prices, availability of credit—have hindered the development and synchronization of brand building among the various stakeholders at Pochampalli. While the Handloom Park has been able to target consumers with brand building, the registered proprietors were unaware and disinterested in the use of the GI as a marketing tool (Vinayan, 2013).

While the craft remains the source of livelihood for many producers, the socio-economic context of the eight products clearly varies. The employment potential at the primary production level is relatively high in the case of Mysore Agarbathis, Machilipatnam Kalamkari, and Pochampalli Ikat. The crafts remain the major source of livelihood for all the artisans involved in them. The number of craftsmen is limited in the case of TP, AM, SBI, and KE (which ranges from 15–250). Besides the direct employment of engaging in the craft, there is a potential of indirect employment in the processing of the product and in further trading of the product. Hence the trends in the GI craft would impact the employment created by the value chain as well. The low profit margin coupled with other opportunities of employment has weaned away the younger generation from the craft, but in the case of textile products, the younger generation was actively involved in marketing and trade.

In the case of Ikat, the process of tie and dye is prevalent in different parts of India (notably in Odisha and Gujarat which also have GIs for their ikats) and this poses a serious problem in highlighting the authenticity of the product. Nonetheless, producers, regular customers, textile lovers, and experts can differentiate between the different types of ikat based on geographical origin, though there has been no in-depth study undertaken to distinguish these in the wake of GI certification. Proper brand-building for the registered GI products, particularly for the textile sector, can tap the potential of product differentiation based on a variety of factors like: (a) technique of ikat; (b) technique of production (in the case of shawls, dyeing, and prints); (c) design (for embroidery, shawls); (d) use of machinery (use of blocks vs. pens; shuttle vs. needle for designs in looms); (e) use or non-use of jacquard or dobby for creating designs, vertical or horizontal looms, pit looms, or frame looms; (f) type of yarn, dyes used; (g) block or hand printing; and (h) use of hand or powerloom.

There exists high competition from similar products for these crafts—Moradabad idol makers for SBI, low quality mirror makers in Aranmula and elsewhere, imitation of ikat weaving by powerlooms and mills, of Kalamkari by screen printers, Kondapalli toys from close substitutes such as Channapatna and Nirmal Toys (which are also registered GI products), and imitation of fragrance in the case of agarbathis.

The promotional and distribution activities are solely the responsibility of the producers though, occasionally, as part of tourism promotion, Aranmula and Ikat are promoted by the state government agencies. Places like Thanjavur, Swamimalai, and Aranmula attract religious tourism, and Mysore is on the tourist map due to its various attractions. A GI tour path should be woven around the local tourism to promote the product and to create awareness.

Moreover, in all the eight cases, one could observe differences in the scale of production, namely, from small scale to large scale producers; highly domestic market oriented to exports to international destinations. However, 'tradition' remains an important component which would motivate different actors to be brought together and this was evident across all the case studies. But these traditions remain popular within a particular region or state. A product very well known in Tamil Nadu may not have been heard of by consumers in Punjab and so on.

Even if there have been gaps in the outcomes, all the proprietors of the product have gone about renewing the GI application. Collective effort at the level of the producers to draw up a uniform CoP and brand building may be helpful in making the GI product realize its potential. The creation of social capital is less as the producers purchase the inputs and sell the products independently.

Overall, irrespective of whether the producers advertise about the 'GI' certification of their product or not, the products would continue to be sold by their 'origin label' like Thanjavur Painting or Pochampalli Sari and so on, which will carry on in the years to come as well.

In the absence of concrete data on employment and income realized, it is not possible to concretely categorize the impact of GI on employment and income impact on livelihood.

The success of the GI as a development tool also depends on the importance of the GI product to the local economy in terms of resources and employment, and so on. Hence, the rural development potential of GI may be exploited in the case of Kondapalli Toys, Mysore Agarbathi, Machilipatnam Kalamkari, and Pochampalli Ikat because of the number of livelihoods dependent on it. Collective strategies to minimize costs, prevent infringement, maintain quality, and brand-building efforts would yield positive results.

Notes

1. The study was conducted in the undivided Andhra Pradesh in early 2014. The study areas Kondapalli and Machilipatnam come under the jurisdiction of present Andhra Pradesh and Pochampalli under the newly formed state of Telangana.

2. An element of secrecy was evident in the case of making of AM, MK, and MA discussed later in the chapter.

3. Shilpa shastras are ancient Hindu texts that describe design principles for a wide range of arts and crafts.

4. Information in this paragraph draws from *Geographical Indications Journal*, Number 4 January 2005.

5. Available at http://www.financialexpress.com/news/survivalatstake/139126/0 and http://missiontelangana.com/two-entrepreneurs-build-handloom-park-in-pochampally/, accessed 28 June 2013. Interview with H. Kopreshachari,

CEO, Handloom Park, 30 January 2013, during a field visit to the Handloom Park.

6. We learnt from the discussion with the GI registry that in its early days, there was no uniformity in filing the logo and hence products filed much earlier, like PI, got the logo registered only in 2017. In recent years, the GI registry has emphasized on getting the logo submitted by the applicant along with the application form.

7. Before the state bifurcation, Lepakshi was the state handicrafts emporium. After bifurcation, Lepakshi remains with Andhra Pradesh while the state emporium of Telangana is known as Golkonda Crafts.

8. It was observed that excellent toys with beautiful crafts and good workmanship were just rolled in newspapers or polythene covers and handed over to the buyers. Among the tourists who were visiting Kondapalli village at that time, it was observed that while some still bought the items, a few did not buy citing the reason of possible damage during transportation.

9. In December 2015, an application for GI in the name of Thikanampallil Aranmula Kannadi was filed by Thikanampallil Aranmula Metal Mirror Nirman Family Charitable Trust. The area of production mentioned is the same as Aranmula and Mallapuzhaseri panchayat, which is the same as the production area of Aranmula Mirror.

10. The study, as mentioned earlier, covered a sample of 354 weavers—136 working with the PHWCS, 152 with the PHTDA, and 66 outside the purview of both.

11. Available at http://dipp.nic.in/sites/default/files/Scheme%20IPR%20 Awareness.pdf, accessed on 13 November 2017.

12. Out of 354 weavers covered under the study, only 24 were women weavers (Vinayan, 2013).

13. A city 40 kilometres from Tanjore.

14. One of the direct exporters was our respondent. His family (of artisans) is said to be the direct descendants of the chief sculptor who built the famous temples in Tarapuram and Gangaikonda Cholapuram in Tamil Nadu and is also credited as being the one who discovered the binding nature of the alluvial soil of Cauvery.

15. At the time of interviews in 2014.

16. One of the respondents has a workshop jointly owned by his brothers which, according to the Poompuhar officials, is bigger in size compared to other such workshops in Swamimalai. Among the idols he supplied, mention should be made of the noteworthy idols supplied by him directly and by his brothers to various Hindu temples around the world: the 108 poses (karnas) of Lord Siva in the temple at Hawaii in the US; the three-foot tall idol of Lord Shanmuga with his consorts, for the Murugan temple in London; a

five-foot high Nataraja kept in the office of the UNESCO in Paris; the idols of Kailasanatha temple in Kabithavathai in Sri Lanka and Perumal temple in Singapore. They are assisted by a team of three master craftsmen and 30 workers. These brothers make the idols according to the Chola tradition and the shilpa shastras. The Census of India, Tamil Nadu, 1961 contains the genealogy map of this family of sculptors.

17. On the fully finished idol, the artisans pore a chemical which provides an antique look and commands a relatively higher price than the idol which is polished and has a glittered finish.

18. Interestingly, the frame makers were also given identity cards as metal mirror craftsperson by the Development Commissioner. The Association brought it to the DC's notice and got it changed.

19. As per the estimates of key informants at Pochampalli during the time of fieldwork conducted by Vinayan in her study in 2011–12 (Vinayan, 2012).

20. Registered proprietors of Pochampalli Ikat GI. The PHWCS was registered in 1955 under the Societies Act 1860. The society has around 800 members. Its jurisdiction is spread over 11 villages. As on March 2012, they had a list of 150 weaver members who have been working with them. The PHTDA was established in 1987 under the Public Societies Registration Act. It is an association of master weavers/traders, in and around Pochampalli, engaged in silk weaving. The main objective of the association is to ensure the development of the members and their business through better understanding, coordination and unity. The association has not been formed with a profit motive and none of the office-bearers are paid from funds from the association. In 2003, there were around 119 members in the association, of whom only around 85 were still engaged in trade/production, while in 2012, the membership had declined to 91 and around 65 members were active in silk sari production and trade. Moreover, it was noted that in the case of both the PHWCS and PHTDA that the spread of their weavers was across the weaving villages in and around Pochampalli in the Nalgonda district and in a few villages in the Warangal district though their offices are located in Pochampalli.

21. Calculated from Vinayan (2013). The study covered a sample of 354 weavers—136 working with the PHWCS, 152 with the PHTDA, and 66 outside the purview of both. Non-GI weavers refer to those weavers who do not weave for master weavers/traders under the PHTDA (35) or who are not members of the PHWCS but other cooperative societies in and around Pochampalli other than the PHWCS (31). In case of the PHTDA, the higher cost of raw material may be attributed to the differences in the designs used, while in the case of non-GI weavers, the lower cost could be because of differences in the type of yarn used, predominantly cotton. Irrespective of the differences, the most discerning feature is that across organization of production, the raw

material component was highest in the total operational cost. The figures refer to March–May 2012 when the field survey was conducted.

22. The weaving of dress materials both in silk and cotton is in vogue; however, their percentage in the sampled weavers is low since the sample selection was based on whether one works under registered proprietors of GI or not.

4

Collective Organizations in GI Implementation
The Unfinished Agenda

GIs are a collective attempt by producers to intervene in a production chain to ensure greater value retention within a particular region (Neilson et al., 2018). The two preconditions required for a fruitful geographical indication are a strong natural claim to a distinct locational identity and strong collective bodies at the local level (Liebl & Roy, 2003). Collective action begins when the producers organize themselves to make strategies (Neilson et al., 2018) to obtain recognition for the value of a GI product that is based on the potential of the local resources (Vandecandelaere et al., 2009–10). In the absence of collective action, GI would not benefit the producers from developing countries (Kher, 2006), and individual producers who operate in the small-scale sector would get discouraged to continue with production if they have to use their individual resources to establish the authenticity of the product and continue to maintain the same. The remuneration of a GI product has to cover the cost of production, which is higher than the industrialized way of production (Vandecandelaere et al., 2009–10). The economic returns on a GI product are proportionate to the awareness of the consumers regarding the same (Gal, 2017).

Collective actions are most helpful in increasing benefits, reducing the transaction costs in marketing, and in accessing resources required for production. In order to manufacture the products that truly reflect the uniqueness associated with the region, there has to be an able governance system that implements certain standards that assures the consumer that indeed they are purchasing a unique product. Implementation of collective strategies requires good governance and institutional capacities (Conejero & Cesar, 2017) as the value of a GI product is influenced by the 'structure of the local community, group reputation, group heterogeneity, way of local governance, control system, entry barriers, and so on' (Gal, 2017). The effectiveness of the collective action also depends on the number of participants (smaller size nurtures cooperation), homogeneity of the group of actors, and fostering of trust (Rosa, 2015). Implicitly, the producers will have to collectively decide the rules regarding the GI product and share responsibilities to implement the rules through exchange of information and knowledge to protect the reputation of the product and to check any conflicting behaviour of the producers. The success of GI is dependent on the extent to which GI is not only institutionalized in terms of recognition, acceptance, and support for GI within the producer community (Neilson et al., 2018) but also to preserve, nurture, and sustain the craft. When there is recognition and support for GI within the producer community, then the chances of free riding and compromising on quality are less.

Collective action is a must in deciding the code of practices (CoP) for different products. The CoP includes the definition of the product (name, characteristics, production, and processing methods), the area under GI, and the guarantee system (control plan) to ensure conformity of a GI product to the specifications. As a consequence, the CoP is both a tool for internal coordination (collective rules for fair competition between producers) and external trust (recognition by society, information on quality available for retailers and consumers) (Vandecandelaere et al., 2009–10, p. 51). In short, implementation of GI rests on the practice of CoP in each of the GI products, and appropriate governance and institutions are mandatory requirements. These institutions can be producer associations converted into cooperatives or appropriate producer companies converted into federations or associations assisted by public or private organizations.

To summarize, collective action is very essential before, during, and after production. In the pre-production stage, collective action is a must for reaching an understanding and formulating CoPs that needs to be followed by diverse groups of producers at the production level. At the post production stage, collective action is required for intensive marketing and market promotion (United Nations Conference on Trade and Development, 2015, p. 14).

In India, the mandatory legal requirement that the GI has to be filed by a collective association[1] has brought an element of collectivism of social capital. However, the collective (which varies across products) that is required to play a crucial role in implementing GI is yet to emerge. Collective action becomes stronger when there is an external agency associated with the producers. On the other hand, even when the products are of significant commercial importance or have potential for higher market returns, the lack of collective action due to the limited awareness of GI at all levels—from the producers, consumers, to policymakers—would add little value to the GI certification position of the product.

This chapter is divided into three sections. The first section discusses the role of collective action in GI implementation from the evidence in India and elsewhere. The second section discusses the steps taken so far by the GI Registry and also discusses the issues that surface in collective action. The third section details the government initiatives. The last section presents the conclusion.

Collective Organizations in Implementing GI: Evidence from Select Cases

Collective efforts are important during the pre and post-GI registration period and involve four phases (Quinones-Ruiz et al., 2016). Phase 1 includes conception and consensus on GI strategy by all the stakeholders involved [also emphasized by (Vandecandelaere et al., 2009–10)]; Phase 2 denotes the definition of and an agreement on the product specification; Phase 3 consists of GI registration in the member country; and Phase 4 consists of GI registration in the EU. Post-GI collective efforts include establishment of a control body, recurrent costs for quality control, and marketing. Based on case studies from Colombia (a developing country), Italy (an EU country with a long GI tradition), and Austria (an EU country with a relatively shorter GI tradition), it emerges that the conception and consensus on GI strategy are very important and time consuming since consensus needs to be arrived at among the stakeholders regarding product specifications.

In the GI Colombian coffee case, where the growers' federation acted on behalf of about 500,000 growers, the study found varying levels of GI knowledge among the supply chain actors as they were not directly involved in the GI decision-making process. Where there were a number of consultations in product specification and area demarcation (in the case of Tuscan olive oil, Sorana bean of Italy, and pumpkin seed oil of Austria) amongst the GI firms (constituted by inter-professional organizations and producer associations), though the overall time spent in the process of GI registration increased, yet there were positive benefits in the form of GI awareness, trust building, and awareness among the GI firms. Importantly, collective action by the end value chain actors is essential in the post registration phase as they have to communicate the origin of the product to the consumers. Quinones-Ruiz et al. (2016) emphasize that a top-down approach, which involves minimum efforts and conflicts at the registration phase, has limited participation by the supply chain stakeholders and leads to very low GI awareness. It could even exclude certain producers from the benefit of GI itself (Gopalakrishnan et al., 2007; Rangnekar, 2011; Vandecandelaere et al., 2009–10). But the involvement of producers and various supply chain actors in the registration phase improves the collective efforts to be taken in the post registration phase, including the governance of the GI. The stronger the collective organization, better will be the GI outcome as realized in some of the GI protected products such as Champagne, Basmati Rice, and Darjeeling Tea.

The case of cherry of Lari, Italy (cited in Vandecandelaere et al., 2009–10), presents a multipronged approach and solidarity among the cherry producers. Here the local GI producers brought in local governments, schools, and industrial associations to join them in promoting the GI image of cherry, along with the rural amenities, landscape, environment, culture and tradition, and the promotion of the area. This effort of involving the players outside the value chain, helped in increasing the awareness of the cherry producers as well as the economic and cultural value of the product. Universities and National Research Councils provided research support to preserve the local native cherry varieties contributing to the preservation of biodiversity. The producer association prepared a logo and set up a collective processing unit to prepare cherry jam. Collective efforts also went into marketing the cherry, based on technical and agronomic values. Mention should be made of educational initiatives of introducing the history of cherry in the local primary schools. Importantly, the local government was influential enough to constitute a national association of cherry municipalities, which is dedicated to research and promotional activities concerning cherries across Italy.

Nyons olive oil from France has a tradition dating back more than 2000 years. When the local producers started facing threats from the large traders who were importing the olive oil from elsewhere and selling it in the name of Nyons olive oil, the local producers organized themselves through an already existing cooperative. This organized effort helped them to define the Nyons olive oil as the one extracted from 'Tanche olive', which can withstand heavy winds and frost. The geographical area was defined clearly. This process helped the local producers to get a GI for Nyons olive oil later (cited in Vandecandelaere et al., 2009–10).

During the GI qualification phase of Kintamani Bali coffee from Indonesia, the creation of the Community for Geographical Indication Protection (CGIP) facilitated the defining of (a) the product area, (b) the CoP, and (c) the specific quality of the product linked with the area, along with the producers and the facilitators. Defining the CoP alone required twelve meetings with the producers over a period of ten months. This qualification phase was supported by the French Agricultural Centre for International Development and the Indonesian Coffee and Cocoa Research Institute, through provision of scientific data and information, facilitation, and mediation. This process ultimately resulted in the GI status for coffee of Kintamani Bali, Indonesia's first GI (cited in Vandecandelaere et al., 2009–10).

Intervention by two Mexican researchers who realized the value of Cotija cheese and its risk of becoming extinct, resulted in the farmers establishing the Regional Association of Producers of Cotija Cheese in 2001, comprising of ninety-three producers. The purpose of this association was to exchange information to identify and define the quality of the product. Over a period of time, this association became a larger civil association with a wide range of stakeholders, including producers, researchers, traders, and professionals from local and regional institutions to develop territorial strategy and to get GI recognition (cited in Vandecandelaere et al., 2009–10).

The Government of Thailand has been promoting GI through its captivating slogan 'One GI One Province', with the idea that each of its seventy-five provinces files at least one GI. With this purpose in mind, the Department of Intellectual Property (DIP) undertakes efforts to disseminate information on GI law and registration system to local community in every province, and also promotes potential GI products of each of the provinces. Out of the seventy-five provinces in Thailand, sixty-three applications have been registered; only sixteen provinces are yet to submit any GI applications.

One of the novel processes of the DIP is to collaborate with the Biodiversity-based Economy Development Office (BEDO), which works with communities to promote their local wisdom-based GIs. The BEDO is engaged in building business opportunities for the local communities of Thailand. It promotes sustainable biodiversity-based economy, together with effective measures of species conservation. The BEDO had been associated with the filing of the GI applications for Sakhon Nakhon natural Indigo dyed fabric and Nam Dok Mai Khung Bang Kachao Mango. The entire process started as a community development programme to bring them to a consensus about whether they wanted to protect their product with a GI. This process of 'public hearing' is conducted with the community and local authorities. Most often the local authorities or communities or researchers working in the area identify the eligible product for filing a GI application. In this public hearing workshop, experts with scientific knowledge, DIP officials, and local government authorities participate. The second stage is to prepare the GI application. The third significant step is to create the internal control system (ICS) that all the producers adhere to in order to get the producers certified by the DIP. Adhering strictly with the ICS has resulted in increasing the price of the mango from 80 Baht a kilo to 200 Baht a kilo. The price of Doi Chaang green coffee bean increased from 12 USD/kg to 65 USD/kg after its GI registration (email communication from a BEDO official on 13 January 2016). The BEDO officials had to work with the mango producers over a period of a year and half to get the GI. The BEDO is also in the process of working with the universities to file GI applications and provide scientific knowledge support. For all these products, the strategy adopted by the BEDO has been to work with the local government (Lalitha, 2016).

Collective Efforts for Expanding Market for GI Products and Brand Building

Market opportunities expand with the awareness of consumers regarding a particular product, popularity, and availability of the product in wider areas, and the value consumers attach to the special characteristics of the product. It should be recognized that GI is not a magic bullet that could address all the issues relating to the markets. Looking at the variety of products registered with GI Registry in India, Das (2010, p. 167) observes that many of the local GIs products would not be recognized in other parts of India, other than their origin of production despite their uniqueness. Hence, she cautions that such products despite their GI status would not be sold at premium price unless they are supported by proper marketing strategies to gain foothold within the country first. In this context, while the demand for products with utility value like textiles and food products with appropriate strategies could gain popularity with GI status, for others, consistent collective efforts has to go into brand building.

GI products like Udupi Mattu Gulla Brinjal, which is cultivated by about 200 farmers in 500 acres in Udupi, and has a localized market in Udupi and Dakshina Kannada districts, may not command a higher premium because of GI, since the local consumers may not appreciate the GI uniqueness at all because they are 'used to it'. Consumers from afar would not recognize the product at all since (1) they have not heard of it, (2) the product does not reach them or, (3) even if the demand exists, the producers are not able to produce more quantity to match the demand. GI protection in this case appears to serve more the purpose of documenting the variety than as a way to create a viable product for the market.

According to Holt (2015), branding becomes a powerful strategy because branding is based on the collective nature of perceptions which are strengthened and re-enforced over time by the organization, its customers, popular culture, and other influencers and becomes a 'brand culture'. Brand cultures are based on the subjective factors which the consumer experiences while consuming and then remembering the experience. In GI products, it is essential to create such brand value for the products.

In order to promote saffron from Taliouine in Morroco, the local cultivators adopted a strategy to invite popular chefs and celebrities to visit the saffron fields. Such dignitaries started patronizing the product, which influenced the consumers preferences and the demand picked up. Similarly to promote Pampa Gaucho da Campanha Meridional meat, the local producers took the help of a butcher, who was well-known for selling only high-quality meat and whose customers did not mind paying a premium to buy the best quality meat. Endorsement and sales by the popular butcher resulted in improving the market for the meat (Vandecandelaere et al., 2009–10).

Immediately after the GI status, Pochampalli received lots of media attention. This boosted the sales significantly by 15 to 20 per cent in the subsequent years. Besides the increase in the productivity of the weavers, introduction of new designs resulted in international trade queries and the incomes of the weavers also increased (Das, 2009; Rout, 2014).

Collective Organization in GI Registered Products[2]

Of the four important phases of GI mentioned by Quinones-Ruiz et al. (2016), the first three, namely, conception and consensus on GI strategy by all stakeholders, definition of area and consensus on product specification, and GI registration in the country are of definite importance in the context of India. The fourth one, namely, GI filing in the EU, takes place only for commodities that are traded in the international markets like Darjeeling Tea and Basmati Rice. Particularly, Phase 1 and 2 are of significant importance. Initially, the Ministry of Commerce, Government of India sent out a letter to all the authorities concerned with the protection of genetic varieties to identify and protect all traditional varieties so that they are not pirated (Marie-Vivien, 2015, p. 111, p. 197). Similarly, the Development Commissioner, Handicrafts, took the initiative to file a number of GI applications for handicrafts while the Textile Committee took the initiative to file a variety of textile related applications. Phase 3 of filing the application with the GI Registry became easy in cases where there was direct state involvement.

Besides the significant role played by the Textiles Committee and the cooperatives, there have been instances of joint applications, especially in the case of Banaras brocades and saris, Paithani saris, and fabrics, there have been nine applicants comprising the state government agencies, associations, NGOs, and cooperatives. Also involved are, apex weaver's societies (such as Boyanika, Poompuhar), individual weaver's societies (representing Kancheepuram Silk, Pochampalli Ikat to quote a few examples), consortium of cooperatives (Cannanore Home Furnishing), corporations (such as Karnataka Silk Industries Corporation Limited), Directorate of Handlooms and Textiles of various state governments, and so on, which indicate the collective efforts in filing applications.

However, in some of the cases, there has been very little producer involvement due to which the GI Registry nowadays insists on producer groups filing the GI applications even if the government or any other group has been involved in the filing of the application, to ensure that the collective producers body is involved in the registration.

Numerous GI applications seeking registration in the agricultural segment involved farmer producer organizations and civil society or other organizations. In the following pages, we discuss the role of UNIDO in the field of GI. A few illustrative examples to demonstrate the GI Registry's emphasis to involve producer associations and promote the use of common logo by producer association and members are also detailed.

Efforts to Promote Collectivism: Role of Government and International Organizations

Since GI aims to qualify quality through geography or region, it is important to strengthen the networks and linkages both at the horizontal and the vertical levels of the value chain. In the case of textiles and related items, the cluster approach as promoted by the United Nations Industrial Development Organization (UNIDO) can be considered as an important mechanism to foster and strengthen collective action (Vinayan, 2007). The interventions encompass trust building through strengthening networks—horizontal and vertical, fostering capabilities of intermediate institutions within the cluster, and strengthening the capacity of the cluster to set strategic development priorities. To do so, UNIDO adopts a participatory approach, oriented towards building a shared vision, promoting collective projects and fostering the emergence of governance mechanisms, which ensure the sustainability of the process. Under this, the Cluster Development Agent (CDA) acts as a temporary catalyst, facilitating the cluster development process and making it sustainable beyond the life span of the project. The main tasks of the CDA includes promotion of the process of trust building among cluster stakeholders, facilitating inter-firm networking, and the development of sustainable institutions of governance. In other words, the underlying outcome of all these interventions is to put in place a sustainable and autonomous governance framework, which is expected to sustain the dynamic momentum in the local economy even after the withdrawal of UNIDO. Thus, the cluster development approach appears best suited to operationalize a GI. On the one hand, higher trust facilitates networking and the building or strengthening of associations. On the other, the emergence of a governance system facilitates the registrations process by raising awareness regarding the issue of quality and, given its strategic coordination capacity, helping ensure uniformity in production through rule setting, monitoring, and enforcement vis-à-vis its members. Moreover, by acting collectively under the umbrella of governance institutions, producers gain greater bargaining capacity for marketing their products.

In India, the interventions of UNIDO with respect to cluster development began as early as 1996 with a detailed mapping of 138 clusters in the country. This was followed by interventions in seven clusters strengthened by several collaborations across the country, with the state and central government agencies or autonomous bodies in different sectors such as textiles (including handlooms), leather, food processing, floriculture and others (which include rubber, coir, engineering, fabrication, brassware, and so on).[3] UNIDO was actively involved in the cluster development programme undertaken in the handloom clusters of Chanderi and Maheshwar in Madhya Pradesh, along with the active involvement of the Department of Rural Industries, Government of Madhya Pradesh and, in Rajasthan, in the Kota Doria cluster. In the clusters of Chanderi and Kota, the registration of geographical indication was a direct outcome of UNIDO interventions as part of strengthening and networking the linkages along the value chain.

In the case of Chanderi handloom cluster, the cluster development intervention spearheaded by the consultancy of UNIDO under the aegis of the government of Madhya Pradesh, led to the formation of the Bunkar Vikas Samiti (a federation of SHGs of weavers) to manage their production and marketing collectively.[4] The consolidated results of the interventions at the cluster also led to the formation of an umbrella organization called the Chanderi Development Foundation (CDF), to manage macro issues at the cluster level. The eleven members of this body (seven weavers, two each of the traders and heads of cooperatives) were the official applicants for the Geographical Indication (GI) registration to protect Chanderi.

One of the important steps taken by the CDF to implement the GI was to develop a logo and distribute the same among the weavers to be used in all their bill books (that was distributed by the CDF) and invoices. Stakeholders in the value chain like retailers and buyers were informed about the GI and also that the products from places other than Chanderi cannot use the GI. Besides conducting sensitization workshops, a website was also created by the CDF to give information about the GI and Chanderi products, along with the list of traders and weavers. An e-commerce portal providing all information about the tradition of Chanderi was also started, besides the extensive use of social media for GI promotion (Sharma & Kulhari, 2015). Sharma and Kulhari also mention that the wages of the weavers increased after they organized themselves into SHGs, which gave them the collective strength to bargain with the traders.

Significant cluster level results could be observed in the Maheshwar handloom cluster due to the interventions of UNIDO.[5] These were carried forward by the Government of Madhya Pradesh, with the Textile Institute or the Handloom Training Institute playing an important role in setting the standard of quality control for Maheshwar Saris. Consequently, the Maheshwar Hathkargha Vikas Samiti was constituted for the sole purpose of protection and enforcement of the GI. It covers 10,000 weavers and 1921 looms and is affiliated to the District Handloom Training Centre at Maheshwar. Thus, while the former is the first applicant of the GI, the latter forms the second applicant.[6]

Kota Doria in Rajasthan, at the behest of the UNIDO interventions, went through several crucial initiatives such as networking across stakeholders, joint market initiatives, linking up with niche market channels, and so on. It also led to the formation of forty-six SHGs of women weavers, of which eleven federated to form the Kota Women Weavers Organization. The programme also led to the formation of an all-weavers organization called the Kota Cluster Development Coordination Committee, to look into the macro issues of the cluster. Across these activities, there were consistent and concerted efforts on the part of the Government of Rajasthan through organizations such as the Rural Non-Farm Development Agency. Such actions and measures also led to greater awareness among the producing villages and different organizations of the stakeholders such as weavers, master weavers, dyers, and so on, to come together to tackle the threat from powerlooms. The application for GI was mooted as an important tool to mitigate the threat of duplication by powerlooms. Through the nominations of village representatives of organizations across stakeholders, the Kota Doria Development Hadauti Foundation (KDHF) came into being in 2003. A meticulous exercise of listing of the weavers by their residence was undertaken by the GI committee of the Foundation, and the contribution for application fee also was collected by the weavers, weaver's union, and the SHGs, which facilitated the registration of the GI for Kota Doria.[7]

An important initiative of Kota handloom weavers to fight the competition from powerlooms was to weave very intricate designs that are preferred by the premium segment of the consumers and weave the GI logo on the corner of the sari. But there is no mention of GI on some of the e-tool platforms that apparently sell kota saris as well as powerloom products (Sharma & Kulhari, 2015).

The NABARD, through its cluster development programme played a crucial role in reviving the Bidri artware. Bidri artware is dependent on the GI factor of sand sourced from the fort of Bidar. This sand gives lustre to artwares created with zinc, copper, and silver inlay. The programme started with setting up of the Bidri colony, which led to the forming of SHGs of artisans. The Karnataka Handicrafts Development Corporation secured the GI for the craft in 2008. The cluster formation and registration as a GI product were instrumental in diversification of production. It also resulted in increasing the demand for the products both in the domestic and international markets (Maheshwari, 2014).

The Tea Board of India is significantly associated in the promotion of the GI of Darjeeling Tea as well as in the prevention of the misuse of the GI. Besides GI, the word and the logo of Darjeeling Tea have also been protected under the Trademark and Copyright Act of India as also under respective laws in different countries. The Tea Board has also hired the services of an international agency to report any misappropriation of the IP rights of Darjeeling Tea. The eighty-seven tea gardens identified in the Darjeeling region have been certified and the certificate of origin is given to each consignment from these gardens. Most importantly, the custom authorities have also been instructed to check the certificate of origin on each of the consignments passing through the ports to ensure authenticity of the export product. Such involvement by the Tea Board and the presence of multiple checks by Custom authorities aid in the prevention of them is use of the GI and help in implementing the GI within the country as well as elsewhere (Sharma & Kulhari, 2015).

The National Institute of Fashion Technology (NIFT), Gandhinagar, Gujarat, has been closely engaged with the revival of the Tangaliya shawl from Gujarat which ultimately led to its GI registration. In 2005, Tangaliya was taken up as one of the products for cluster development under the Swarna Jayanti Gram Swarojgar Yojana (SGSY) of the Ministry of Rural Development, GOI, with NIFT acting as the implementing agency. Tangaliya shawl, which uses beadwork, was suffering from narrow product line and lack of pooled procurement of raw materials. This led to higher prices paid individually by the weavers which did not match with the final price of the finished product. It also resulted in repetitive design and poor market potential. Intervention by NIFT resulted in newer designs and product lines, and better product visibility. NIFT felt the need to arrange for market compensation for the Tangaliya community through commercial gain from their traditional craft and thus the idea to protect it with GI was born. An association was subsequently formed with 226 Tangaliya artisans, which got protection in the year 2009. The media coverage following the GI registration resulted in increased trade queries from abroad, NGOs from Gujarat, as well as from the state sales emporiums. However, as NIFT has been associated with this initiative on a project mode, after the project is over, continued assistance will be required to face the challenges in infrastructure, quality, and product design (Pal & Das, 2014).

Similarly, in agriculture, NABARD and the Small Farmers' Agribusiness Consortium (SFAC) (as part of the Department of Agriculture and Cooperation at the Ministry of Agriculture) have created a Producers' Organization Development and Upliftment Corpus (PRODUCE) Fund, with a corpus of Rs. 200 crores for the promotion of 2000 FPOs by March 2016. This was a major intervention aimed at facilitating the aggregation of inputs supplies and output marketing, besides village-level value addition. NABARD also facilitated the formation of 2200 FPOs against the target of 2000 (NABARD, 2016). For the GI protected agricultural products, such FPOs would be very useful. However, not all FPOs have become successful in their operation due to lack of training and clear strategies (Singh & Singh, 2013). Discussions with an NGO based in Ahmedabad[8] pointed out another dimension for a collective organization like FPO to be successful and, importantly, in GI registered high value crops. According to this NGO, if the FPO consists of a majority of large farmers, the value for collective action remains less as the large farmers have their own network providing credit and market. But if the FPO consists of a majority of small farmers and a few progressive farmers, then the FPO functions well because the FPO would be driven by the demand of the small farmers and the presence of a few large farmers would act as a source of guidance and inspiration.

Role of the GI Registry in Forming Collectives

In this section, the role of the GI Registry in encouraging producers to form collectives is documented. As indicated in the GI law and rules, the emphasis is on the ability of the applicant or the registered proprietor to demonstrate their capacity to 'represent the interests of the producers'. Given this, the GI Registry through the consultative meetings of the individual applications and also through the opposition filed by the concerned parties have evolved certain mechanisms over the years to encourage the formation of collectives to ensure that the applications are filed by producer associations, which would make the producers more accountable for the functioning of their association. Select cases of such instances have been documented below:

i. In the case of Payyanur Pavithra Ring (PPR), the application for GI was filed by the Payyanur Pavithra Ring Artisans and Development Society (PPRADS), which was in business by the name of Lakshmi Jewellery (LJ) in 2004. This was opposed by the proprietor of Sree Lakshmi Jewellery (SLJ) on the following grounds: (1) it is the family of SLJ which first invented the ring in 1794; (2) the PPRADS does not protect the interests of the producers as only one person in the PPRADS was a producer and the rest were traders; and (3) importantly, due to the existence of religious sentiments and several artisans in Payyanur who knew the art of making the PPR, the opposition got strengthened. The opposition and the exchanges which continued over a period of six years were not sustained by the Registry including on the ground that the traders may not always adequately represent 'the interest of the producers'. The GI was finally granted in the year 2010.[9] An appeal to stay the grant of GI was made by one Subash Jewellers (SJ) directly to the Madras High Court and, later, before the Intellectual Property Appellate Board (IPAB), with the photographs of the misuse of GI by LJ for its own benefits. The fact of the pending cases of the rightful owners of PPR before the courts of Payyanur was also brought before the IPAB. The IPAB directed LJ to issue a public notice in the local newspapers for the benefit of all those who were engaged with PPR. This resulted in further appeals against the proprietorship of PPR. Though the IPAB recognized the regional link of the PPR, it nevertheless ruled that the applicant of the PPR did not represent the interests of the producers as evident from the response to the public notice. It also took objection to the PPRADS falsely reporting that they represented the interest of the producers. The status now is that the GI is recognized but the proprietorship matter is still sub judice (Vinayan, 2017).

ii. The Export Commissioner (EC), Export Promotion Bureau (EPB), Government of Uttar Pradesh, filed a number of products for GI registration in the later part of 2009. Three of the cases are discussed here due to the subtle differences in them. The application for GI of Moradabad Metal Craft (MMC) shows the process whereby the initial application from the government progressed to be owned by the Moradabad Handicraft Exporters Association (MHEA). MMC's application was filed by the EC, EPB, and Government of Uttar Pradesh in the year 2009. In the subsequent examination of the application, and on the question of the appropriateness of EC representing the interest of the producers, the EC entered into an agreement for sharing the rights as co-proprietor of the GI with the MHEA, subject to a few conditions, where the EC reserved the right to (1) include any other party as co-applicant and to register anybody as GI users; (2) decide the quality and standards, with the MHEA holding the rights to make recommendations. The consultative group meeting (CGM) that met in late 2009 suggested that any producer in the GI area should be aware of the benefit of the GI registration. It further sought clarification on the legal status of the applicant and recommended that a representative organization of producer group to be included as co-applicant. In August 2010, the MHEA was included in the amended application. However, the subsequent letter from the GI Registry to the EC recommends that the EC should act as a facilitator and assist the representative producer group in forming an association of producers, with its by-laws registered with the appropriate authority. Subsequently, in 2012, the MHEA was registered, when the eligibility to the membership was open to export firms, industrial units and export houses located in Moradabad district. Export organizations outside Moradabad would be included, subject to a limit of 20 per cent of the total strength of the membership. Thus, here the membership includes all types of industrial units and exporters (both direct and merchandise exporters).

iii. Saharanpur Wood Craft is another application filed by the EPB of Uttar Pradesh, jointly with the Saharanpur Woodcraft Industries Group in August 2009. The registration was accorded in March 2014. The reasons for the delay were due to the GI Registry and the CGM emphasizing that the proprietorship of GI should rest with the producer association rather than any government agency. The first CGM meeting recommended the EPB to be a facilitator and also sought documentary evidence of the representative producer group and linkage with the area. In response to this, the EPB, while co-opting the Woodcraft Design and Development

Agency, Saharanpur (consisting of artisans, exporters, and traders) as another applicant, requested the Registry to allow the EPB to be one of the applicants in order to safeguard the interests of the grass root artisans and craftsmen. The subsequent amendment included the Handicraft Welfare Society, Saharanpur, as another applicant. The amended application in 2013 has been sent in the name of the Woodcraft Design and Development Agency, Handicraft Welfare Society, and Export Commissioner, UP. The final registration, however, has been in the name of the Woodcraft Design and Development Agency facilitated by the Export Commissioner, UP.

iv. The EPB filed the application for Kannauj Attar in February 2009 and the registration materialized on 31 March 2014. In response to the GI Registry's first compliance report on the absence of industry/producer association, the EPB responded by stating that the EPB had taken the initiative to file the application as no industry association had come forward to file the GI application. Subsequent to the insistence by the GI Registry, the EPB agreed to add the Attar and Perfumers Association (APA) as a co-applicant, but only after the second report of the CGM. This modified report was again examined by the CGM which recommended that the EPB be the co-applicant and the producers association be the main applicant. The CGM also mentioned that the by-laws of the registered association should mention the clause relating to the protection and promotion of the GI product.[10] Accordingly, the revised statement of the case mentions the APA as the main applicant (with the membership open to all people and organizations relating to the perfumery manufacturing industry in that area). On further examining the amended application, the CGM recommended and suggested that the EPB function as a facilitator of the GI instead of being the co-applicant. One of the post-GI registration activities recommended by the GI authority is to file fifty producers as authorized users within three months of filing the application while the rest are similar to the case of MMC.

v. The GI for the Pattamadai pai was filed by Poompuhar in January 2010, and the registration was accorded in March 2013. There are about 300 artisans working on this craft, with an annual turnover of Rs. 25 to 30 lakhs. The consultative group in this case also recommended Poompuhar be a facilitator and form a representative group of producers who would be the applicant. Poompuhar responded by saying that the Tamil Nadu Legislative Assembly had directed Poompuhar to file the GI applications on behalf of the artisans, thus indicating the political directives to file the GIs. However, Poompuhar further insisted that it is an agency working for the promotion of crafts and welfare of the artisans, and 'to safeguard the interest of the Pattamadai pai Artisans, the Government of Tamil Nadu has announced during the Assembly Session in 2009, that the Tamil Nadu Handicrafts Development Corporation has to file GI Application for Pattamadai pai before the GI Registry'. It further assured the GI Registry that it would take the responsibility of filing the authorized user applications.[11] Finally, in February 2013, Poompuhar became the proprietor of the Pattamadai pai GI. However, till June 2017, there were no registered authorized users of this craft.

vi. The Director Horticulture, Government of Karnataka, filed an affidavit in the case of Udupi Hadagali jasmine, stating that the farmers cultivating the Udupi jasmine would be formed into an association. Further, the role of the horticulture department would remain as a facilitator and it would assist the association in the development of the infrastructure required for the production and supply of genuine planting material, value addition, marketing, and brand development of the flowers. In the case of the Vazhakulam pineapple GI, initially the application was filed by the Nadukkara Agro Processing Company, a public limited company, where the shares were held by the member farmers. However, in the first formality report, the GI Registry asked the company to bring in the farmer association as the co-applicant. Eventually, the Vazhakulam GI was filed and is owned by the Nadukkara Company, Vazhakulam Pineapple Farmers Association, and the Kerala Agricultural University.

vii. During the study on Pochampalli, it emerged that in the Pochampalli cluster, the Handloom Park had initiated discussion on the application for authorized user status of GI. However, the registered users did not give consent (as envisaged in the GI Rules).[12] This point to the absence of a collective organization which could foster trust among the various stakeholders. While the Handloom Park has been heralded as an important activity in the post-GI phase, the brand building has not percolated to the non-Handloom Park producers and stakeholders, though the former has been able to establish specific trademarks for both the domestic and export markets (mentioned in Chapter 3).

viii. A logo creates a distinct identity for the product and helps the producer connect with the consumer by reducing information asymmetry. As mentioned elsewhere in the book, earlier, separate applications used to be filed for product and logo registrations with the GI Registry of India. It was found that out of 260 products, there were about 29 products (or 12 per cent of the total products) for which separate applications had been registered for the logo. Discussions with the GI Registry on related issues yielded that, in the initial years of registering the GI, some of the applicants sought to register the logo separately and some of the applicants, even after repeated reminders from the Registry, did not respond. However, in the recent years, the GI Registry insists on merging the application for logo to be submitted along with the application for the GI registration itself.[13] The images of the product that are submitted along with the GI application to the Registry include the logo of the product. The advantage of the logo is to distinguish the product from similar products, and it would be very useful when the value chain and the list of authorized users who are eligible to use the logo are identified. However, mere registering of the logo is not sufficient for the promotion of logos. Once the logo is registered, the concerned association/proprietor should work towards popularizing the logo amongst the consumers in order to boost the sales of the product. Here again, collective action will be helpful in creating a collective brand or logo and market positioning the same.

In the EU, the mandatory requirement to use symbols to signify the PDO/PGI on all registered products came about in 2009 (See Box 4.1). In Thailand too, there is a common logo for GI which is prominently advertised and is also associated in the minds of the consumers (Vinayan, 2015).

While a common logo will be helpful for small producers who cannot spend on brand building, some firms choose to use their

Box 4.1   Logo for Geographical Indications Abroad

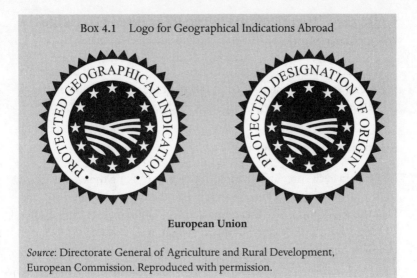

European Union

Source: Directorate General of Agriculture and Rural Development, European Commission. Reproduced with permission.

individual logo along with the common logo to differentiate their product. The Prosciutto di Parma (PDO) of Italy uses two logos, one of the collective brand and the other, the individual company. In such cases, the common logo complements the individual promotion of the product with GI.

Use of a GI logo is not in vogue in India as it was evident from the case studies discussed in Chapter 3 in the cases of Swamimalai Bronze Icons, Mysore Agarbathi, and Machilipatnam Kalamkari work. Less than 5 per cent of the Pochampalli weavers believed that a logo would be useful for marketing. As GI awareness is still evolving in India, individual product logos without any of them mentioning GI may not improve the awareness about it and will not serve as a marketing strategy. Instead, if one common logo is publicized, any product from any corner of India with the common logo will instantly create a regional identity in the minds of the consumers (like hallmark which is applicable for any gold jewellery by any producer). In August 2018, the Government of India has unveiled a logo and a tag line 'Invaluable treasures of incredible India'.[14] Once the logo is adequately publicized and modus operandi for the use of logo is decided, it could usher in a sea of change.

Collective Organizations in the Registered GIs: Issues to be Addressed

In this section, based on the case studies, the observations of the authors regarding encouragement of collectivism in the use, as well as issues in implementation of, GI registration are discussed.

Swamimalai Bronze Icon

As detailed in the previous chapter, at the time of filing the GI, the office of the Development Commissioner, Handicrafts, took the lead and filed the application. The Swamimalai Icon Manufacturers Cooperative Cottage Industrial Society Limited, which was started in 1958 and is functioning for the benefit of artisans, was not involved in the process. The Society has 500 members who live in and around the ten km radius of Swamimalai and produce and sell bronze idols. The purpose of the society is to (a) facilitate better sales deals and earn profit for the artisans, (b) get orders, and (c) execute the orders by the members. The society charges an entry fee of Rs. 25 for the membership. Shares are priced at Rs. 500 each. The Tamil Nadu Government has also provided capital and the society has an elected body. When a society member wants to sell an idol through the society, the society would pay 50 per cent of the cost of the idol and the remaining amount is paid after the sale is done. When the metal price was less, the society used to pay full money for the idol to the members. This practice helped the producers to avoid distress selling. As the government emporia provide payment on the idols only after the sales take place, members try to sell their idols through the society, though, at times of urgent economic needs, producers sell the idols through utensil shops or private traders too. The society operates for the benefit of small producers and, hence, does not extend the marketing assistance to those producers whose idols are above forty kilos, the logic being that if an artisan can invest in the raw material for an idol of forty kilos, he/she has the resources to market it as well.

In order to encourage sales through the society, it does not levy sales tax. The society does not play a role in buying the raw materials for the artisans, nor does it engage in any training activity for the members. The Society does not have a separate showroom and sells the icons from its office. With a little focus on brand-building activity, the society could become very beneficial for the artisans in marketing the GI-tagged SBI products.

Bhavani Jamakkalam

The GI for Bhavani Jamakkalam (carpets) has been obtained by the Department of Handlooms, Government of Tamil Nadu, and the various cooperatives are recognized as the authorized users for the GI. This product, like many other handloom products, faces severe competition from the powerloom products. Weavers get assistance from the cooperatives to get yarn, and they weave the product in the looms set up either at home or elsewhere. The cooperatives themselves suffer from lack of demand and innovations in designs. All the carpet creations have the uniform horizontal lines design, which is easily replicated in the powerloom sector at a relatively cheaper cost, affecting the demand for the handloom carpets. The cooperatives themselves do not engage in publicity related activities and depend on the government orders and the exhibitions organized for sales. A few innovative weavers, a handful in number, are working with silk yarns and produce wall hangings which due to a lack of publicity and marketing have not yet reached a wider market to create adequate demand. Hence, in this case, introduction of new designs and diversification could help the weavers but the larger issue of competition from powerlooms remain.

Kondapalli Toys

In the absence of collective organization, it is possible that a few persons with better resources are able to secure advantage than those with fewer. The lack of a showroom that could display all the artisanal creations has led individual artisans to use the front portion of their house as a shop; however, it lacks attractive display. In such a scenario, a single artisan with better resources to display the creations in a better location, like closer to the entrance of the village, is likely to get more footfalls than other artisans. Collective efforts in this case could lead to creation of a shop cum exhibition centre in the society building which can be utilized by all.

Aranmula Mirror

The Parthasarathy Handicraft Society, formed for the purpose of getting the GI for the Aranmula Mirror, was started with five members at that time, which over a period have increased to eight members. Recently, the society also renewed the Part A certificate of Aranmula Mirror. Membership fee for the association is Rs. 50. Other than this, the society has not built any share capital among the members. The members themselves noted that very little activity takes place in the association in general and nothing on GI in particular. Interestingly, though the price is not uniformly fixed by the members of the association, presently, the members of the association do not sell the product beyond a certain floor level. Though the members are also aware of a few artisans riding on the reputation of the mirror, no action has been taken so far. Discussions with the members revealed that the association lost an opportunity to utilize the funds under the cluster development plan due to lack of cooperation and vision. If they had utilized the opportunity then, there would have been a common facility centre to purchase materials, common showrooms, and sales, where uniform prices would have prevailed and the returns would have been equal. However, the association members have decided to come together to oppose another application for metal mirror from a different panchayat in August 2016.

Kasuti Embroidery

As the GI registration for Kasuti Embroidery (KE) was done by the State Directorate of Handicrafts and Handlooms, an artisan association was not formed. Later, in the Kalghatagi taluka, twenty workers took training from an NGO in KE and formed an association. Under the National Programme for Rural Industries project, NABARD had sanctioned Rs. 1,50,000 for their association. Work orders for KE were distributed among the members and the money received for the work was also distributed equally. Over a period, it was realized by the members that while some members finished the work on time, others did not. This resulted in (a) the cloth given by the customers not being returned on time, (b) the quality of the work not being satisfactory, and (c) the cloth returned also being dirty as KE was practised by spreading the cloth on the floor and some artisans did not take care to spread any paper or fabric underneath the cloth on which the embroidery was to be made. Of the twenty odd members, only three people were serious about the craft, and the orders were completed mainly by these three. But the rest of the members wanted the money to be distributed equally among all the members. This created a rift and some people lost their interest to continue in the association. A few of the trained women migrated to other villages after their marriage and the number of people who knew and practised KE dwindled. The association disintegrated due to a lack of cooperation and interest among the members. This is a case of a lack of cooperation among workers and a few free-riding on the capacities of others.

Pochampalli Ikat

The Pochampalli Ikat Weavers Private Limited (PIWPL), formed to support and promote Ikat weaving, faces constraints in working capital. Though their annual turnover increased from Rs. 1 crore in 2009–10 to Rs. 3 crores in 2012–13, their revenue was grossly inadequate to meet the debt repayments on term loans. In this context, the company requested the state and central government to lend their support. For the first two years, the weavers were paid salaries; later they were given wages at piece rate. This has been a major hurdle in attracting more weavers. The Park is situated far away from the residential settlements of the weavers and transport facilities are not so frequent. The weavers are brought to the Handloom Park in chartered auto rickshaws and a few state road transport buses. Moreover, weaving being a quintessentially family activity, the Handloom Park has not been able to attract weavers per se, especially since the remuneration is based on piece-rate and not based on monthly salaries.

Mysore Agarbathi

Mysore Agarbathi is a classic case, where the rules and regulations and CoP designed by the All India Agarbathi Manufacturers Association (AIAMA) would have been the model for many other GI products, had it been successful in implementing it. The AIAMA had stipulated rules and conditions for the use of GI by its members. As per the amendments/additions made to the memorandum of the AIAMA on 26 November 2006,[15] the following CoP needed to be adhered to by the manufacturers:[16] the essential ingredients to be used in the manufacture of agarbathis to qualify for use of GI mark Mysore Agarbathi was that the product should be manufactured using some of the natural substances that are traditionally used for the manufacture of agarbathi. In order to be an authorized user of the GI, the manufacturer should be enrolled as a life member of AIAMA, with either the registered office or the manufacturing unit in the state of Karnataka (as per this clause, a manufacturer in Gujarat can be a member of AIAMA, but unless either the production unit or the registered office is in Karnataka, he/she will not get the authorized user status). The manufacturer should have in-house bathi rolling facility and all essential manufacturing process should be done in-house. The inspection body identified as Fame R&D Centre promoted by AIAMA and the Government of Karnataka would inspect and approve the samples and products of those members whose membership has been scrutinized by the AIAMA. The geographical indication is Mysore Agarbathi, consisting of a pictorial representation. A manufacturer who wishes to be an authorized user of the GI in his/her products has to apply separately for each product and get the authorization specifically for each product. The GI has to be accompanied by a statement to the effect that the registered proprietor of the GI is AIAMA and the manufacturer is an authorized user of the mark. The authorized user should always display the GI on the specified product along with its trademark. The authorized user shall not use the GI as its trademark or as its company name. The authorized user is not permitted to print or affix the GI hologram on the display packets of its specified products. The GI hologram has to be purchased from AIAMA by paying the prescribed fees and only such a purchased GI hologram can be pasted onto the authorized user's display packages.

However, according to unconfirmed information from the members of AIAMA, these rules are yet to be implemented as there is a divided opinion among the members on the use of the word 'Mysore Agarbathi' by producers who are operating from places like Bengaluru in Karnataka. The option to go for another GI in the name of Bengaluru or any other place is difficult because the raw materials for both are sourced from the same place. Further, the fragrance difference is not maintained for long as it gets infringed due to fierce competition.

Lack of collective action to prevent competition from powerlooms which infringes the designs of Banaras saris indicates the lack of agency among the GI holders (Pai & Singla, 2016). On the other hand, even the Banaras weavers have started producing cheaper materials to cut down costs and to compete with the powerloom weavers (Pai & Singla, 2016).

In the case of Tangaliya shawl, the number of weavers engaged in the craft, including those who are involved in it as a secondary occupation, is estimated at 230–50. But the number of weavers actively engaged in the craft would not be more than fifty. GI registration has led to the increased visibility of the product and also resulted in business opportunities from companies like Fab India. However, the limited number of weavers could not complete the task with quality and these business opportunities were available only for a limited period of time. Hence, sustained hand holding is required to sustain the craft in the years to come.[17] Similar has been the experience with Pochampalli when Air India placed bulk orders with the Pochampalli weavers, capacity constraints came in the way of timely completion, with quality and uniformity of the small manufacturing units. This subsequently resulted in the setting up of the Handloom Park (Das, 2009).

The lesson from these cases is that, external agencies which get involved in registering the GI or reviving the craft have to be associated with the craft at least for a decade to ensure that the craft has grown sufficiently to sustain on its own. This is because, most often, such products are buried in a variety of problems like lack of raw materials and credit, delay in payments for the products made, inadequate marketing, and so on. GI alone cannot help in that situation. As the initial few years are spent in pulling the craft out of its troubles, the external agency should extend assistance for another term till the producers have learnt to implement the GI standards on their own or able to run their producer company/association on their own.

Summary and Way Forward

Evidence from India and elsewhere emphasizes that collective action is a must for GI filing and GI implementation. The discussion in this chapter also showed that in the GI cases from India, the involvement of a promotional agency, be it the UNIDO in the case of Chanderi or Tea

Board of India in the case of Darjeeling Tea, have been very helpful in implementing the GI. It is also noted that the GI Registry is doing its best to bring in collectivism and hence it encourages the producers to take the lead in filing the applications. Wherever a top-down approach has been adopted in GI filing, like in the cases of it being done by the government or government board for products like bronze idols (Development Commissioner Handicrafts, Government of India), Bhavani Jamakkalam (GI filed by Department of Handlooms and Textiles), and Kasuti (Karnataka State Handicraft Development Corporation Limited), there has been very little follow-up for the promotion of the GIs later. In fact, in the Pochampalli case, though two committees at the state and district level respectively were constituted to look into the implementation of the GI, the district level committee did not function in this matter due to a want of human resources (Chapter 3). The GI registration process gives an opportunity to build on the social capital of producers and create awareness regarding GI and formulate strategies. But in the hurry to register GIs by agencies other than the producers, this opportunity has been missed in many products or it remains with a few stakeholders (Kumar & Bahl, 2010). In cases like Kondapalli Toys and Aranmula Mirror, where the producer associations were involved in the filing of the application, lack of collectivism was obvious. Collective action in these cases could reduce the cost of materials and increase the net income for the producers. In any case, except for a few products that have a sizeable market presence in the domestic and in the export market, the efforts so far have stopped at only mobilizing a few producers to file the GI application. This should change.

A few suggestions in this direction are as follows: The topmost priority of the different state governments may be to identify an existing department like culture and tourism which may be given the responsibility of taking forward the different GI products beyond their registration stage. As the GI registration so far consists of products with utility and decorative value which will have the potential of economic returns from the domestic and / or export markets, all the products at once may not be taken up for promotion at the same time. Careful considerations should be done in deciding 'who to sell and where to sell and how to sell and when to sell' (Vandecandelaere et al., 2009–10, p. 105). These decisions will help in focusing and effectively spending the resources for strategic marketing. Depending on the demand assessment and the probable consumer appeal for the products, a few products from each segment (agriculture, handicrafts, textiles, and so on) may be taken up for market development by the state government, on a public–private partnership basis. As a first step, taking into consideration the type of product, constraints in the raw material availability or modern skill and so on, the CoP should be drawn, and the different producer groups should be sensitized about the importance of adopting the CoP. To reduce wide heterogeneity in the products produced, assistance may be given in the form of design development, raw material procurement, and technology, processing or value addition. There are a number of existing schemes for the handicrafts, handlooms, micro and small industries, and for the agricultural sector. Some of these schemes could be effectively targeted for the provision of raw material, credit, or technology assistance for the promotion of select GI products.

Once there is sufficient conviction among the producers to adopt and implement the CoP, the next step is to inform the consumers about the adherence to quality, and to attract the consumers to differentiate the product based on its quality. While there are a number of third party certifications available in India, as they involve considerable amount of paperwork, involvement of an external agency would become a must and the entire process could prove costly for the small producers. Hence, the participatory guarantee (PGS), as prescribed for the organic producers by the Central Government, could be adopted for different sectors. Under the PGS, 'a system of open, group appraisals is carried out ... to ensure complete physical checks of the farm and, equally importantly, to verbally re-confirm that the farmer understands organic growing practices and what they are committing to' (Khosla, 2007, p. 12).

The use of the local farmers as part of the peer appraisal groups helps in considerable social control. Under the PGS, any farm that tests positive for pesticide residue means that the entire group gets suspended. Such a check encourages the farmers to help each other and address the issues collectively. Further, under the PGS, the entire farm of the farmer gets certified, which increases the marketability of the different products. Once the farmers with PGS are familiar with adopting and adhering to certain standards, then they may slowly progress to adopting the certifications by third parties (Lalitha & Vinayan, 2017).

The next step is the most challenging part of marketing and reaching out to the consumers. Here, the Culture and Tourism Department may play a significant role in advertising frequently in the print and electronic media about the heritage products of the state and also in organizing festivals that would help in the promotion of the GI products. Importantly in such trade fairs, the producers should be encouraged to sell only the GI products and such fairs should not encourage sales of counterfeit products. Adherence to CoP and following a PGS would increase the bargaining power of the GI producers, particularly when the GI products are the fundamental raw materials or important in the final stage of the product.

Such collective initiatives would improve the visibility and marketability of the product and result in improved economic returns for all the producers. Evidences from successful GIs should be discussed with the producers to create more awareness about GI and to learn from such products to create CoP. External help from different stakeholders, both within and outside the value chain, would help in implementing the GIs and reap benefits from the same.

In the Indian context, the term 'producer' is defined very widely and includes the trader and dealer as well. In the absence of collective action, the dealer or the trader in the end stream of the value chain will get maximum economic benefits rather than the producer. As the trader or dealer in the end stream of the value chain is the link in communicating with the actual consumer, it is essential that they are appropriately sensitized about the GI. As the benefits received by them would be different than the actual producer, the sharing of the returns should be discussed *a priori* to benefit the downstream producers. Though this point is applicable when the value chain and benefit sharing are defined, it is essential that such strategies are thought of when a few products are identified by the government for promotion.

Notes

1. As discussed in the earlier chapter, the government has filed the GI application in many cases even though it has not been a direct producer.

2. The discussion in this section is applicable both to handicrafts and agricultural GIs and hence it uses the term producer to mean both producer of agricultural and handicraft goods respectively.

3. For details, see http://www.dcmsme.gov.in/clusters/unido/listassit.htm, accessed on 10 October 2017. The list covers 23 clusters wherein UNIDO assisted Cluster Development Programme has been undertaken across the mentioned sectors.

4. For more details, see the link available at: https://www.google.co.in/url?sa=t&rct=j&q=&esrc=s&source=web&cd=1&cad=rja&uact=8&ved=0ahUKEwiBgZ_rjjWAhUDvo8KHZhoB3kQFggnMAA&url=http%3A%2F%2Fwww.clusterobservatory.in%2Fcase%2Fcase6.doc&usg=AOvVaw2tPpDhyXQfx-9irJMZyLo4, accessed on 10 October 2017.

5. Refer Annexure 1b of the End of Project Report under the project 'Support to Country Effort for SME Cluster Development' of UNIDO (US/IND/01/193) during 2002–5, available at http://clusterobservatory.in/report/EPR%20Madya%20Pradesh.doc, accessed on 11 October 2017.

6. For details, refer to the documents filed by the applicants with the GI Registry. See the following links. http://ipindiaservices.gov.in/GI_DOC/197/197%20-%20GI%20-%20ppt%20-%2013-08-2010.pdf, accessed on 10 October 2017; http://ipindiaservices.gov.in/GI_DOC/197/197%20-%20Form%20GI-1%20-%2008-02-2010.pdf, accessed on 10 October 2017.

7. For details, refer http://clusterobservatory.in/report/Fianl%20Kota%20EPR.doc, accessed on 10 October 2017.

8. Discussion with the executives of Development Support Centre, Ahmedabad on 24 October 2017.

9. For details see (Vinayan, 2015).

10. For details, see http://ipindiaservices.gov.in/GI_DOC/157/157%20-%20GI%20-%20Minutes%20of%20CGM%20-%2024-08-2013.pdf, accessed on 17 August 2016.

11. For details, see http://ipindiaservices.gov.in/GI_DOC/195/195%20-%20GI%20-%20Filing%20of%20Authorised%20User%20Application%20-%2002-02-2012.pdf, accessed on 17 August 2016.

12. Section 56 (1) of the GI rules clearly indicate that the application for the authorized user should be jointly moved by the registered proprietor and the proposing authorized user. Further, Section 56 (2) indicates that a consent letter of the registered proprietor may accompany the application and where it is not complied with, a copy of the application shall be endorsed to the registered proprietor and the Registry may be informed in due course.

13. Discussion with GI officials on 16 August 2016. In the pending GI cases, the GI Registry recommends the merger of the GI and logo application for the product.

14. For more details, see https://www.thehindu.com/news/national/gi-logo-tagline%20launched/article24575474.ece https://www.thehindu.com/news/national/gi-logo-tagline launched/article24575474.ece

15. There is a long list of various practices and here only a few relevant to the topic of GI are presented.

16. For details see, http://ipindiaservices.gov.in/GI_DOC/13/13%20-%20GI%20-%20Enclosure%20of%20Annual%20General%20Body%20Meeting%20-%2011-08-2004.pdf accessed on October 6, 2018

17. Discussion with Rajesh Gupta, an expert involved in the cluster programme of Tangaliya shawl.

5

Conclusion and the Way Forward

GIs are a distinct form of intellectual property rights, held collectively by those producers who, by and large, practise such crafts and cultivation in rural areas. So far, the Indian sui generis system has appropriately recognized and registered products belonging to agriculture, handicraft, natural, manufactured, and foodstuff category with the GI Registry. The registered products range from the well-known Basmati Rice, Darjeeling Tea, Kancheepuram Silk Saris, to the relatively lesser known Kaipad Rice, Appemidi Mangoes, and Puneri Pagadi. The market reach of the products also ranges from the local (village, taluka, or district) to the state, national, and international level. As a community property right, the development potentials associated with this IPR can benefit the producers whose livelihood is woven around such crafts and farm practices. This book in its different chapters provided an overview of the issues concerned with GI, opportunities and challenges before the GIs, the outcomes and impact realized by a few registered products so far, the potentials that remain untapped, and the role of collective organizations in implementing the GIs. In this chapter a brief summary of the chapters is presented. In the second section, 'Policy Suggestions for the Promotion of Rural Livelihoods', policy suggestions and strategies to achieve the desired results are discussed.

The first chapter, an overview of GIs, explained the role of the government in and the development potentials of the GIs. One of the important requirements for GI to serve its development potential is the degree of involvement of the local economy and its resources in the making of the product, and consumer awareness about the product. In such cases, the economy revolves around the GI product and gives rise to other associated activities, which is known as the extended territorial strategy, where 'localism' plays a crucial role in the sustainability of local livelihoods and paves the way for rural development. Such regions also attract tourists, who provide further dynamism to the local economy, with tourism leading the demand for other 'place goods' or goods that are produced in the region. If the value chain of the GI is located in different fragmental parts, then the benefits generated could vary, depending on its position in the value chain ladder. All these involve costs and depend on the governance strategies to protect the uniqueness and popularity of the product.

The second chapter presented the prevailing status of the registered products in terms of categories. It highlighted the opportunities and challenges that the registered GIs of India face. It also stressed on the governance issues with reference to the (a) coverage of geographical area, (b) stakeholders, (c) prevailing codes of practice (CoPs), (d) status of the inspection body, (e) prevalence of infringement, and (f) quality of products. For a majority of the products, an inspection mechanism to check the quality of the product has not been set up.

The third chapter, based on case studies conducted by the authors, brought out the impact of GI registration. In this chapter, assuming the efforts towards filing the GI registration as inputs, we discussed the outputs generated by the input efforts followed by the different outcomes due to outputs, and the resultant impact on society, the producer, and the consumer.. The case studies consisted of products which were purely based on human skills and products which were dependent on both natural resources and human skills. The quality of the product was taken care of by the individual producers, who did the inspection by themselves while the institutional buyers had their own norms of deciding the quality parameters. In each of the products, the approach to the market has been both direct sales to the consumers through state-owned emporiums and traders. Neither the market demand nor the market channels have changed after GI certification. All the products are completely handcrafted and hence environment friendly, except for the chemical dyeing part of the Pochampalli craft. The rural development potential is also evident in crafts like Pochampally Ikat,

Machilipatnam Kalamkari, and Swamimalai Bronze Icons, which create sizeable employment opportunities and also use natural resources.

The fourth chapter discussed the importance of collective actions that range from maintaining the reputation of the product to reaching the market, and, further, in implementing the GI. The authors also note that the involvement of professional agencies in the early stages of cluster formation proved to be helpful for the GI craft, particularly in organizing the artisans, facilitating documentation, and securing the legal rights. However, the artisans engaged in these crafts require hand-holding for a longer period. The use of the logo and the role of the participatory guaranteeing a system of reaching the local markets, was also emphasized. However, collective actions in setting up CoP and fighting infringement have not yet emerged in the Indian context. The need for a dedicated government body to promote the implementation of GI was also emphasized in this chapter.

Policy Suggestions for the Promotion of Rural Livelihoods

In the context of GI products of India, a strong intermediary marketing agency is required in order to realize the market potential. The word 'marketing' means organizing collective efforts to improve quality and popularizing the products' uniqueness among the wider public to create or improve the demand for the products and create brand image of the products. As GI products are manufactured in majority by small producers, they cannot engage in market promotion activities, as spending time on such things may reduce the time they devote to crafts, as their actual means of livelihood is craft making. Hence, an intermediary marketing institution with clearly defined strategies might be thought of by the government.

As mentioned in Chapter 2, the agricultural GIs consist of high value crops such as fruits and vegetables. Using GIs as a marketing tool, highlighting the uniqueness, rarity, and quality component would help in doubling farmers' income. The successful implementation of GIs in the EU countries is the result of stakeholder participation at all stages of GI implementation, including in the specification and monitoring of production standards and the enforcement and defending of GIs rights (Dagne, 2012, p. 400). Particularly for the agricultural GIs, emphasis on the CoPs to ensure quality and uniqueness would ensure repeat purchases from the consumers who are guided by quality rather than price. It must be noted here that the CoPs are emphasized to drive home the point that in the case of agricultural products, farmers should adhere to the specified plant protection mechanism to make the product safe and of good quality.

Role of the Government

Unlike the other individually held IPRs, where the owner can license the right to another to exploit the potential and still benefit from the license fee or milestone payments, the community form of rights like GI cannot be transferred to anyone else due to its link with the geographical features. But by teaching the craft to others outside the craft community, the GI 'knowhow' is spread to others thanks to efforts by special institutions like National Institute of Design, National Institute of Fashion Technology, and so on. While the knowhow may enable the learners to reproduce the craft, the uniqueness of the craft will be maintained only if the geographical link is maintained. Especially in case of crafts which are based only on human skills, teaching crafts outside the community could lead to conflicts as the new learner might practice it outside the specified geographical territory.

Besides the training in the advanced nuances including contemporarization of the craft, the artisans require training inputs in newer designs and colours, pricing, display, documentation, and procedures relating to exports. Training in these areas will help the artisans to be market-savvy.

Except in cases where the applications were filed by the government or government departments, the cost of the application is borne by the association along with the documentation charges, and the renewal charges have also been borne by the producers. In view of this, it is essential that strategies are made to provide incentives to those producers who maintain the tradition of continuing with production. Towards this end, each state government should set up an exclusive department. Or perhaps the culture and tourism department, in coordination with the agriculture and cottage industries, should widely publicize the GI products of the state in the media and also be in charge of GI implementation.

We do acknowledge that the local governments do not have adequate resources to carry out their routine tasks. But the local governments of each state should be involved in facilitating the filing of the GI and in setting up the governance system since they are located in the place of action. Presently, a few of the local governments, while being aware of the traditional association of the product with the region, are not aware of the GI status. As many of the GI products are produced in rural areas, the local governments should be involved in building the institutional mechanisms, maintaining the quality of the natural resources, records of different economic activities going on in the vicinity, and reporting infringements.

The role of local governments in facilitating social cohesion is very important for producing crops such as Bhalia wheat, where unless there is cooperation among farmers in terms of the timing of draining, preparation, and irrigation of the field, cultivation cannot take place.

Some of the agricultural products require technical assistance to improve productivity which is an issue due to climate change and other conditions that were discussed in Chapter 2. The central government launched a scheme 'My Village, My Pride (MVMP)' in 2015, under which the scientists of the Indian Council of Agricultural Research (ICAR) could adopt a village each and implement best farming practices and government policies there. MVMP could be an ideal tool to actively promote GI products of the villages, where productivity could be an issue due to a variety of reasons, forcing the farmers to look for alternatives. In such cases, technical guidance would help the farmers to continue/revive the product again.

Perishables like horticulture and floriculture products require cold storage facilities. So farmers would be able to get better economic returns if they are able to store the goods and market it later. This will fetch better returns and prevent poor returns due to bumper harvest. This will also help the farmers to reduce the dependency on the traders and realize higher returns.

With the aim to promote the cottage and rural industries of the state, the Government of Gujarat announced the Cottage and Rural Industries Policy 2016. Specific mention has been made about the promotion of languishing crafts and adoption of the One-Village-One-Product concept to promote the same. There are already numerous products identified under GI from different states of the country.

Taking into consideration the amount of resources used from the location, the number of livelihoods dependent on it, the knowhow, the type of technology used, and the quality of the product, targeted promotion of one or more products from the region may be undertaken.

The Government of India has launched several schemes to promote the handicrafts sector. But often the artisans are not aware of such programmes and do not benefit from them. Awareness regarding the same should be created among the craftspersons. It was observed in the context of Gujarat that there is no institution beyond the District Industries Centre to provide information/assistance to the artisans who often operate from small talukas, towns, or villages thereby experiencing hurdles in their communication with the government . This might be true for other states too.

GI product promotion could be done through public private partnership and with the help of the corporate sector. As a prior step, the corporate sector should be sensitized about GI and the need for their involvement in GI promotion. Under the amendments made to the Indian Companies Act, it is mandatory for the corporate sector to set aside a certain percentage of their profit for meeting its responsibilities towards society. Such Corporate Social Responsibility (CSR) activities can be focused on helping the local community to file the GI application, or promoting languishing crafts in specific regions, which will give a boost to the sector to grow. Corporates could be encouraged to adopt a village where the GI product/crop is grown and contribute to the promotion of the product. Further, in order to increase the GI-centric activity within the village/locality, CSR could be linked to providing technological assistance in adding value to the product. For instance, the Anglong Ginger producing areas of the North-Eastern states could aim to produce candies and beverages that would appeal to different age groups. But, at the same time, as Soam and Hussain (2011) observe, social, business, and scientific vigour is required to convert such localized production activities into viable commercial ventures. The involvement of the LANCO Institute of General Humanitarian Trust in the promotion of Kondapalli Toys is a good example of CSR activity in this context. Besides handholding the community to get the GI recognition for Kondapalli Toys, LANCO also promoted the craft by placing large orders of Kondapalli Toys to be distributed during social events celebrated by the company.

Mention may be made here of the Hira Laxmi craft park in Bhuj, Kutch, Gujarat set up by the Ashapura Foundation. The uniqueness of this park is that artisans from different crafts (selected through a lottery system) are invited to occupy a space in the park for a period of one month, free of charge. During this period, they are required to demonstrate the craft to the visitors and also sell their creations. Artisans are also given free boarding and lodging at the park for the duration of their stay. As this park is in Bhujodi which attracts lots of visitors, the artisans benefit a lot by way of increased sales. Such initiatives in different states would help the artisans a lot.

Registered GIs apart, there are numerous crafts and agricultural products that need to be protected with GI. Speeding up the work of local biodiversity management committees and organizing the peoples' biodiversity register through the local governments would also help in identifying the potential GIs to be filed. In any case, efforts should not stop with protection but proceed further to create market impact and earn economic returns for the producers.

Logo

The lack of a common logo for GI in India has been one of the major issues highlighted by several researchers. The recently set up Cell for IPR Promotion and Management (CIPAM) announced a competition for designing a logo and tagline for the GI products of India on 17 October 2017.[1] In August 2018, the logo for GI with an impressive tag line has been introduced. However, the officials are not yet decided on who should be able to use the logo. The definition of producer as envisaged in the legal framework is wide and hence it is important to institutionalize the network and linkages within the value chain before the logo is available for use. Moreover, the government should launch a campaign in print and electronic media to promote local products and consumer awareness, in the same spirit with which the cleanliness mission 'Swachh Bharat' of the government has been popularized. It should be made mandatory for each of the registered GI products to use the common GI logo within a stipulated timeframe.

A few products like Mysore Sandal Soap carry the printed message that it is a 'Geographical Indication Registry Product' on the cover, which could create at least a curiosity value in the minds of the consumers who care to read the printed contents. A common logo, on the contrary, will help the consumers to instantly recognize the product as is the case with the ISI, Agmark and Hallmark (associated with jewellery). In the earlier days, when radio was the main means of mass communication, repeated messages about ISI[2] marks on goods taught people to differentiate the standard good from the substandard product. It is hoped that as and when the common logo use is finalized by the Government of India, similar efforts will be launched to popularize the GI products of the country.

Certification and Capacity Building

As mentioned elsewhere, presently there are a few handicraft and agricultural products that are exported abroad. Exports through organized channels will have to be compliant with various procedures set up by the Export Promotion Council of Handicrafts. For instance, export regulations require that provisions of statutes dealing with wages, bonus, contract labour, child labour, and so on, be obeyed by the producers. Agricultural exports through APEDA should follow the specifications laid down by it. For instance, for Basmati rice, Basmati.net provides the protocol to be followed, which includes the requirement to register the farmer, the land, and the variety that is cultivated under the name Basmati.

As the trend of third-party certifications is catching up with the EU, there are many certifications that are to be complied with by the Indian exporters. For instance, the EU timber regulations require that the wood required for the craft should not have been harvested illegally; Vriksh demands that the wood has been procured from well-managed forests; the Oeco Tex certificate insists on getting the assurance from the textile producers that there has been no hazardous process or products used in the production of textiles; the REACH (Registration, Evaluation, Authorization, and Restriction of Chemicals) regulation requires that no hazardous chemicals be used in the production process; the Children's Toxic Metal Act (2010) ensures that the products are safe for the children to use and so on. Adherence to such statutes and having certifications to that effect will widen the prospects in the overseas market, where conscious consumers pay attention to the process of producing the product and are willing to pay a premium for adherence to social and environmental norms (Das & Lalitha, 2015). Compliance with such regulations also requires capacity-building of the artisans in the required field in order to sensitize them to follow the requirements. For all these purposes, it is essential that there is an inspection body which meticulously checks the raw materials/ingredients used for GI production.

Role of the GI Registry

A commendable role has been played by the GI Registry in the recent years as evident from the significant differences in the content and quality of application between the early years and now. It is obvious that the system is beginning to evolve, and each case of GI registration brings with it a different kind of issue and challenge to be addressed.

Evidently, despite the requests for more details like inspection, turnover, producer, association, and so on by the GI Registry (after the first examination report or after the consultative group meeting), compliance is not cent per cent. However, the GI Registry is not initiating any tough action like rectification of registration for non-compliance issues and so on, based on the apprehension that it could prevent filing of GI altogether. Justifiably, at this juncture it is required that more products are identified for the purpose of filing the GI.

The growing body of empirical case studies suggests that not only do production techniques evolve, the process of arriving at an official product definition and method is usually controversial. Tradition and authenticity are moving targets. The extent to which any certification system can formally guarantee them is doubtful at best. Examination by public authorities does not extend to scrutinizing these 'behind the scenes' choices, so it is naive to accept that the registration system actually verifies 'the authentic and unvarying local methods' of production (Gangjee, 2012, p. 8). Even in the Indian context, it can be said that while in a few cases the GI factor is very strong and, hence, the authenticity could be established without any complication, in case of handicrafts it could be difficult and challenging for the Registry and the applicant.

It is suggested that the GI Registry can mandate economic information pertaining to the craft. If there is appropriate information on the (a) type of market catered to, (b) involvement of women in the craft, and (c) turnover generated at the time of submitting the application and so on, it would serve a valuable purpose as a baseline and would yield itself for potential comparison with any follow-up study. Presently, such information is severely lacking. A few baseline studies have been done by the National Institute of Design and National Institute of Fashion Technology for a few textile products, but more analysis for different products could provide an idea about the directions in which strategies could be initiated. For instance, at the time of registration of Pochampalli Ikat, it was suggested by the expert from NIFT that it is important to carefully document the different types of ikat weaving in different parts of the country and examine the influences they have on each other and, thereby, highlight the uniqueness.

The GI Registry, like any other IP registering offices, advertises only on its website when a particular application has been filed and the same is open for any opposition. But unlike the patents or trademarks, where the interested parties and competitors would keep a watchful eye on the applications and opposition, due to the limited awareness about GI, applications filed may not get the desired attention. Given the diversity across the country and the fact that the GI deals with communities which may not be conversant in English or Hindi, the two languages followed by the website, and the fact that a person will have to take efforts to visit the Registry's website to update oneself, the information published on the GI website might not get the desired attention from different stakeholders. Unless publicity is given in the vernacular language papers, the concerned stakeholders might not be aware of a particular application that has been filed with the Registry. Perhaps due to the lack of awareness, not many GI applications were opposed. The importance of advertisement in the regional languages got highlighted in the Payyanur Pavithra Ring case discussed in this volume (Chapter 4). Giving publicity in the vernacular papers will also help in identifying the authorized users.

Tourism Around GI

In the European countries, tourism paths are drawn around the protected product route. Vandecandelaere et al. (2009–10) provides the example of Lardo di Colonnata of Italy and Morocco for promoting tourism. It is a fine example where the GI registered pig fat matured in marble tubs became famous in the 1990s, leading to increased tourism, resulting in emigrants returning to Colonnata and setting up restaurants and grocery stores, revitalizing the village economy. In Morocco, tourism routes have been developed around the production places of saffron and argan oil, which provides an opportunity to see the production process, indulge in tasting sessions and buy the products. Slowly, some of the village groups started offering homestay, contributing to the village economy, besides improving cleanliness and hygiene.

International civil society organizations, like the Slow Food Foundation, the Earth Markets, and Ark of Taste, organize traditional and origin-linked food fairs to provide market openings for small producers (cited in Vandecandelaere et al., 2009–10).

A few GI related food festivals are organized in different parts of the country. In Arunachal Pradesh, Orange Festivals are held coinciding with the harvest season, creating additional demand by the tourists. Strawberry festivals are held in Mahabaleshwar, which offer strawberry tasting sessions that have generated good publicity and sales for the farmers.[3] The Government of Gujarat has been popularizing the Rannutsav in Kutch for the past few years, which is creating a new demand for the Kutch crafts.

GI Awareness

It was mentioned elsewhere in this volume that the value of the GI product increases with the awareness on the part of the consumers about the product. It is true that despite the potential of quite a few local products, the concept of GI has not been properly grasped by several governments, particularly in the developing economies and LDCs (Vittori, 2010). The GI registry conducts workshops in different places, but these are not regular events. Awareness creation is required at different levels for consumers, producers, traders, and retailers, corporates, governments, and amongst the law enforcing agencies, to identify uniqueness and reputation, and to check infringement practices.

Awareness creation is essential, particularly in the context of globalization, where 'brands' gain more popularity than non-branded goods. Hence, if efforts are not taken to create awareness about these national heritage products with different sections of society, some of the regionally known crafts and agricultural crops might get erased from the production scenario as well as from the minds of people.

In the trade fairs and exhibitions, GI pavilions need to be created, with the description of the crafts and the artisans who have created it. Craftsmen practising Thanjavur Painting, Swamimalai Bronze Icon, and Aranmula Mirror talked about the highly positive outcome of the Festival of India conducted in Paris, London, and the US in the 1980s, where they demonstrated the making of the craft to the consumers in the US, France, and other European countries. Particularly, an Aranmula artisan said he sold all the pieces that he had taken along and came back with a good number of orders that became a big turning point in his life. Such festivals should be organized at regular intervals abroad, giving a boost to the exports. Similarly, regional food festivals involving the locally cultivated crops and vegetables are conducted in some places coinciding with the harvest season. Popularizing such festivals would also be very beneficial for the producers. There is a need for a separate marketing intermediary for the GI products as marketing and creating demand through awareness is very essential for GI promotion. While the state handicrafts corporations can devise a strategy to highlight the GI products of their state with appropriate descriptions, the agricultural and horticultural departments of each state should organize the seasonal food festival.

The panchayats and the municipalities should widely publicize through billboards and tourism routes about the GI registered products of that locality. There are two major concerns regarding the GIs in India: one is the status of languishing crafts/crops, and the second is the fact that the younger generation is keeping away from such professions. A couple of suggestions mentioned here could address these issues. To create awareness, at all levels of school education, lessons should be introduced about the craft and agricultural heritage of India. One innovative publisher, 'Tara Books', has brought out a picture book titled *8 Ways to Draw an Elephant*. In this, the Italian designer Paola Ferrarotti has worked with several Indian artists to imagine and render the Indian elephant in eight different art styles, including Saura, Meena, Patua, Pithora, and Mata-ni-Pachedi (Dasgupta, 2016). Mata-ni-Pachedi (Kalamkari work of Ahmedabad, Gujarat) has recently filed a GI application. Such strategies can create curiosity and revive interest among the younger generation to learn and pursue such crafts. Universities and technology development centres of the states should encourage more studies on GIs and publicize such studies.

Liebl and Roy (2003) mention about the involvement of young designers in using the master artisans of Orissa Pattachitra to create their art on modern furniture. Titan watches used traditional rangoli designs on their watches. Such depiction of art would also revive the crafts.

In this context, as has been discussed in the volume, when the government was involved in the filing of GI, pre-registration activities took centre stage and the post-registration activities were not given focus, with the result that the different stakeholders did not know about the GI grant for the product. When the association was involved in filing the GI, the necessity to convene meetings resulted in information flowing across the groups.

The organization which filed the application for legal protection of GI should also be in charge of the promotion of the GI. When these two entities are different, the awareness, promotion, and marketing become an issue. Awareness creation could also check infringement, as consumers could take efforts to assure themselves of the authenticity of the product. But not all the producers have the wherewithal to prevent infringement. Investment is required to check infringement. It is hoped that the CIPAM would invest in creating measures for preventing infringements. For instance, the Tea Board has spent more than $200,000 fighting infringement cases of Darjeeling Tea which may not be possible for all the registered GI proprietors. The twin strategies adopted by Kota Doria weavers, that of concentrating on intricate heavier designs in handlooms instead of competing with powerlooms, and to weave the Kota Doria logo in each of the saris (Sharma & Kulhari, 2015), are very innovative strategies to combat fraudulent practices and to create a niche market for the products.

Data

The Sixth Economic Census collected information on the number of handicrafts and handloom enterprises (using the central government's list of handicrafts to identify the craft enterprises) for the first time in India. The data provides a rough estimate of the number of people dependent on crafts and handlooms.

There are very few products in India for which data are available on livelihoods, production, and volume transacted in the domestic and export market. The export data on crafts and agricultural products indicate the possibility of the presence of GI-registered products and the potential opportunities in the future. It is not clear whether the GI-registered products among the exported goods carry the GI tag and inform the end stream consumers about the region of origin. If it is done that way then besides addressing the 'nostalgic value' of the Indian diaspora, it could also attract the attention of the consumers who are interested in consuming authentic products.

The unorganized nature of the craft and agricultural sector is one of the reasons for the lack of data on these sectors, which prevents any targeted intervention. Creating databases would be of immense value to assess the impact of GI and could serve as a model for potential products and in undertaking corrective course of action.

Potential Ways of the New Use of the GIs

The intensity and the direction of the GI impacts directly depend on the level of awareness, active participation, and cooperation of the producers and other stakeholders in the value chain in safeguarding the collective reputation.

Creative destruction of old styles to cater to the modern contemporary demand could help promote and revive the craft by infusing new demand. Bhavani Jamakkalam (handloom floor carpet) weavers traditionally produced carpets with monotonous horizontal broad lines with set colours and, as mentioned elsewhere in the volume, the demand for such designs has reduced a lot. Competition from the powerlooms contributes to the decline of the craft further. Hence, some of the artists started using the same technique of carpet weaving to introduce new designs that can be used as wall hangings. Wall hangings with alphabets are used as teaching material in schools and adult education centres. Since the GI for Bhavani Jamakkalam has been filed in the broad category of Class 24 (textile and textile goods) and Class 26 (carpets, rugs, mats, and matting), the newer creations also belong to the GI protected category of goods only.

There are several aromatic GI protected rice varieties in India, which may be exploited for their (1) market potential as rice is the staple diet for a sizeable segment of the population, and (2) specific nutritional qualities to target specific health conscious consumers. India is rich in many scented rice varieties but due to the importance given to Basmati, the existence of more than 300 non-Basmati scented rice varieties in India has been overshadowed (Mishra, 2014). Such varieties should be identified and protected under GI.

GI Implementation for Promoting Livelihoods

In the sui generis system, the potential involvement of public authorities helps in authenticating the product (Marie-Vivien, 2015) and in ensuring that (a) all the producers comply with all the requirements of production and (b) no third party misuses the GI recognition in the marketplace (Gangjee, 2012). But due to a lack of post GI efforts by the government, except in a few cases like Basmati and Darjeeling Tea and a few that are traded in the organized segment, measures to check authenticity and prevention of misuse of GI are not in place so far. The recently formulated CIPAM's mandate seems to focus more on awareness creation. With reference to GI, such awareness promotion should not stop with pre-registration activities alone which focuses on filing more GI applications. There should be more emphasis on creating awareness regarding the post-GI activities (or the actual implementation part of GI) to reap benefits out of GI registration. Such studies could highlight any interventions at local level, if any, which could be scaled up to be adopted in other regions with GI products.

It appears that producers from India have limited interests in joining the international coalition of GI producers known as the Organization for an International Geographical Indications Network (OriGIn), an NGO based in Geneva, for the international protection of GI and to develop it as a tool for sustainable development (Vittori, 2010). Around eighty-five members representing more than two million producers from about forty countries are members of OriGIn.[4] OriGIn helps in exchanges of best practices between the producers. Interactions with such bodies will help in improving the capacities and adopting suitable strategies to promote the products.

There are about 125 foreign and 139 Indian national applications waiting for approval with the GI Registry. As the foreign applications are for wines, spirits, and food stuffs, currently the presence of Indian nationals in that arena is almost non-existent. Nevertheless, they could influence the local consumption pattern. Compared to this, there are

139 applications from Indian nationals waiting for a decision. Tamil Nadu, with thirty-one applications, is leading the rest of the states in the number of applications pending approval, followed by West Bengal, Uttar Pradesh, and Maharashtra, with thirteen, eleven, and ten applications respectively. There could be a healthy competition among the states to secure GIs for the unique products of their states. But in that competition, the quest for defining GI uniqueness should not be lost. While filing applications, care should be taken to include all the eligible producers as stakeholders, and the production area as contiguous and not widespread. When the GI areas are widespread, there could be wide heterogeneity in the product, leading to reduced uniqueness and challenges in clearly defining CoPs, which reduce the 'unique selling point' of the product.

Similar to the Basmati and Rasgulla controversy where Odisha is claiming the GI title, another interstate conflict is likely to come up with Madhya Pradesh and Chattisgarh claiming GI title for the Kadaknath chicken,[5] which is known for its unique meat. While such interstate conflicts show the increasing awareness, it also highlights the challenges in defining the GI area. Very similar to the interstate situation, inter country contests could also arise. India adopting GI has led to interest in GI by Sri Lanka and Bangladesh (Calboli, 2017). For instance, filing of Uppada Jamdani sarees from Andhra Pradesh has triggered a controversy in Bangladesh as Bangladesh claims that Jamdani originates from Dhaka (Karim, 2016). Karim raises concerns about the Indian GIs besides the Uppada Jamdani on, Fazli mango and Nakshi katha embroidery, claiming these products belong to Bangladesh. Bangladesh enacted the GI of Goods (Registration and Protection) Act 2013 and the GI Goods Rules in 2015. Uppada Jamdani application was filed in 2008 and GI was granted in 2013 in India. Karim points out that though both the countries recognize the homonymous GI applications, but GI on Uppada Jamdani could create confusion in the minds of consumers. However, it should be recognized that Jamdani is a weaving style like tie and dye or ikat. There are GIs on different types of ikats in India, Thailand, and Indonesia and they cannot be considered as infringing the GI protection of each other.

GOI (2011, p. 99) states that 'in France, Champagne, took as long as 150 years to build up reputation and goodwill globally'. It might take long years for Indian GIs also to achieve such position. A wide variety of products have been filed for GI. Targeted efforts of selecting a few products for promotion at a time (may be using the formula for selection as under one product per village/taluka), assessing the quality and improving the quality, creating awareness and demand based on quality and not on price, and providing the support for marketing would help in realizing the development potential of GI products. A changing consumption pattern that emphasizes more on the 'local goods' than on imported goods is the key to promote GI goods and efforts towards this would encourage the producers to continue with their production and support the livelihoods dependent on these products.

Notes

1. See http://pib.nic.in/newsite/PrintRelease.aspx?relid=171786, accessed on 22 November 2017.

2. Indian Standards Institution earlier now known as Indian Bureau of Standards.

3. Interaction with Ganesh Hingmire who has initiated the efforts to file GIs for Maharashtra's important products.

4. From India, the Tamil Nadu Technology Development and Promotion Centre is a member.

5. See https://www.ndtv.com/india-news/madhya-pradesh-and-chhattis-garhs-new-bone-of-contention-the-kadaknath-chicken-1825390, accessed on 22 March 2018 and thanks to Gargi Chakrabarti for bringing it to our attention.

References

Acharya, S.S. 2015. 'Second Phase of Agricultural Marketing Reforms and Research Issues'. *Indian Journal of Agricultural Marketing* 29 (2): 41–9.

All India Artisans and Craftsworkers Welfare Association (AIACA). 2017. *National Handicrafts Policy Report*, supported by the Ministry of Textiles, Government of India. Retrieved from http://www.aiacaonline.org/wp-content/uploads/2018/06/National-Handicrafts-Policy-Report_Full-version_Final.pdf.

Arfini, F. 1999. 'The Value of Typical Products: The Case of Proscuitto di Parma and Parmigiano Reggiano Cheese No. 241032'. 67th Seminar, European Association of Agricultural Economists (EAAE), 28–30. October. LeMans, France.

Barjolle, D. and B. Sylvander. 1999. 'Some Factors of Success for Origin Labeled Products in Agri-food Supply Chains in Europe: Market, Internal Resources and Institutions'. In B. Sylvander, D. Barjolle, and F. Arfini (Eds), *Proceedings of the 67th EAAE Seminar*, pp. 46–71. France: LeMans.

Barjolle, D., P. Marguerite, and P. Anna. 2009. 'Impacts of Geographical Indications: Review of Methods and Empirical Evidences'. International Association of Agricultural Economists Conference, 16–22 August. Beijing.

Basole, A. 2015. 'Authenticity, Innovation, and the Geographical Indication in an Artisanal Industry: The Case of Banarasi Sari'. *The Journal of World Intellectual Property Rights* 18 (3–4): 127–49.

Belletti, G. 1999. 'Origin Labelled Products, Reputation and Heterogeneity of Firms, No. 240135'. 67th Seminar, European Association of Agricultural Economists (EAAE), 28–30 October. LeMans, France.

Belletti, G. and A. Marescotti. 2006. 'I Percorsi di Istituzionalizzazione delle Produzioni Agroalimentari Tipiche'. In B. Rocchi and D. Romano (Eds), *Tipicamente Buono: Concezioni di Qualità Lungo la Filiera dei Prodotti Agro-alimentari in Toscana*, pp. 121–47. Milano: Franco Angeli.

Belletti, G. and A. Marescotti. 2009. 'Monitoring and Evaluating the Effects of the Protection of Geographical Indications: A Methodological Proposal'. In *The Effects of Protecting Geographical Indications: Ways and Means of their Evaluation, Publication No. 7*. Bern: Swiss Federal Institute of Intellectual Property.

Belletti, G., A. Marescotti, M. Paus, S. Reviron, A. Deppeler, H. Stamm, and E. Thévenod-Mottet. 2011. 'The Effects of Protecting Geographical Indications Ways and Means of their Evaluation'. *Swiss Federal Institute of Intellectual Property 7*. Retrieved from https://flore.unifi.it/retrieve/handle/2158/606197/18700/Belletti-Marescotti-%20et%20al%20-%20Effects-of-Protecting-Geographical-Indications.pdf.

Belletti, G., A. Marescotti, and S. Scarmuzzi. 2001. *Paths of Rural Development Based on Typical Products: A Comparison between Alternative Strategies*. Department of Economics, University of Florence, pp. 384–95.

Berenguer, A. 2004. 'Geographical Origins in the World'. Paper presented at the workshop 'Promoting Agricultural Competitiveness through Local Know-how'. *Proceedings of the Montpellier Workshop*. Washington DC; Paris; Montpellier: World Bank Group; MAAPAR; CIRAD.

Bonnet, C. and M. Simioni. 2001. 'Assessing Consumer Response to Protected Designation of Origin Labeling: A Mixed Multinomial Logit Approach'. *European Review of Agricultural Economics* 28 (4): 433–99.

Bowen, S. 2010. 'Development from Within? The Potential for Geographical Indications in the Global South'. *The Journal of World Intellectual Property Rights* 13 (2): 231–52.

Bramley, C. 2011. 'A Review of the Socio-Economic Impact of Geographical Indications: Considerations for the Developing World'. Paper prepared for presentation at the WIPO Worldwide Symposium on Geographical Indications. Lima.

Bramley, C. and J. Kirsten. 2007. 'Exploring the Economic Rationale for Protecting Geographical Indicators in Agriculture'. *Agrekon* 46 (1): 69–93.

Bramley, C., E. Bienabe, and J. Kirsten. 2009. 'The Economics of Geographical Indications: Towards a Conceptual Framework for Geographical Indication Research in Developing Countries'. *The Economics of Intellectual Property: Suggestions for Further Research in Developing Countries and Countries with Economies in Transition*. Geneva: World Intellectual Property Organisation.

Bramley, C., E. Bienabe, and J. Kirsten (Eds). 2013. *Developing Geographical Indications in the South: The South African Experience*. Heidelberg: Springer.

Buhler, A., E. Fischer, and M.L. Nabholz. 1980. *Indian Tie-Dyed Fabrics* (Vol. 4). Michigan: University of Michigan.

Calboli, I. 2013. 'Of Markets, Culture, and Terroir: The Unique Economic and Culture Relted Benefits of Geographical Indications of Origin'. (Final draft).

Retrieved on 25 March 2018. Available at https://papers.ssrn.com/sol3/papers.cfm?abstract_id=2329566.

Calboli, I. 2017. 'Geographical Indications between Trade, Development, Culture, and Marketing:Framing a Fair(er) System of Protection in the Global Economy'. In I. Calboli and N.-L. Wee Loon (Eds), *Geographical Indications at the Crossroads of Trade, Development, and Culture Focus on Asia-Pacific*, pp. 3–35. Cambridge University Press.

Chand, R. 2017. *http://agricoop.nic.in/sites/default/files/NITI%20Aayog%20Policy%20Paper.pdf.* Retrieved on 12 July 2017. Available at www.agricoop.nic.in.

Chatterjee, A. 2003. *www.craftrevival.org.* Retrieved on 6 October 2015. Retrieved from http://www.craftrevival.org/voiceDetails.asp?Code=351.

Conejero, M.A. and A.D. Cesar. 2017. 'The Governance of Local Productive Arrangements (LPA) for the Strategic Management of Geographical Indications (GIS)'. *Ambiente & Sociedade* 20 (1): 293–314.

Coombe, R.J. 2005. 'Legal Claims to Culture in and Against the Market: Neoliberalism and the Global Proliferation of Meaningful Difference'. *Law, Culture and the Humanities* 1 (1): 35–52.

Dagne, T.W. 2012. 'Intelletucal Property, Traditional Knowledge and Biodiversity in the Global Economy: The Potential of Geographical Indications for Protecting Traditional Knowledge-based Agricultural Products'. Thesis submitted to Dalhousie University. Nova Scotia.

Das, K. 2009. 'Socio Economic Implications of Protecting Geographical Indications in India'. New Delhi: Centre for WTO Studies. Retrieved from http://wtocentre.iift.ac.in/Papers/GI_Paper_CWS_August%2009_Revised.pdf.

Das, K. 2010. 'Prospects and Challenges of Geographical Indications in India'. *Journal of World Intellectual Property* 13 (2): 148–201.

Das, K. and N. Lalitha. 2015. *The Handicraft Sector of Gujarat: Policy Concerns.* Government of Gujarat, Cottage and Rural Industries Commissionerate, Gandhinagar.

Dasgupta, U.M. 2016. 'Our Plot Against Evil—Stories Remain Among the Best Ways to Teach Children How to Cultivate Empathy and Mutual Respect'. *The Hindu, Weekend Edition*, November 20: 9.

Datta, T.K. 2010. 'Darjeeling Tea in India'. In A. Lecocent, E. Vandecandelaere, and J.J. Cadilhon (Eds), *Quality Linked to Geographical Origin and Geographical Indications: Lessons Learned from Six Case Studies in Asia*, pp. 113–60. Bangkok: Food and Agricultural Organization.

Dharmaraju, P. 2006. 'Angara and Koyyalagudem: Marketing in Handloom Cooperatives'. *Economic and Political Weekly* 41 (31): 3385–7.

Dikshit, R. 2014. 'Narendra Modi's Dilemma: Surat vs Banarasi Saris'. *The Times of India*, March 27. Retrieved on 27 October 2017. Available at https://timesofindia.indiatimes.com/news/Narendra-Modis-dilemma-Surat-vs-Banarasi-saris/articleshow/32742485.cms.

Durand, C. and S. Fournier. 2017. 'Can Geographical Indications Modernize Indonesian and Vietnamese Agriculture? Analysing the Role of National and Local Governments and Producers Strategies'. *World Development* 98: 93–104. http://dx.doi.org/10.1016/j.worlddev.2015.11.022.

Folkeson, C. 2005. *Geographical Indications and Rural Development in the EU.* Lund: Department of Economics, University of Lund.

Fotopoulos, C. and A. Krystallis. 2003. 'Quality Labels as a Marketing Advantage: The Case of the PDO Zagora Apples in the Greek Market'. *European Journal of Marketing* 37 (10): 1350–74.

Gal, P. 2017. 'Factors Influencing the Success of Geographical Indications'. Paper presented at the 24th Conference of European Association of Wine Economists. Bologna, Italy.

Gangjee, D.S. 2012. *Relocating the Law of Geographical Indications.* Cambridge: Cambrdige University Press.

Garcia, C., D. Marie-Vivien, C.G. Kushalappa, P. Chengappa, and K. Nanaya. 2007. 'Geographical Indications and Biodiversity in Western Ghats'. *Mountain Research and Development* 27 (3): 206–10.

Gopalakrishnan, N.S., P.S. Nair, and A.K. Babu. 2007. *Exploring the Relationship between Geographical Indications and Traditional Knowledge: An Analysis of the Legal Tools for the Protection of Geographical Indications in Asia.* Geneva: International Centre for Trade and Sustainable Development.

Government of India. 2011. *Working Group Report on Handicrafts for 12th Five Year Plan.* New Delhi: Ministry of Textiles.

———. 2012. 'Chettinad Kottan—GI Application No. 200'. *Geographical Indications Journal* 47: 33–41.

———. 2015. *Annual Report of the Office of the Controller General of Patents, Designs, Trademarks and Geographical Indications.* New Delhi: Department of Industrial Policy and Promotion, Ministry of Commerce and Industry.

Government of Maharashtra. 2010. World Bank funded Maharashtra Agricultural Competitiveness Project (MACP): Project Implementation Plan. Retrieved on 2 August 2016. Available at HYPERLINK "https://vanamati.gov.in/pdf/MACP_PIP%5b1%5d.pdf" https://vanamati.gov.in/pdf/MACP_PIP[1].pdf.

Hassan, D. and S. Monier-Dilhan. 2006. 'National Brands and Store Brands: Competition through Public Quality Labels'. *Agribusiness* 22 (1): 21–30.

Hayes, D.J., S.H. Lence, and A. Stoppa. 2003. *Farmer-Owned Brands?* Iowa: Center for Agricultural and Rural Development, Iowa State University.

Holt, D. 2015. 'Brands and Branding'. Retrieved from http://testconso.typepad.com/files/brands-and-branding-csg2.pdf.

Hughes, J. 2009 *Coffee and Chocolate: Can We Help Developing Country Farmers through Geographical Indications*. Washington D C: International Intellectual Property Institute. Retrieved on September 2017. from http://iipi.org/wp-content/uploads/2010/09/Coffee-and-Chocolate-J.-Hughes.pdf.

Insight Consulting, OriGIn, REDD. 2013. *Study on Geographical Indications Protection for Non-Agricultural Products in the Internal Market.* Switzerland.

Jay, T. and M. Taylor. 2013. 'A Case of Champagne: A Study of Geographical Indications'. *Corporate Governance Ejournal*, Paper 29. Retrieved on 28 October. Available at http://epublications.bond.edu.au/cgi/viewcontent.cgi?article=1028&context=cgej.

Jena, P.R. and U. Grote. 2010. 'Changing Institutions to Protect Regional Heritage: A Case for Geographical Indications in the Indian Agrifood Sector'. *Development Policy Review* 28 (2): 217–36.

Kapur, A. 2016. *Made Only in India—Goods with Geographical Indications*. New Delhi: Routledge.

Karim, M.A. 2016. 'Indian Claims over Geographical Indications of Bangladesh: Sustainability Under Intellectual Property Regime'. *Queen Mary Journal of Intellectual Property* 6 (1): 75–91.

Kher, A.W. 2006. 'Enjoying a Good Port with Clear Conscience: Geographic Indicators, Rent Seeking and Development'. *The Estey Centre Journal of International Law and Trade Policy* 7 (1): 1–14.

Khosla, Ron. 2007. 'A Participatory Gurantee System for India', *The Organic Standard* © *Grolink AB*, 69: 11–14.

Kolady, D.E., W.H. Lesser, and C. Ye. 2011. 'The Economic Effects of Geographical Indications on Developing Country Producers: A Comparison of Darjeeling and Oolong Teas'. *The WIPO Journal* 2 (2): 157–72.

Kumar, G. and N. Bahl. 2010. 'Geographical Indications of India: Socio Economic and Development Issues'. *Policy Brief No. 2*, September. India: All India Artisans and Craftworkers Welfare Association.

Kumar, R., V. Nelson, A. Martin, D. Badal, A. Latheef, B.S. Reddy, ... M. Hartog, 2015. 'Draft Evaluation Design, for the "Evaluation of Early Impacts of the Better Cotton Initiative on Smallholders Cotton Producers in Kurnool District"'. London: Submitted to ISEAL Alliance and Better Cotton Initiative.

Lalitha, N. 2014. *Socio-economic Implications of Protecting Handicrafts through Geographical Indications: A Case Study of Selected Products from Southern States.* New Delhi: Report submitted to the Indian Council of Social Science Research.

———. 2016. *Creating Viable Markets Through Use of Geographical Indications: What Can India Learn from Thailand?* ICSSR-NRCT Bilateral Scholars Exchange Programme, Thammasat University, India Studies Centre, Bangkok.

Lalitha, N. and S. Vinayan. 2017. 'GIs for Protecting Agro Biodiversity and Promoting Rural Livelihoods: Status, Strategies and Wayforward'. *GIDR Working Paper No. 240*, 17 January. Ahmedabad.

Libery, B. and M. Kneafsay. 1998. 'Product and Place: Promoting Quality Products and Services in the Lagging Rural Regions of the European Union'. *European Urban and Regional Studies* 5: 329.

Liebl, M. and T. Roy. 2003a. 'Handmade in India: Preliminary Analysis of Crafts Producers and Crafts Production'. *Economic and Political Weekly* 38 (51/52): 5366–76.

———. 2003b. *Handmade in India: Traditional Craft Skills in a Changing World.* World Bank. Retrieved on 25 October 2017. Available at http://www.aiaca-online.org/resources-other-studies.

Lourerio, M.L. and J.J. McClusky. 2000. 'Assessing Consumer Response to Protected Geographical Identification Labeling'. *Agribusiness* 16 (3): 309–20.

Maheshwari, A. 2014. 'Building Brands through GIs'. In T.K. Rout and B. Majhi (Eds), *WTO, TRIPS and Geographical Indications (GIs)*, pp. 75–89. New Delhi: New Century Publications.

Marie-Vivien, D. 2013. 'The Protection of Geographical Indications for Handicrafts: How to Apply the Concepts of Natural and Human Factors to All Products'. *The WIPO Journal* 4 (2): 191–205.

Marie-Vivien, D. 2015. *The Protection of Geographical Indications in India: A New Perspective on the French and European Experience.* New Delhi: Sage Publications.

Marie-Vivien, D. and E. Bienabe. 2017. 'The Multifaceted Role of the State in the Protection of Geographical Indications: A Worldwide Review'. *World Development* October, 98: 1–11. Available at http://dx.doi.org/10.1016/j.worlddev.2017.04.035.

Marie-Vivien, D., L. Be'rard, J. Boutonnet, and F. Casabianca. 2017. 'Are French Geographical Indications Losing Their Soul? Analyzing Recent Developments in the Governance of the Link to the Origin in France'. *World Development* 19: 25–34. doi:http://dx.doi.org/10.1016/j.worlddev.2015.01.001.

McGinnis, M.D. and E. Ostrom. 2014. 'Social Ecological System Framework: Initial Changes and Continuing Challenges'. *Ecology and Society* 19 (2): 30.

Menapace, L., G. Colson, C. Grebitus, and M. Facendola. 2009. *Consumer Preferences for Country-of-origin and Geographical Indications, and Protected Designation of Origin Labels.* Iowa: Iowa State University-Department of Economics.

Mishra, S. 2015. 'Kalanamak: The Future of Indian scented Rice'. Down to Earth. June 7. Retrieved on 21 June 2016. Available at http://www.downtoearth.org.in/coverage/kalanamak-10106.

Moran, W. 1993. 'Rural Space as Intellectual Property'. *Political Geography* 12 (3): 263–77.

Mubayi, Y. 2016. *Policy Gaps Study on the Crafts Sector in India.* New Delhi: All India Artisans and Craftworkers Welfare Association.

Mulik, K. and J.M. Crespi. 2011. 'Geographical Indications and the Trade Related Intellectual Property Rights Agreement (TRIPS): A Case of Basmati Rice Exports'. *Journal of Agricultural & Food Industrial Organization* 9 (1). Retrieved from http://www.bepress.com/jafio/vol9/iss1/art4.

NABARD. 2016. *Doubling Farmer's Income by 2022.* Mumbai: NABARD.

Naidu, G.C. 2014. 'Geographical Indications of India—Icons of our Cultural Heritage', *IP Expressions*, 1 (1), Office of the Controller General of Patents, Designs, and Trademarks, Government of India.

Naidu, T. A. (2013a). 'Pedana Kalamkari Art form gets GI Tag'. *The Hindu.* August 18. Retrieved on 20 February 2014. Available at HYPERLINK "http://www.thehindu.com/news/national/andhra-pradesh/pedana-kalamkari-art-form-gets-gi-tag/article%205033067.ece" http://www.thehindu.com/news/national/andhra-pradesh/pedana-kalamkari-art-form-gets-gi-tag/article 5033067.ece.

———. 2013b. 'French couple to showcase Kalamkari works in Paris'. *The Hindu.* November 18. Retrieved on 20 February 2014. Available at http://www.thehindu.com/news/cities/Vijayawada/french-couple-to-showcase-kalamkari-works-in-paris/%20article5363999.ece.

———. 2013c. 'Black jiggery scarcity forces Kalamkari units to down shutters'. *The Hindu.* December 4. Retrieved on 20 February 2014. Available at http://www.thehindu.com/news/cities/Vijayawada/black-jaggery-scarcity-forces-kalamkari-units-to-down-shutters/article5421154.ece.

———. 2013d. 'Kalamkari Union Told to Apply for Permanent Trade Licence'. *The Hindu.* December 14. Retrieved on 20 February 2014. Available at http://www.thehindu.com/todays-paper/tp-national/tp-andhrapradesh/kalamkari-union-told-to-apply-for-permanent-trade-licence/article5458371.ece.

Nair, L. 2016. 'Making India GI Brand Conscious'. *The Hindu*, March 17. Retrieved on 6 October 2017. Available at http://www.thehindu.com/opinion/op-ed/comment-article-by-latha-r-nair-making-india-geographical-indications-gi-brand-conscious/article8361576.ece.

Nair, L.R. and R. Kumar. 2005. *Geograhical Indications: A Search for Identity.* Butterworth: Lexix Nexis.

Nanda, N., I. Barpujari, and N. Srivastava. 2013. 'The Protection of Geographical Indications in India: Issues and Challenges'. TERI Briefing Paper.

Neilson, J., J. Wright, and L. Aklimawati, 2018. 'Geographical Indications and Value Capture in the Indonesia Coffee Sector'. *Journal of Rural Studies* 59 (2018): 35–48.

OECD. 2000. *Appellations of Origin and Geographical Indications in OECD Member Countries: Economic and Legal Implications.* Working Party on

Agricultural Policies and Markets of the Committee for Agriculture. Paris: OECD.

Pacciani, A., G. Belletti, A. Marescotti, and S. Scaramuzzi. 2001. 'The Role of Typical Products in Fostering Rural Development and the Effects of Regulation (EEC) 2081/92'. 73rd Seminar. European Association of Agricultural Economists (EAAE), 28–30. Ancona, Italy. Available at https://www.researchgate.net/profile/Giovanni_Belletti/publication/228776258_The_role_of_typical_products_in_fostering_rural_development_and_the_effects_of_regulation_EEC_208192/links/0fcfd5090c9234971b000000/The-role-of-typical-products-in-fostering-rura.

Pai, Y. and T. Singla. 2016. '"Vanity GIs": India's Legislation on Geographical Indications and Missing Regulatory Framework'. Retrieved on 20 April 2017, available at SSRN: https://ssrn.com/abstract=2856549.

Pal, D. and A. Das. 2014. 'Integrating GIs with Development'. In T. Rout and B. Majhi (Eds), WTO, TRIPS and Geographical Indications, pp. 90–110. New Delhi: New Century Publications.

Panda, N. 2015. 'Stone Artisans Stare at Bleak Future'. The Telegraph, August 25. Retrieved on 6 October 2016. Available at https://www.telegraphindia.com/states/odisha/stone-artisans-stare-at-bleak-future/cid/1470693.

Paus, M. and S. Reviron. 2009. 'Evaluating the Effects of Protecting Geographical Indications: Scientific Context and Case Studies'. The Effects of Protecting Geographical Indications: Ways and Means of Their Evaluation, Publication No. 7.

Quinones-Ruiz, X.F., M. Penkar, G. Belletti, A. Marescotti, S. Scarmuzzii, E. Barzini, ... L.F. Samper-Gartner. 2016. 'Insights into the Blackbox of Collective Efforts for the Registration of Geographical Indications'. Landuse Policy, pp. 103–111. Retrieved on 17 September 2017. Available at https://www.researchgate.net/profile/Xiomara_Quinones-Ruiz/publication/303873992_Insights_into_the_black_box_of_collective_efforts_for_the_registration_of_Geographical_Indications/links/576ee5a808ae62194746bc44.pdf.

———. 2004. The Socio-economics of Geographical Indications: A Review of Empirical Evidence from Europe. Geneva: UNCTAD-ICTSD Project on IPRs and Sustainable Development.

Rangnekar, D. 2011. 'Remaking Place: The Social Construction of a Geographical Indication for Feni'. Environment and Planning A: Economy and Space. 43 (9): 2043–59. doi:10.1068/a43259.

Reddy, N.D. 2007. 'Handloom Sector in India—The Current Status and Shape of Things to Come by 2015'. In J. Vyas (Ed.), Indian Textiles 2015, pp. 363–378. Ahmedabad: Textile Review.

Reviron, S., E. Thevenod-Mottet, and N. El Benni. 2009. Geographical Indications: Creation and Distribution of Economic Value in Developing Countries. NCCR Trade Regulation Swiss National Centre for Competence in Research.

Rich, K.M. 2011. 'Trajectories of Value Chain Governance and Geographical Indications: Issues for Upgrading Handicrafts Goods in India'. *CUTS CITEE Working Paper No. 1/2011.*

Rosa, M.D. 2015. 'The Role of Geographical Indication in Supporting Food Safety—A Not Taken for Granted Nexus'. *Italian Journal of Food Safety* 4 (4931): 186–91.

Rout, T.K. 2014. 'GI as Instument for Sustainable Development: A Case of Pochampally Ikat'. In T.K. Rout and B. Majhi (Eds), *WTO, TRIPS and Geographical Indications (GIs)*, pp. 51–64. New Delhi, India: New Century Publications.

Sarkar, D. 2016. 'Famous Malda Mango Facing Major Export Crisis'. *The Economic Times*, May 24. Retrieved on 23 June 2016. Available at http://economictimes.indiatimes.com/news/economy/agriculture/famous-malda-mango-facing-major-export-crisis/articleshow/52418917.cms.

Seetisarn, P. and Y. Chiaravutthi. 2011. 'Thai Consumers Willingness to Pay for Food Products with Geographical Indications'. *International Business Research* 4 (3): 161–70.

Sharma, R.W. and S. Kulhari. 2015. *Marketing of GI Products: Unlocking their Commerical Potential.* New Delhi: Centre for WTO Studies, Indian Institute of Foreign Trade.

Singh, S. and T. Singh. 2013. *Producer Companies in India: A Study of Organisation and Performance, CMA Publication No. 246.* Ahmedabad: Centre for Management in Agriculture, Indian Institute of Management.

Singhal, S. 2008. 'Geographical Indications and Traditional Knowledge'. *Journal of Intellectual Property Law and Practice* 3 (11): 732–8.

Soam, S.K. and K.R. Sastry. 2008. *Socio-Economic Implications of GI Registration for Agricultural and Non-Agricultural Commodities/Products in India.* Hyderabad: National Academy of Agricultural Research Management.

Soam, S. and M. Hussain. 2011. 'Commercialisation of Indigenous Health Drinks as Geographical Indications'. *Journal of Intellectual Property Rights* 16 (2): 170–5.

Soam, S., P.S. Tiwari, and K.R. Sastry. 2007. 'Sustainable Use and Conservation of Agro-biodiversity through Protecting as Goods of Geographical Indications'. In S. Kannaiyan, and A. Gopalam (Eds), *Crop Genetic Resources and Conservation*, pp. 229–41. New Delhi: Associated Publishing Company.

Stiglitz, J. 1989. 'Imperfect Formation in the Product Market'. In R. Schmalenesse and R.D. Willig, *Handbook of Industrial Organization* (Vol. I). Amsterdam: Elsevier.

Sylvander, B. 2004. *Development of Origin Labelled Products: Humanity, Innovation and Sustainability (DOLPHINS). Final Report. Synthesis & Recommendations.* Retrieved on 20 April 2014. Available at http://www.origin-food.org/pdf/wp7/dol_d8.pdf.

Thiedig, F. and B. Sylvander. 2004. 'Welcome to the Club? An Economical Approach to Geographical Indications in the European Union'. *Agrarwirtschaft* 49 (12): 428–37, November 7.

Tirole, J. 1988. *The Theory of Industiral Organization*. Cambridge: MIT Press.

Tregear, A., A. Torok, and M. Gorton. 2016. 'Geographical Indications and Upgrading of Small-scale Producers in Global Agro-food Chains: A Case Study of the Mako Onion Protected Designation of Origin'. *Environment and Planning A: Economy and Space* 48 (2): 433–51. doi: 10.1177/0308518X15607467.

Tueber, R. 2009. 'Producers' and Consumers' Expectations toward Geographical Indications—Empirical Evidence for Hessian Apple Wine'. 113th Seminar, European Association of Agricultural Economists (EAAE), 3–6 September. Chania, Crete, Greece.

Tyabji, L. 2008. 'Tandoori Chikan, Polyster Khadi'. *India International Centre Quarterly* 35 (3–4): 250–9.

UNCTAD. 2015. *Why Geographical Indications for Least Developed Countries*. Geneva: UNCTAD.

United Nations Industrial Development Organization (UNDP). 2010. *Adding Value to Traditional Products of Regional Origin*. Vienna: United Nations Industrial Development Organization.

Vandecandelaere, E., F. Arfini, G. Belletti, ———— (n.d.) Available at http://www.undp.org/content/dam/undp/library/corporate/brochure/SDGs_Booklet_Web_En.pdf Retrieved on 5 October, 2018. and A. Marescotti. 2009–10. *Linking People Places and Products—A Guide for Promoting Quality Linked to Geographical Origin and Sustainable Geographical Indications*. Rome: Food and Agriculture Organisation.

Vattam, S. 2003. 'The Colours of Kasuti'. *The Deccan Herald*, October.

Vinayan, S. 2006. *Liberalisation and Handloom Industry: The Interface between Handlooms and Powerlooms in Andhra Pradesh*. Hyderabad: Unpublished PhD Thesis submitted to the University of Hyderabad.

————. 2007. *Geographical Indications and Cluster Development in Indian Handloom Sector: Opportunities for Poverty Reduction*. Bonn: Internship Report at UNIDO, Vienna submitted to the German Development Institute as part of the Managing Global Governance Programme (MGG).

————. 2012. 'Intellectual Property Rights and Handloom Sector: Challenges in Implementation of Geographical Indications Act'. *Journal of Intellectual Property Rights* 17 (1): 55–63.

————. 2013. *Socio-economics of Geographical Indications in the Indian Handloom Sector: A Case Study of Pochampally*. New Delhi: Report submitted to the Indian—Council of Social Science Research.

————. 2015. 'Willingness to Pay for GI Products in India: The Case of Darjeeling Tea and Pochampally Ikat'. *Hyderabad Social Development Papers* 3 (1–3): 1–21.

————. 2017. 'Geographical Indications in India: Issues and Challenges—An Overview'. *Journal of World Intellectual Property* 20 (3–4): 119–32.

Vittori, M. 2010. 'The International Debate on Geographical Indications: The Point of View of Global Coalition of GI Producers OriGIn'. *The Journal of World Intellectual Property* 13 (2): 304–14.

Wekesa, M. 2006. *What Is Sui Generis System of Intellectual Property Protection?* Technopolicy Brief No. 13. Nairobi: The African Technology Policy Studies Network.

Index

About the Authors

N. Lalitha is professor at the Gujarat Institute of Development Research (GIDR), Ahmedabad, India. She began her career at GIDR in 1994. She holds a PhD in economics from Bangalore University through the Institute for Social and Economic Change, Bengaluru. Her research focuses on issues around globalization, trade, and development. In tracing the impact of globalization, she concentrates on issues related to intellectual property rights in pharmaceuticals and biotechnology.

Soumya Vinayan is assistant professor at the Council for Social Development (CSD), Hyderabad, India. She holds a PhD in economics from the University of Hyderabad. Her core research areas are political economy of financing higher education and the emergence of the private player; and theory and praxis of intellectual property regimes and its interplay in realizing distributive 'rent' to artisanal mode of production.